40 Reading Intervention Strategies for P-6 Students

Elaine K. McEwan-Adkins

Hawker Brownlow EDUCATION

Republished in Australia by

Hawker Brownlow
EDUCATION

P.O. Box 580, Moorabbin, Victoria 3189, Australia
Phone: (03) 8558 2444 Fax: (03) 8558 2400
Toll Free Ph: 1800 334 603 Fax: 1800 150 445
Website: www.hbe.com.au
Email: orders@hbe.com.au
Code: SOT4749
ISBN: 978 1 74239 474 9
1209
© 2009 Hawker Brownlow Education
This work is copyright. Apart from any fair dealings for the purposes of private study, research, criticism or review, or as permitted under the Copyright Act, no part should be reproduced, transmitted, stored, communicated or recorded by any process, without written permission. Any enquiries regarding copyright or permissions for reproduction must be made to Hawker Brownlow Education.
Printed in Australia
Originally published in 2010 by Solution Tree Press

Solution Tree

© 2010 Solution Tree Press

Table of Contents

Problem-Solution Table of Contents ix
Year-Level Grid Table of Contents xiii
Topical Table of Contents xv
About the Author xix
Preface xxi
    The Goals of This Book xxii
    Who Needs This Book xxii
    Overview of the Contents. xxii
Introduction 1

PART 1
Interventions for Improving Instruction 3

    What the Research Says About Effective Instruction for Students at Risk 5

INTERVENTION 1
Implementing Research-Based Instruction for Intervention Groups
(Years P–6) 7
    Background Knowledge. 12
    How to Design Lessons for Intervention Groups 12
    Sample Lesson for Teaching Main Idea 12

INTERVENTION 2
Reducing Cognitive Load and Increasing Cognitive Processing
(Years P–6) 15
    Background Knowledge. 15
    Research-Based Learning Principles for Intervention Groups 16
    Sample Lesson for the Think-Pair-Share Routine 17

INTERVENTION 3
Practising Beyond Perfection (Years P–6) 21
    Background Knowledge. 21
    Providing Practice in Intervention Groups and Differentiated Centres 22

INTERVENTION 4
Teaching Task Engagement, Time Management
and Self-Control (Years P–2). 25
    Background Knowledge. 25
    Sample Lessons for Teaching Classroom Routines 25

PART 2
Interventions for Building Phonemic Awareness 29

    What the Research Says About Phonemic Awareness Instruction 31

INTERVENTION 5
Blending Sounds to Make Words (Years P–1) 33
    Background Knowledge. 33
    Sample Lessons for Blending Sounds 34

INTERVENTION 6
Segmenting Words Into Sounds (Years P–1) 37
    Background Knowledge. 37
    Sample Lessons for Teaching Segmenting 37

PART 3
Interventions for Building Word Identification Skills. 41

    What the Research Says About Word Identification Instruction 43

INTERVENTION 7
Mastering Letter-Sound Correspondences (Years P–1) 45
    Background Knowledge. 45
    Sample Lessons for Teaching Letter-Sound Correspondences 49

INTERVENTION 8
Reading Regular Words (Years P–2) 53
    Background Knowledge. 53
    Sample Lessons for Reading Regular Words 53

INTERVENTION 9
Reading Irregular (Exception) Words (Years P–3) 57
    Background Knowledge. 57
    Sample Lesson for Teaching Exception Words 58

INTERVENTION 10
Facilitating Advanced Word Reading (Years 2–6) 61
    Background Knowledge. 61
    Instructional Activities for Advanced Word Reading 62

INTERVENTION 11
Reading Decodable Books (Years P–1) 67
    Background Knowledge. 67
    Sample Lesson for Teaching Decodable Books. 67

INTERVENTION 12
Building Mental Orthographic Images for Keywords
or Frequently Misread Words (Years 2–6) 71
    Background Knowledge. 71
    Sample Lesson for Teaching Key Words or Frequently Misread Words. 72

PART 4
Interventions for Building Fluency 75

    What the Research Says About Fluency Instruction. 77

INTERVENTION 13
Crossing the Fluency Bridge (Years 1–3) 79
    Essential Program Components for Building Fluency by the End of Year Two. 79

INTERVENTION 14
Facilitating Fluency in Your Reading Groups (Years 1–2) 83
    Background Knowledge. 83
    Sample Lessons for Facilitating Fluency 83

INTERVENTION 15
Structuring Repeated Oral Reading Activities Using Prosody as a
Motivator or Indicator of Text Comprehension (Years 3–6) 87
    Background Knowledge. 87
    Repeated Oral Reading Performance Activities to Improve Comprehension. 88
    Remediating the Robotic Reader With or Without Comprehension 89

INTERVENTION 16
Choosing Books for Independent Reading (Years 3–6) 91
    Background Knowledge. 91
    Sample Lesson for Teaching Book Selection 92

INTERVENTION 17
Teaching the Fastest Way to Read Words (Years 3–6) 97
    Background Knowledge. 97
    Sample Lesson for Teaching the Fastest Way to Read Words 98

PART 5
Interventions for Building Vocabulary. 101

    What the Research Says About Vocabulary Instruction. 103

INTERVENTION 18
Using Context to Infer Word Meanings (Years 2–6) 105
    Background Knowledge. 105
    Sample Lesson for Teaching How to Use Context to Infer Word Meaning 106

© 2009 Hawker Brownlow Education • SOT4749

INTERVENTION 19
Teaching More Vocabulary Every Day (Years 2–6) 109
- Background Knowledge 109
- Sample Lessons for Teaching Vocabulary 109

INTERVENTION 20
Using Read-Alouds to Teach New Words (Years P–2) 117
- Background Knowledge 117
- Use a Daily Read-Aloud with a Classroom Connection to Teach New Words 117
- Use Nonfiction Read-Alouds to Teach Word and World Knowledge 118

INTERVENTION 21
Organising Vocabulary for Understanding and Retention (Years 4–6) . . . 119
- Background Knowledge 119
- Sample Lesson for Teaching a Graphic Organiser 120
- Teaching Students to Construct a Semantic Word Map 120
- Teaching Students to Construct a Word Structure Map 120
- Teaching Students to Construct a Frayer Model 123

INTERVENTION 22
Writing Sentences to Show You Know (Years 4–6) 125
- Background Knowledge 125
- Sample Lesson for Teaching Show You Know Sentences 125

INTERVENTION 23
Teaching Contextual Information About Words (Years 4–6) 129
- Background Knowledge 129
- Sample Lesson for Teaching the Concept Map 129

INTERVENTION 24
Facilitating Content Vocabulary Instruction (Years 4–6) 131
- Background Knowledge 131
- Sample Weekly Lessons for Small-Group Intervention 132

INTERVENTION 25
Playing the Word Power Game (Years 4–6) 137
- Background Knowledge 137
- Sample Lesson for Playing the Word Power Game 138

PART 6
Interventions for Facilitating Comprehension 143
- What the Research Says About Reading Comprehension 145

Table of Contents

INTERVENTION 26
Scaffolding Year-level Reading Texts for
Struggling Students (Years 3–6) 147
    Background Knowledge. 147
    Daily Schedule for Pull-Aside Homogeneous Reading Groups 148

INTERVENTION 27
Teaching the Seven Cognitive Strategies of Highly Effective Readers
(Years 3–6) 151
    Background Knowledge. 151

INTERVENTION 28
Teaching Students About Inferences (Years 3–6) 153
    Background Knowledge. 153
    Sample Lesson for Teaching Inference. 154

INTERVENTION 29
Teaching Pronouns to Improve Inferential Comprehension
(Years 2–6) 159
    Background Knowledge. 159
    Sample Lesson for Teaching Pronouns. 160

INTERVENTION 30
Thinking Aloud to Teach Inference (Years 3–6) 165
    Background Knowledge. 165
    Thinking Aloud for Students 165
    Thinking Aloud With Students to Solve Their Comprehension Difficulties 167

INTERVENTION 31
Facilitating Cooperative Comprehension (Years 3–6) 171
    Background Knowledge. 171
    Sample Lesson for Teaching Cooperative Comprehension 171

INTERVENTION 32
Mastering the Five Cs of Summarising (Years 4–6) 177
    Background Knowledge. 177
    Sample Lesson for Teacher-Directed Small-Group Intervention 178

INTERVENTION 33
Using Graphic Organisers to Summarise Stories (Years P–2) 187
    Background Knowledge. 187

INTERVENTION 34
Teaching Students How to Monitor Their Silent Reading
Comprehension (Years 4–6) 191
    Background Knowledge. 191
    Sample Lesson for Teaching Monitoring. 191

INTERVENTION 35
Coding Text to Improve Comprehension (Years 4–6) 197
- Background Knowledge. 197
- Sample Lesson for Teaching Text Coding 198

INTERVENTION 36
Asking and Answering Questions (Years 3–6) 203
- Background Knowledge. 203
- Sample Lesson for Teaching Questioning 204

INTERVENTION 37
Previewing Text to Improve Comprehension (Years 3–6) 209
- Background Knowledge. 209
- Sample Lesson for Using Text Previews 210

PART 7
Interventions for Teaching Students to Read a Lot 213

- What the Research Says About Reading a Lot 215

INTERVENTION 38
Teaching Reading a Lot (Years P–2) 217
- Background Knowledge. 217
- Sample Plan for Whole-Class (or Whole-School) Intervention 217

INTERVENTION 39
Facilitating REAL Reading in the Classroom (Years 1–3) 221
- Background Knowledge. 221

INTERVENTION 40
Teaching Reading a Lot (Years 4–6) 225
- Background Knowledge. 225
- Sample Lesson for Choosing Comfort Zone Books. 225

Conclusion 229
Glossary 231
References 239

Problem-Solution Table of Contents

When Students Have Difficulty Hearing and Manipulating Sounds
- Intervention 5: Blending Sounds to Make Words (Years P–1) 33
- Intervention 6: Segmenting Words Into Sounds (Years P–1) 37
- Intervention 7: Mastering Letter-Sound Correspondences (Years P–1) 45

When Students Have Difficulty Learning the Letters
- Intervention 7: Mastering Letter-Sound Correspondences (Years P–1) 45

When Students Are Painfully Slow Readers
- Intervention 7: Mastering Letter-Sound Correspondences (Years P–1) 45
- Intervention 8: Reading Regular Words (Years P–2) 53
- Intervention 10: Facilitating Advanced Word Reading (Years 2–6) 61
- Intervention 11: Reading Decodable Books (Years P–1) 67
- Intervention 13: Crossing the Fluency Bridge (Years 1–3) 79
- Intervention 14: Facilitating Fluency in Your Reading Groups (Years 1–2) 83
- Intervention 16: Choosing Books for Independent Reading (Years 3–6) 91

When Students Need to Hear the Story Read Aloud Before They Can Understand It
- Intervention 11: Reading Decodable Books (Years P–1) 67
- Intervention 39: Facilitating REAL Reading in the Classroom (Years 1–3) 221

When Students Have Fluency but Don't Comprehend Well
- Intervention 15: Structuring Repeated Oral Reading Activities Using Prosody as a Motivator or Indicator of Text Comprehension (Years 3–6) 87
- Intervention 27: Teaching the Seven Cognitive Strategies of Highly Effective Readers (Years 3–6) 151

When Students Are Eager Volunteers, but Always Have the Wrong Answers
- Intervention 31: Facilitating Cooperative Comprehension (Years 3–6) 171
- Intervention 34: Teaching Students How to Monitor Their Silent Reading Comprehension (Years 4–6) 191
- Intervention 35: Coding Text to Improve Comprehension (Years 4–6) 197
- Intervention 36: Asking and Answering Questions (Years 3–6) 203

When Students Can't Make Inferences
- Intervention 28: Teaching Students About Inferences (Years 3–6) 153
- Intervention 29: Teaching Pronouns to Improve Inferential Comprehension (Years 2–6) 159
- Intervention 30: Thinking Aloud to Teach Inference (Years 3–6) 165
- Intervention 31: Facilitating Cooperative Comprehension (Years 3–6) 171

© 2009 Hawker Brownlow Education • SOT4749

When Students Are Unable to Summarise
  Intervention 32: Mastering the Five Cs of Summarising (Years 4–6) 177
  Intervention 33: Using Graphic Organisers to Summarise Stories (Years P–2) 187

When Students Are English Language Learners or Have Limited Vocabulary and Background Knowledge
  Intervention 18: Using Context to Infer Word Meanings (Years 2–6) 105
  Intervention 19: Teaching More Vocabulary Every Day (Years 2–6) 109
  Intervention 20: Using Read-Alouds to Teach New Words (Years P–2) 117
  Intervention 21: Organising Vocabulary for Understanding and Retention (Years 4–6) 119
  Intervention 22: Writing Sentences to Show You Know (Years 4–6) 125
  Intervention 23: Teaching Contextual Information About Words (Years 4–6) 129
  Intervention 24: Facilitating Content Vocabulary Instruction (Years 4–6) 131
  Intervention 25: Playing the Word Power Game (Years 4–6) 137

When Students Can Read but Can't Spell
  Intervention 9: Reading Irregular (Exception) Words (Years P–3) 57
  Intervention 12: Building Mental Orthographic Images for Keywords or
    Frequently Misread Words (Years 2–6) 71

When Guessing Is Your Students' First Strategy When They Can't Identify a Word
  Intervention 10: Facilitating Advanced Word Reading (Years 2–6) 61
  Intervention 16: Choosing Books for Independent Reading (Years 3–6) 91

When Upper-Grade Students Can't Read Multisyllabic Words
  Intervention 10: Facilitating Advanced Word Reading (Years 2–6) 61

When You Teach It, but Students Still Don't Get It
  Intervention 1: Implementing Research-Based Instruction for Intervention Groups (Years P–6) . . 7
  Intervention 2: Reducing Cognitive Load and Increasing Cognitive Processing (Years P–6) 15
  Intervention 3: Practising Beyond Perfection (Years P–6) 21
  Intervention 4: Teaching Task Engagement, Time Management
    and Self-Control (Years P–2) 25

When Students Don't Read a Lot Either In or Out of School
  Intervention 13: Crossing the Fluency Bridge (Years 1–3) 79
  Intervention 17: Teaching the Fastest Way to Read Words (Years 3–6) 97
  Intervention 38: Teaching Reading a Lot (Years P–2) 217
  Intervention 39: Facilitating REAL Reading in the Classroom (Years 1–3) 221
  Intervention 40: Teaching Reading a Lot (Years 4–6) 225

When Students Are Barely On Year Level and Struggling to Maintain That Status
  Intervention 26: Scaffolding Year-level Reading Texts for Struggling Students
    (Years 3–6) 147
  Intervention 27: Teaching the Seven Cognitive Strategies of Highly
    Effective Readers (Years 3–6) 151

Problem-Solution Table of Contents

When Students Do Not Orally Read With Prosody
Intervention 15: Structuring Repeated Oral Reading Activities Using Prosody as a Motivator or Indicator of Text Comprehension (Years 3–6) 87

When Students Read Carelessly and Often Zone Out During Reading
Intervention 34: Teaching Students How to Monitor Their Silent Reading Comprehension (Years 4–6) 191

Intervention 35: Coding Text to Improve Comprehension (Years 4–6) 197

When Students Have Difficulty Telling What a Story Is About
Intervention 33: Using Graphic Organisers to Summarise Stories (Years P–2) 187

When Students Have Difficulty Writing a Sentence Summarising a Story or Article On Their Independent Reading Level
Intervention 32: Mastering the Five Cs of Summarising (Years 4–6) 177

When Students Are Unable to Answer Even the Most Basic Comprehension Questions
Intervention 35: Coding Text to Improve Comprehension (Years 4–6) 197

When Students Are Overwhelmed by Too Much to Learn
Intervention 2: Reducing Cognitive Load and Increasing Cognitive Processing (Years P–6). 15

When Students Need More Practice
Intervention 3: Practising Beyond Perfection (Years P–6) 21

Intervention 26: Scaffolding Year-level Reading Texts for Struggling Students (Years 3–6) 147

When Students Lack the Background Knowledge to Understand Text
Intervention 19: Teaching More Vocabulary Every Day (Years 2–6) 109

Intervention 24: Facilitating Content Vocabulary Instruction (Years 4–6) 131

Intervention 26: Scaffolding Year-level Reading Texts for Struggling Students (Years 3–6) 147

When Students Don't Like to Read
Intervention 17: Teaching the Fastest Way to Read Words (Years 3–6). 97

Intervention 37: Previewing Text to Improve Comprehension (Years 3–6) 209

Intervention 40: Teaching Reading a Lot (Years 4–6). 225

When Students Activate Irrelevant Prior Knowledge
Intervention 35: Coding Text to Improve Comprehension (Years 4–6) 197

When You Teach It but Students Still Don't Get It
Intervention 1: Implementing Research-Based Instruction for Intervention Groups (Years P–6) . . 7

Intervention 2: Reducing Cognitive Load and Increasing Cognitive Processing (Years P–6) 15

Intervention 3: Practising Beyond Perfection (Years P–6) 21

When Students Fail to Monitor Their Comprehension
Intervention 34: Teaching Students How to Monitor Their Silent Reading Comprehension (Years 4–6) 191

Intervention 35: Coding Text to Improve Comprehension (Years 4–6) 197

© 2009 Hawker Brownlow Education • SOT4749

Year-Level Grid Table of Contents

Intervention Number and Title	Topic	P	1	2	3	4	5	6
1. Implementing Research-Based Instruction for Intervention Groups	Instruction	x	x	x	x	x	x	x
2. Reducing Cognitive Load and Increasing Cognitive Processing	Instruction	x	x	x	x	x	x	x
3. Practising Beyond Perfection	Instruction	x	x	x	x	x	x	x
4. Teaching Task Engagement, Time Management and Self-Control	Instruction	x	x	x	x	x	x	x
5. Blending Sounds to Make Words	Phonemic Awareness	x	x					
6. Segmenting Words Into Sounds	Phonemic Awareness	x	x					
7. Mastering Letter-Sound Correspondences	Word Identification	x	x	x				
8. Reading Regular Words	Word Identification	x	x	x				
9. Reading Irregular (Exception) Words	Word Identification	x	x	x				
10. Facilitating Advanced Word Reading	Word Identification		x	x	x	x	x	x
11. Reading Decodable Books	Word Identification	x	x	x				
12. Building Mental Orthographic Images for Keywords or Frequently Misread Words	Word Identification			x	x	x	x	x
13. Crossing the Fluency Bridge	Fluency		x	x	x			
14. Facililtating Fluency in Your Reading Groups	Fluency		x	x				
15. Structuring Repeated Oral Reading Activities Using Prosody as a Motivator or Indicator of Text Comprehension	Fluency				x	x	x	x
16. Choosing Books for Independent Reading	Fluency				x	x	x	x
17. Teaching the Fastest Way to Read Words	Fluency				x	x	x	x
18. Using Context to Infer Word Meanings	Vocabulary			x	x	x	x	x
19. Teaching More Vocabulary Every Day	Vocabulary	x	x	x	x	x	x	x
20. Using Read-Alouds to Teach New Words	Vocabulary	x	x	x	x			
21. Organising Vocabulary for Understanding and Retention	Vocabulary					x	x	x
22. Writing Sentences to Show You Know	Vocabulary					x	x	x
23. Teaching Contextual Information About Words	Vocabulary					x	x	x
24. Facilitating Content Vocabulary Instruction	Vocabulary				x	x	x	x

© 2009 Hawker Brownlow Education • SOT4749

Intervention Number and Title	Topic	P	1	2	3	4	5	6
25. Playing the Word Power Game	Vocabulary					x	x	x
26. Scaffolding Year-Level Reading Texts for Struggling Students	Comprehension				x	x	x	x
27. Teaching the Seven Cognitive Strategies of Highly Effective Readers	Comprehension	x	x	x	x	x	x	x
28. Teaching Students About Inferences	Comprehension				x	x	x	x
29. Teaching Pronouns to Improve Inferential Comprehension	Comprehension		x	x	x	x	x	x
30. Thinking Aloud to Teach Inference	Comprehension				x	x	x	x
31. Facilitating Cooperative Comprehension	Comprehension				x	x	x	x
32. Mastering the Five Cs of Summarising	Comprehension					x	x	x
33. Using Graphic Organisers to Summarise Stories	Comprehension	x	x	x				
34. Teaching Students How to Monitor Their Silent Reading Comprehension	Comprehension					x	x	x
35. Coding Text to Improve Comprehension	Comprehension					x	x	x
36. Asking and Answering Questions	Comprehension					x	x	x
37. Previewing Text to Improve Comprehension	Comprehension				x	x	x	x
38. Teaching Reading a Lot (Years P–2)	Reading a Lot	x	x	x				
39. Facilitating REAL Reading in the Classroom	Reading a Lot		x	x	x			
40. Teaching Reading a Lot (Years 4–6)	Reading a Lot				x	x	x	x

Topical Table of Contents

Accessible Text
- 13. Crossing the Fluency Bridge. 79
- 14. Facilitating Fluency in Your Reading Groups 83
- 16. Choosing Books for Independent Reading. 91

Cognitive Apprenticeships
- 30. Thinking Aloud to Teach Inference 165

Cognitive Processing
- 2. Reducing Cognitive Load and Increasing Cognitive Processing 15

Cognitive Strategy Instruction
- 27. Teaching the Seven Cognitive Strategies of Highly Effective Readers 151

Comprehension
- 26. Scaffolding Year-Level Reading Texts for Struggling Students 147
- 28. Teaching Students About Inference. 153
- 29. Teaching Pronouns to Improve Inferential Comprehension 159
- 30. Thinking Aloud to Teach Inference 165
- 32. Mastering the Five Cs of Summarising 177
- 34. Teaching Students How to Monitor Their Silent Reading Comprehension 191
- 35. Coding Text to Improve Comprehension. 197
- 36. Asking and Answering Questions 203

Cooperative Learning
- 31. Facilitating Cooperative Comprehension. 171

Graphic Organising
- 21. Organising Vocabulary for Understanding and Retention. 119
- 33. Using Graphic Organisers to Summarise Stories. 187

Exception Words
- 9. Reading Irregular (Exception) Words 57

Fluency Instruction
- 13. Crossing the Fluency Bridge. 79
- 14. Facilitating Fluency in Your Reading Groups 83

Instructional Effectiveness
- 1. Implementing Research-Based Instruction for Intervention Groups 7
- 2. Reducing Cognitive Load and Increasing Cognitive Processing 15
- 3. Practising Beyond Perfection 21
- 4. Teaching Task Engagement, Time Management and Self-Control 25

Mental Orthographic Images
    9. Reading Irregular (Exception) Words 57
   12. Building Mental Orthographic Images for Keywords
       or Frequently Misread Words 71

Monitoring Comprehension
   34. Teaching Students How to Monitor Their Silent Reading Comprehension 191

Motivating Students to Read
   38. Teaching Reading a Lot (Years P–2) 217
   39. Facilitating REAL Reading in the Classroom 221
   40. Teaching Reading a Lot (Years 4–6) 225

Oral Reading
   14. Facilitating Fluency in Your Reading Groups 83
   15. Structuring Repeated Oral Reading Activities Using Prosody as a Motivator
       or Indicator of Text Comprehension 87
   39. Facilitating REAL Reading in the Classroom 221

Phonemic Awareness
    5. Blending Sounds to Make Words 33
    6. Segmenting Words Into Sounds. 37

Phonics: See Word Identification

Questioning
   36. Asking and Answering Questions 203

Silent Reading
   34. Teaching Students How to Monitor Their Silent Reading Comprehension 191

Summarising
   32. Mastering the Five Cs of Summarising 177

Thinking Aloud by Teachers
   22. Writing Sentences to Show You Know 125
   28. Teaching Students About Inferences 153
   30. Thinking Aloud to Teach Inference 165
   31. Facilitating Cooperative Comprehension. 171
   36. Asking and Answering Questions 203

Vocabulary Instruction
   18. Using Context to Infer Word Meanings. 105
   19. Teaching More Vocabulary Every Day. 109
   20. Using Read-Alouds to Teach New Words. 117
   22. Writing Sentences to Show You Know 125
   23. Teaching Contextual Information About Words 129
   24. Facilitating Content Vocabulary Instruction. 131
   25. Playing the Word Power Game 137

Word Identification

7. Mastering Letter-Sound Correspondences 45
8. Reading Regular Words 53
10. Facilitating Advanced Word Reading 61
11. Reading Decodable Books. 67
17. Teaching the Fastest Way to Read Words 97

About the Author

Elaine K. McEwan-Adkins is a partner and educational consultant with the McEwan-Adkins Group offering professional development in literacy and school leadership.

A former teacher, librarian, principal and assistant superintendent for instruction in a suburban school area, Elaine is the author of more than thirty-five books for parents and educators. She has also written such titles as *Teach Them All to Read: Catching Kids Before They Fall Through the Cracks,* and *Ten Traits of Highly Effective Schools*.

She received an undergraduate degree in education and both a master's degree in library science and a doctorate in educational administration.

Preface

Not very long ago, I was shocked to learn that my granddaughter, whose year four teacher had recommended her for placement in year five advanced English and maths classes, was reading at only a year three level at the end of this "enriched" experience. She had gotten all As in years 3 and 4 at one of the finest schools in one of the best areas, but she still fell through the cracks. How was she able to keep this astonishing lack of reading ability under wraps for so long? I suspected that she did it with clever guessing, highly developed social and verbal skills, well-above-average writing skills, a little help from her friends and a total lack of accountability for understanding anything she read. An online reading test, given as an afterthought in her year five English class, revealed this appalling academic deficiency. The teacher was stunned and embarrassed but had no suggestions for how to remediate the problem. The school offered no programs that might help her.

Days before school was to adjourn for the holidays, her mother called me in a panic. My husband and I dropped everything and flew to see them. I gave Abigail some simple tests and then had her tested by an expert who had more reliable assessments. She confirmed what I already knew: Abigail didn't have a good grasp of long and short vowels, and she was vague about quite a few consonant blends and digraphs as well. Multisyllabic words threw her into a panic. She readily admitted that she hadn't read an entire book for more than two years. Her fluency, vocabulary and comprehension were all stuck in year three.

Abigail is a whiz at soccer and softball, is a member of a fantastic dance team, writes wonderfully imaginative stories and is well liked by a wide circle of friends, but nobody was holding her accountable for comprehending what she read. She was getting by on sheer bravado. Abigail's mother ended up paying for private tutoring throughout the summer holidays. Although Abigail complained bitterly about attending "summer school", she filled in all of her word identification gaps and was so grateful for the experience that she wrote a testimonial for the tutor's website. However, catching up on the fluency, vocabulary and comprehension aspects of reading is almost impossible. She missed two years of reading the number of books she should have by her age, and all of her peers passed her by in terms of word and world knowledge. She will likely never read *Harry Potter*, *The Secret Garden* or *Little Women*. Abigail is one of the reasons I have written this book: to give primary educators a research-based menu of intervention strategies to help students the minute they show signs of falling through the cracks. I also want educators to understand that they don't have to "wait and see" when students are floundering in prep/reception. They can intervene immediately and with confidence.

The interventions in this book are designed for general educators to use with individuals or small groups of students who simply cannot keep up with the pace of instruction. Struggling students need a different kind of instruction, more time and ample amounts of guided practice to help them become confident readers. Some of the strategies are more preventive in nature—for example, ways that year-level teams or entire schools can become more proactive about reaching students at risk. All of the strategies in this book are grounded in research.

The Goals of This Book

The goals of this book are as follows:

- To provide a well-rounded collection of research-based reading intervention strategies that can be used by classroom teachers, interventionists, special educators and ESL teachers seeking to support struggling readers in their classrooms and schools

- To provide teacher-friendly sample lesson plans and miniroutines that the classroom teacher can readily understand and adapt

- To provide citations and descriptions of current research educators can use to substantiate their strategy choices

Who Needs This Book

I wrote this book for prep to year 6 educators in various positions. Most educators are deeply concerned with literacy levels in their schools. Everyone is feeling the relentless pressure of high-stakes testing and the need to provide the highest levels of instruction. This book is intended for the following groups:

- Primary teachers of all kinds and levels—preP–6 regular classroom, special education, bilingual education and other reading teachers—who are looking for ways to teach *all* students to read

- Literacy coaches, interventionists, speech pathologists and other educational specialists who are designing interventions and teaching individual students and intervention groups in the regular classroom

- Special education, bilingual and other administrators who need resources for their teachers and coaches

- Tertiary educators who are looking for a research-based collection of intervention strategies as a resource in their classrooms

Overview of the Contents

The intervention strategies are numbered 1 to 40 and are grouped into seven sections: instruction, phonemic awareness, word identification, fluency, vocabulary, comprehension and reading a lot. Each of the seven topical sections is preceded by a short research summary, and each of the 40 intervention strategies is presented in the following format:

- A description

- A brief discussion of essential background knowledge and more specific research

- Sample lessons, think-alouds, mini teaching routines or instructional aids to support instruction

Highly effective teachers often use these intervention strategies during whole-group instruction, since many of them will not only scaffold struggling readers but will also motivate and accelerate average and above-average students. Many of the interventions gain exponential power when implemented across a year level or throughout the school.

© 2009 Hawker Brownlow Education • SOT4749

You will find the following special features in this book:

- Strategies for thinking aloud to scaffold challenging comprehension skills like inferencing, summarising and monitoring
- Ways to teach inference with sample lessons using authentic text examples
- Ways to teach more vocabulary in less time with greater understanding and retention
- Ways to increase the vocabulary and background knowledge of ESLs and students with overall low vocabulary and language skills
- Both historical and up-to-date research citations to inform and support your intervention decisions
- More than thirty sample lessons with step-by-step instructions and teaching formats that include modelling, ways to build in student practice and suggestions for keeping students engaged
- Routines to facilitate student practice of key reading skills
- Interventions to help students cross the fluency bridge from word identification to comprehension
- Year-level notations to help determine which strategies work best at specific year levels
- A topical table of contents to help you find strategies by subject

Just ahead, the introduction provides background knowledge on how the 40 strategies can be implemented in your classroom or school. Once you have read it, you will be prepared to explore the seven different categories of intervention strategies in this book and determine where you want to begin in your efforts to help all of your students become proficient, confident and motivated readers.

Introduction

We will never teach all of our students to read if we do not teach our students who have the greatest difficulties to read. Another way to say this is: Getting to 100% requires going through the bottom 20%.

—Torgesen (2006, p. 1)

More than twenty-five years ago, effective schools guru Ron Edmonds (1981) said the following:

> We can, whenever and wherever we choose, successfully teach all students whose schooling is of interest to us. We already know more than we need to do that. Whether or not we do it must finally depend on how we feel about the fact that we haven't done it so far. (p. 53)

Although Edmonds was writing in a broad sense about student achievement, his statement aptly describes the current state of affairs in reading. Today, more educators than ever before are feeling empowered to teach *all* children to read. They are working collaboratively to build collective efficacy and instructional capacity in their schools. They have moved beyond personal feelings of doubt to become energised by the success of their students. My optimism about the possibilities of teaching all students to read is bolstered by a body of experimental intervention research carried on since the 1980s. However, we must be very clear about what *all* means when we commit to teaching them all to read. According to Torgesen (2002), although "intensive preventive instruction can bring the average word-reading skills of children at risk for reading disabilities solidly into the average range, even under the best-known instructional conditions, a substantial proportion of children (6 per cent) will remain relatively impaired in word-level reading skills at the conclusion of the intervention" (p. 96). Some students will not respond to the very best we have to offer in our classrooms. However, because you and your colleagues cannot be sure which students are having serious reading difficulties that do not respond to intensive and specialised interventions until you intervene, you have a moral imperative to teach all children using research-based instructional methods from their first enrolment in your school or classroom. Meanwhile, you must maintain a firm belief that all of your students will learn to read until you see solid data that show that they can't. This approach to teaching reading is similar to the measures taken by the best physicians when they are confronted with seriously ill patients. Dedicated doctors do not give up until they have exhausted all of their treatment options. We can do no less for our students at risk.

Teaching them all to read is a highly complex undertaking that requires the skilful management of time, data, instructional programs and human resources at levels previously unseen in many primary schools. It also requires knowledgeable and passionate school leaders, highly effective teachers, high-quality embedded professional development and a school culture that *expects* all students to succeed and provides multiple opportunities for those students to learn (McEwan, 2008, 2009).

The 40 intervention strategies in this book are designed to maximise your instructional effectiveness with struggling students. They can be used in two ways: (1) in whole-group instruction if you are working in a very low-performing school with many disadvantaged students, or (2) in small intervention groups as a supplement to the whole-group instruction you are providing during your core reading lesson.

You will find there are several ways to organise the classroom or school to provide highly effective initial instruction in a large group setting combined with small-group interventions—both in and out of the classroom—with various specialists (for example, speech pathologists, reading teachers or special education teachers).

As you skim the tables of contents, you may find that some of the interventions are similar to what you are already doing. However, if you examine them more closely, you might discover some subtle differences:

1. Instruction is meant to be delivered in small groups.

2. Students are more directly and explicitly taught.

3. More built-in practice and review routines are provided.

4. You are expected to build more modelling and thinking aloud into your instruction.

5. A variety of presentation techniques, such as signalling and choral response, are provided to ensure that students are engaged and on task during instruction. These strategies are meant to provide increased opportunities to learn and to close the gap between students at risk and their more advantaged counterparts, but they are not enough by themselves. Although the interventions are based on solid research, they still need the magic touch of talented teachers to bring them to life in the classroom and to tweak them here and there to meet the students' needs. Your success at implementing these interventions depends on several variables:

   - Your willingness to differentiate classroom instruction to provide what students at risk need: differentiated, explicit, systematic, supportive instruction

   - The effectiveness of your assessments in diagnosing what types of interventions students need

   - The level of your expectations for students

   - The alignment between the intervention and your assessment tools in terms of assessing a student's response to the intervention

   - The amount of time you are willing to devote to teaching and practice

   - Your skill at using the various research-based presentation techniques

   - Your ability to motivate and energise students who may be discouraged and frustrated by their failure

   - The degree to which you are able to collaborate with your administrators and colleagues to implement a strategy across a year level or even schoolwide

Part 1

Interventions for Improving Instruction

What the Research Says About Effective Instruction for Students at Risk

In the pages ahead, you will find brief research summaries and a set of intervention strategies for each of the components of a balanced reading program: phonemic awareness, word identification, fluency, vocabulary, comprehension and reading a lot. The intervention strategies can be used in several ways:

- As interventions in a response to intervention implementation

- As a supplement or "boost" to students who need extra help to keep up with whole-group reading instruction

- As schoolwide interventions in low-performing, high-poverty schools

However, these research summaries on the various aspects of a balanced reading program do not address the most critical question: What type of instruction is most effective for the struggling readers in your school? By *struggling readers*, we mean students with suspected as well as documented reading and language disabilities, English language learners and students who acquire skills and knowledge more slowly than their peers. Three discrete bodies of research tell us what types of instruction are most effective: *differentiated, explicit, systematic* and *supportive*. The evidence for what works to ensure that students at risk learn to read is well documented (figure P.1). The four interventions presented in Part 1 are equally applicable to all year levels, but space precludes providing sample lessons or examples for every year level.

As you investigate the four instruction-focused intervention strategies in Part 1, reflect on your current teaching practices as they relate to whole-group instruction. If you want more of your students to achieve year-level proficiency, implementing one or more of these interventions for a small group of struggling readers will help you achieve that goal.

Figure P.1: Research summary for differentiated, explicit, systematic and supportive instruction.

Type of Study	Description of Findings
Experimental research in primary year classrooms	Differentiated instruction based on students' assessed literacy levels and delivered with the most effective type of instruction for their documented needs at specific points in time is more effective than less diagnostic and more intuitive whole group instruction. Researchers found that children who began year one with below-average letter–word reading skills demonstrate greater improvement with greater amounts of time in explicit teacher-managed code-focused instruction while students who begin school with strong letter-word reading skills make more improvement in their overall reading ability when they spend less time in code-focused activities (Connor, Morrison, Fishman, Schatschneider, & Underwood, 2007; Connor, Morrison, & Katch, 2004; Connor, Morrison, & Petrella, 2004; Connor, Morrison, & Slominski, 2006; Connor, Schatschneider, Fishman, & Morrison, 2008; Connor et al., 2009).
Experimental, evaluative and meta-analysis reviews on direct instruction	Research on the power of direct instruction to get results with students at risk has been ongoing for more than thirty years (Adams & Carnine, 2003; Swanson & Hoskyn, 1998). Direct instruction as an instructional model differs from *Direct Instruction*, the curriculum, but they share many characteristics in common, such as the lesson design in figure 1.1 and the presentation techniques described in figure 1.3.
Meta-analyses and reviews of research on effective instruction	The following instructional practices are known to improve student achievement generally (Brophy, 1999; Marzano, Gaddy, & Dean, 2000; Walberg & Paik, 2003) and can be found in many of the intervention strategies in this book: (1) teaching summarising and note taking; (2) using graphic organisers; (3) questions and discussion about important concepts and big ideas in content learning; (4) scaffolding (the provision of help for struggling students); (5) comparing and classifying; (6) facilitating cooperative learning that is carefully structured and monitored; (7) providing direct instruction to include sequencing of lessons, guided practice and immediate feedback; (8) making connections between past and present learning and alerting students to main ideas; (9) insisting that students master foundational concepts and skills before moving on to new learning; (10) combining approaches like tutoring, mastery learning, cooperative learning and strategic instruction; and (11) focusing instruction on specific learning objectives.

© 2009 Hawker Brownlow Education and Elaine McEwan-Adkins.

INTERVENTION 1

Implementing Research-Based Instruction for Intervention Groups (Years P–6)

> *No amount of good feeling is adequate without that pedagogical dimension, without students actually knowing more and being able to do more at the end of a school year than they could at the beginning.*
>
> —Kohl (1998, p. 27)

This intervention strategy describes an instructional model that, if implemented with fidelity, will enable your students at risk to learn to read. Figure 1.1 illustrates how it works. The model is based on a well-designed lesson that includes direct and explicit instruction, teacher modelling and multiple opportunities for students to engage in guided and cumulative practice. The lesson is delivered with research-based teaching moves (figure 1.2) and is further enhanced by proven presentation techniques (figure 1.3). The result is differentiated, explicit, systematic and supportive (scaffolded) instruction that provides what students at risk need to be academically successful (figure 1.4).

Figure 1.2 contains a list of the teaching moves that are routinely used by highly effective teachers (McEwan, 2007). The degree to which teachers can integrate multiple teaching moves into every lesson will increase their effectiveness. For example, teachers who do not regularly model and think aloud for their students reduce the likelihood that struggling students will be able to achieve the objective. Failing to scaffold instruction by providing more time or more accessible materials for struggling students also limits their learning opportunities. If you intentionally build in moves like attributing, affirming and coaching, students will be more engaged and motivated (especially those who are struggling).

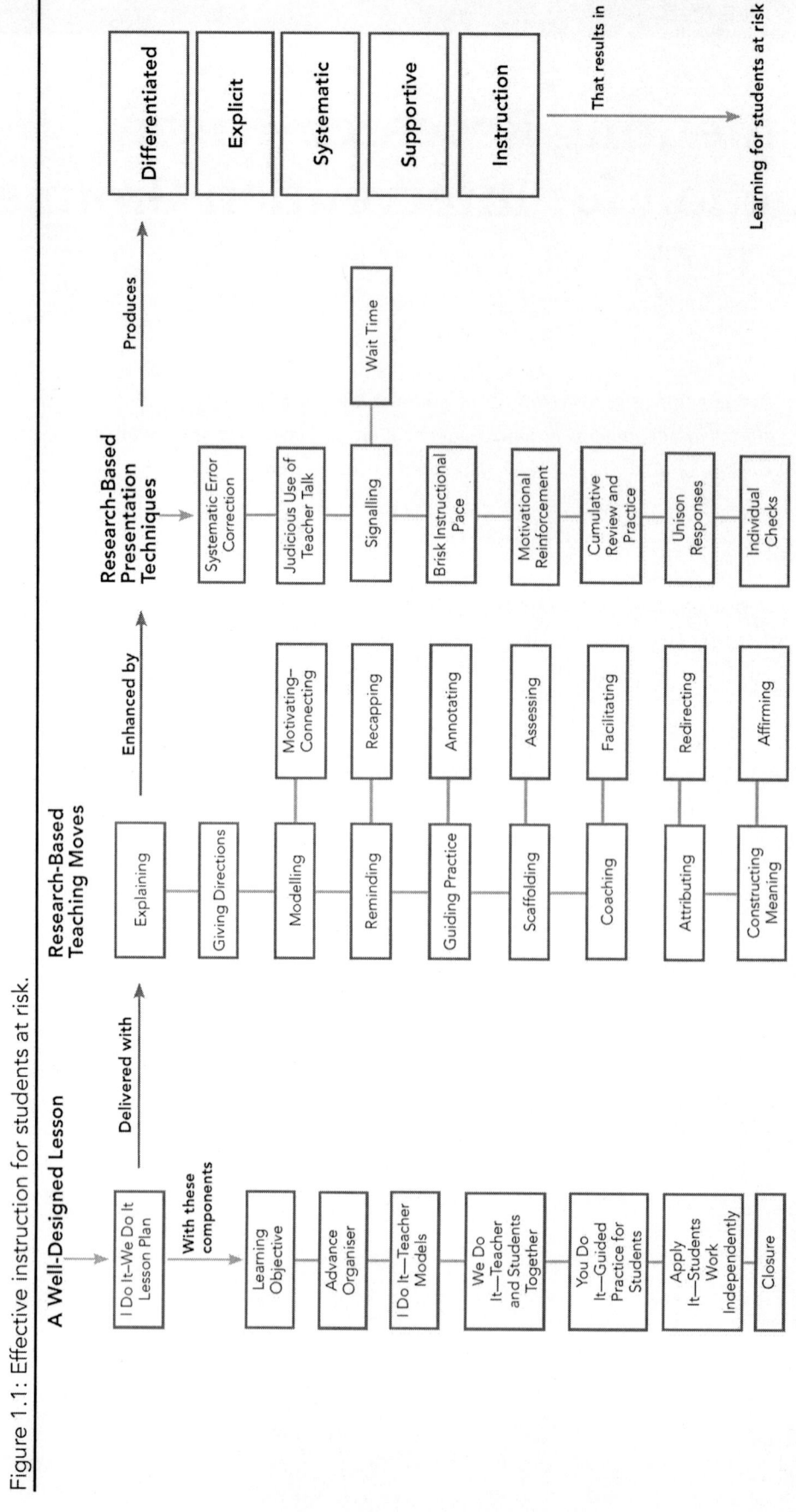

Figure 1.1: Effective instruction for students at risk.

A Well-Designed Lesson → Delivered with → **Research-Based Teaching Moves** → Enhanced by → **Research-Based Presentation Techniques** → Produces → Differentiated / Explicit / Systematic / Supportive / Instruction → That results in → Learning for students at risk

A Well-Designed Lesson:
- I Do It–We Do It Lesson Plan
- With these components:
  - Learning Objective
  - Advance Organiser
  - I Do It—Teacher Models
  - We Do It—Teacher and Students Together
  - You Do It—Guided Practice for Students
  - Apply It—Students Work Independently
  - Closure

Research-Based Teaching Moves:
- Explaining
- Giving Directions
- Modelling
- Reminding
- Guiding Practice
- Scaffolding
- Coaching
- Attributing
- Constructing Meaning
- Motivating–Connecting
- Recapping
- Annotating
- Assessing
- Facilitating
- Redirecting
- Affirming

Research-Based Presentation Techniques:
- Systematic Error Correction
- Judicious Use of Teacher Talk
- Signalling
- Wait Time
- Brisk Instructional Pace
- Motivational Reinforcement
- Cumulative Review and Practice
- Unison Responses
- Individual Checks

© 2009 Hawker Brownlow Education and Elaine McEwan-Adkins.

Figure 1.2: Research-based teaching moves.

Move	Description
Explaining	Providing verbal input about what will happen in a lesson, what the goals are, why it's being done, how it will help students, and what the roles of the teacher and students will be during the lesson
Giving directions	Providing unambiguous and concise verbal input that seeks to give students a way to get from where they are at the beginning of a lesson, task or unit to the achievement of a specific task or outcome; providing wait time for students to process directions, time for students to respond and opportunities to ask clarifying questions
Modelling	Thinking aloud regarding cognitive processing (for example, making connections with prior knowledge to something that is read in the text, showing how an inference was made and demonstrating how to write a summary)
Reminding	Causing students to remember or think about something they have been taught previously or restating in a different way something they have been taught previously so they will remember it
Guiding practice	Leading students through a supervised rehearsal of a skill, process or routine to ensure understanding, accuracy and automaticity
Scaffolding	Providing instructional support (for example, further explanation, modelling, coaching or additional opportunities to learn) at students' independent learning levels that enables students to solve problems, carry out tasks, master content and skills, or achieve goals that would otherwise be impossible without teacher support
Coaching	Asking students to think aloud; cueing them to choose strategies that have been taught (for example, cognitive strategies for monitoring, summarising or organising)
Attributing	Communicating to students that their accomplishments are the result of effort, wise decision making, attending to the task, exercising good judgment and perseverance, rather than their intelligence or ability
Constructing meaning	Working collaboratively with students to extract and construct multiple meanings from conversations, discussions and the reading together of texts
Motivating–connecting	Generating interest, activating prior knowledge and connecting instruction to the real world or the solution of real problems
Recapping	Summarising what has been concluded, learned or constructed during a given discussion or class period, as well as providing statements regarding why it is important and where it can be applied or connected in the future
Annotating	Adding additional information during the course of reading or discussion—information that students do not have but need to make sense of the discussion or text
Assessing	Determining both formally (through testing) and informally (through questioning) what students have learned and where instruction needs to be adjusted and adapted to achieve mastery
Facilitating	Thinking along with students and helping them develop their own ideas, rather than managing their thinking, explaining ideas and telling them what to do and how to do it
Redirecting	Monitoring the level of student attention and engagement and using a variety of techniques, prompts and signals to regain or redirect students' attention and focus on the learning task, transitioning students from one activity to another with minimal time loss
Affirming	Encouraging, praising or rewarding students' actions, attitudes, thinking processes, verbal statements and work products

Source: Adapted from Pressley, El-Dinary, Gaskins, et al., 1992.

Figure 1.3 contains a variety of what I call *proven presentation techniques*. They were developed, tested with students and refined for the power they demonstrated to improve student learning with the direct instruction curricula (Adams & Carnine, 2003), but they have made their way, in one form or another, into the repertoire of thousands of teachers. The techniques are particularly valuable when working with struggling students because they will help zero in with laser-like precision on the task or skill and the needs of the learner.

Figure 1.3: Proven presentation techniques.

Technique	Description
Systematic error correction	The teacher provides immediate corrective feedback to students by modelling the correct answer, guiding students to the correct answer as needed and then asking the corrected student to give the answer independently. The teacher then uses delayed testing by asking the student to repeat the correct answer later in the lesson.
Judicious use of teacher talk	The teacher presents the lesson in concise statements using language the students are able to understand. The teacher does not present information unrelated to the task the students are to complete or provide verbose explanations. Nor does the teacher distract herself (or her students) with comments unrelated to the lesson.
Signalling	The teacher gives a cue that tells the students when to respond. The cue can be visual (pointing to a letter or running a hand underneath a word), verbal ("Get ready") or auditory (a hand clap or pencil tap). The purpose of signalling is to give all students an opportunity to think about the answer to a question, thereby eliminating the calling out of answers by students who can retrieve answers more quickly.
Wait time	A thinking pause is provided by the teacher immediately after giving the directions. It lasts for as many seconds as the teacher feels are needed to give all students a chance to figure out the answer. Without the wait time, more advanced students will shout out the answer.
Brisk instructional pace	Keeping a "perky" pace is important to minimise the amount of time between activities and the amount of time between a student's answer and the teacher's next question or prompt. Students need to feel the energy to pay attention.
Motivational reinforcement	The teacher strengthens appropriate academic and social behaviours by using positive reinforcement. The teacher increases social behaviours (staying in seat, raising hand before talking, keeping hands to self) by delivering consistent praise for these behaviours. The goal is to maintain a 3:1 ratio of praise for appropriate behaviour to a correction of criticism for problem behaviour. The teacher also delivers reinforcement to peers who are displaying appropriate behaviour. For academic behaviours, the teacher adjusts the level of reinforcement to fit the difficulty level of the task.
Cumulative review and practice	The teacher maximises opportunities for practice by increasing the number of practice items and finding additional time during the school day for practice. The cumulative aspect of practice ensures that previously introduced skills are constantly included with new material during practice.
Unison responses	The teacher signals all students to answer together to maximise practice and regularly monitor student progress. The teacher asks questions of individual students as an additional check of progress only after the whole group is correctly answering all of the questions together.
Individual checks	After the teacher is assured that all students are answering correctly, he or she will then begin to check in with individual students to see if they can answer the question without the support of the group. If students cannot, the teacher will then go back to unison responding and practice to build confidence and avoid embarrassing the student.

Source: McEwan & Damer, 2000. An excellent summary of the research can be found in Adams & Carnine, 2003.

Figure 1.4 describes the attributes of effective instruction for students at risk. Average and above-average students are more able to compensate for ineffective instruction. Students at risk must have differentiated, explicit, systematic and supportive instruction in order to keep up with their average and above-average classmates. A little-known secret that I share from my own experience as a teacher, parent and primary school principal is that average and above-average students are also capable of achieving far more when they experience this type of instruction.

Figure 1.4: Attributes of effective instruction for students at risk.

Attribute	Description
Differentiated	**Specifically designed to match the different instructional needs of students with a variety of instructional approaches and programs** Differentiated instruction can only be provided if teachers have data from reliable assessments regarding students' specific needs. Although models are available that differentiate instructional approaches based on pathways to the brain (Sprenger, 1999), multiple intelligences (Gardner, 1983) or various learning styles (Gregorc, 1985; McCarthy, 1997; Sternberg, 1996), when differentiating in the context of teaching the core program, differentiation of student centres based on the task difficulty or reading level is advisable. However, differentiated instruction should focus on particular weaknesses of students who have failed to respond to whole-group instruction and need more explicit, systematic and supportive instruction in a small group—or, failing progress in the classroom, more intensive and specialised instruction outside the classroom.
Explicit	**Plain in language; distinctly expressed; clearly stated; not merely implied** Explicit instruction is characterised by conspicuous sequences of instruction (Dixon, Carnine, & Kame'enui, 1992). For example, adequate teacher modelling (I do it) should be used so students can see, hear and understand the task or the skill, and ample opportunities to practise with both group and teacher support (we do it) should be provided before moving to the final phase of the instructional sequence, when students demonstrate the task or skill on their own (you do it). Explicit instruction does not overload students' working memories with too much information or too many new skills at once. Explicit instruction gives students the time they need to elaborate, review, summarise or otherwise cognitively process new material to move it from short-term memory to long-term memory (Rosenshine, 1986). According to Torgesen (2005), nothing is left to chance; all skills are taught directly; student practice activities are carefully guided with "instructive" error correction; and practice activities are carefully engineered to produce mastery.
Systematic	**Characterised by the use of a method or plan** Systematic instruction is organised and sequential. The skills that are needed to become a fluent reader cannot be taught sporadically or planned on the spur of the moment.
Supportive	**To uphold by aid, encouragement or countenance; to keep from failing or declining** The educational version of support is called *scaffolding*. Scaffolding can be provided in many ways: further explanation, modelling, coaching, or additional opportunities to learn at students' independent learning levels. Scaffolded instruction enables students to solve problems, carry out tasks, master content and skills, or achieve goals that would be impossible without teacher modelling, prompting and support.

© 2009 Hawker Brownlow Education and Elaine McEwan-Adkins.

Background Knowledge

The teaching moves described in figure 1.2 include both teacher-centred moves (such as explaining, giving directions and reminding) and student-centred moves (such as constructing meaning, motivating–connecting and facilitating). The teacher-centred and student-centred instructional paradigms are not mutually exclusive. Both behaviourist and cognitive teaching models are essential in every classroom. However, when considering how to design instruction for struggling students, it is important to be aware of the special needs of students at risk and consider differentiated, explicit, systematic and supportive instruction as the most effective way to teach them all to read.

How to Design Lessons for Intervention Groups

As you design lessons for intervention groups, keep in mind that what is working for your average and above-average students may not create a climate of success for your struggling students. For example, suppose you have a small group of students who seem unable to grasp the concept of *main idea*. Think about how your original lesson may have missed the learning target for your struggling students. You may not have provided a clear definition of what a main idea is or modelled numerous times how to identify it. Perhaps you assumed that by year four or five, students knew how to find a main idea, so you gave an abbreviated lesson. Maybe you quickly mentioned "getting the gist", demonstrated with only one example that was ambiguous at best, expected only the most advanced students to answer your questions for fear of embarrassing your struggling students, and then assigned a year-level worksheet that was inaccessible to your students at risk and ESL students. Chances are, these struggling students lost you at the very beginning. Don't consider their blank stares a personal criticism of your teaching; you just have to make the lesson easier for everyone to understand.

Figure 1.5 shows a sample first lesson for teaching *main idea*. Note how carefully the teacher selects her words, how simple and student-friendly the definitions are, and how often the teacher expects students to simply repeat or write down something that is important to remember. The lesson contains repetition and choral responding to keep students engaged, and there is absolutely no extraneous teacher talk to confuse students. Second-language learners or students with reading disabilities can readily follow the lesson format and become more familiar with new vocabulary each time a choral response is required. Note also that the passage is easy to understand. Many of the intervention strategies in this book are based on similar lesson designs in which students are provided with increased opportunities to learn through teacher modelling and thinking aloud, unison responses to practise new learning and the teacher's high expectations. This is just the first in a series of main idea lessons, and it explains how to identify the main idea when it is not explicitly stated in the text. After several opportunities to write a main idea sentence with this type of short article, the teacher will transition to short stories in which the main idea is explicitly stated.

Sample Lesson for Teaching Main Idea

The upcoming sample lesson—as well as all of the sample lessons in this book—is designed to be used with a small intervention group that is struggling to keep up with the whole-group lessons in the core program. However, there may be some instances when your whole class could benefit from an intervention, and the sample lessons can be used that way as well. This lesson illustrates many of the presentation techniques described in figure 1.3.

Figure 1.5: Sample lesson for teaching the main idea.

Lesson Objective	Students will be able to write a short summary sentence that tells the main idea when reading text that does not explicitly state the main idea.
Advance Organiser	**Teacher Says:** Today we are going to learn a skill that will help you become a better reader. We will learn how to identify the main idea of a story.
Direct Explanation of Definitions	**Teacher Says:** The main idea tells about a whole story in just a few words. What is the main idea? **Students Say:** The main idea tells about a whole story in just a few words. **Teacher Says:** Every story has a main idea and details. The details are the different parts of the story. What are the details? **Students Say:** The details are the different parts of the story. **Teacher Does:** Write definitions for the terms *main idea* and *details* on the board, and students copy the definitions into their vocabulary notebooks. [AUTHOR'S NOTE TO TEACHER: *Main idea* and *details* are two important vocabulary words. Their definitions must be memorised.]
I Do It: Teacher Models Picking Out Details	**Teacher Does:** Put the story on the overhead. **Teacher Says:** First, I am going to read this short story and show you how to pick out the details in this story. **Teacher Does:** Read the story aloud while students follow. **Teacher Says:** Every year, drovers come to town and ride horses and rope calves. There is a big parade through the centre of town. The children wear their drover outfits to school.
Review of the Definitions	**Teacher Says:** First, I am going to pick out the details in this story. Details are the different parts of the story. What are details? **Students Say:** Details are the different parts of the story.
Teacher Models Picking Out the Details	**Teacher Says:** Read the first sentence with me. **Choral Reading:** Every year, drovers come to town and ride horses and rope calves. **Teacher Says:** "Every year, drovers come to town and ride horses and rope calves" is a detail. It tells only part of the story. Let's read the next sentence. **Choral Reading:** There is a big parade through the centre of town. **Teacher Says:** "There is a big parade through the centre of town" is a detail. It tells only part of the story. **Teacher Says:** Let's read the last sentence together. **Choral Reading:** The children wear their drover outfits to school. **Teacher Says:** "The children wear their drover outfits to school" is a detail. It tells only part of the story.

continued →

We Do It: Teacher and Students Pick Out Details Together	**Teacher Says:** What are details? **Students Say:** Details are different parts of the story. **Teacher Says:** Let's read the story and pick out the details together. Ready. First sentence: "Every year, drovers come to town and ride horses and rope calves." Tell me the first detail. **Students Say:** Every year, drovers come to town and ride horses and rope calves. **Teacher Says:** Let's read the second sentence: "There is a big parade through the centre of town." Tell me the second detail. **Students Say:** There is a big parade through the centre of town. **Teacher Says:** Let's read the last sentence: "The children wear their drover outfits to school." What's the last detail in this story? **Students Say:** The children wear their drover outfits to school.
Teacher Models Identifying the Main Idea and Writing a Main Idea Sentence	**Teacher Says:** Now I am going to show you how to identify the main idea. What is a main idea? **Students Say:** A main idea tells about the whole story in just a few words. **Teacher Says:** Right. Remember, a detail is never a main idea. So I have to look at the details and figure out what this story is about. To do that, I ask myself, "Who or what is being talked about in this story?" I can answer that question: "What is being talked about is a country festival." Next, I have to ask myself, "What is this story saying about a country festival?" One detail told me that the country festival happens every year when drovers come to town. I know that things that happen every year are important. Another detail told me that one of the activities was a parade. That tells me that when the festival is in town, people have lots of fun. Another detail told me that students get dressed up in their drover outfits to go to school. That tells me that everybody in the town is involved. Now that I have thought about all of the things the story said about a country festival, I am ready to identify the main idea in just a few words. I have to remind myself that the main idea tells about the whole story in just a few words and that the details are never the main idea. So I have to use my own words to identify the main idea. The story is about a country festival, so I'm going to start my main idea with the words *the country festival*. Then, I'm going to choose some other words that mean about the same thing as a country festival. The words *celebration* and *event* work. Then, I'm going to choose some words that describe or tell what a rodeo is like—words like *exciting*, *droving* and *yearly*. Now I'm going to connect all of those words to write a sentence that tells the story's main idea. **The country festival is an exciting, droving celebration that happens yearly in our town.**

Source: Baumann, 1984; Bursuck & Damer, 2007; Carnine, Silbert, Kame'enui, & Tarver, 2004; Dixon, Klau, Rosoff, & Conrad, 2002; Kame'enui, 1986; and personal communication with M. Damer, February 17, 2009.

INTERVENTION 2

Reducing Cognitive Load and Increasing Cognitive Processing (Years P–6)

> *Students understand and remember ideas better when they have to transform those ideas from one form to another. Apparently it is in this transformation process that the author's ideas become [the] reader's ideas, rendering them more memorable. Examined from a teacher's perspective, what this means is that teachers have many options to choose from when they try to engage students more actively in their own comprehension: summarising, monitoring, . . . engaging visual representation, and requiring students to ask their own questions all seem to generate learning.*
>
> —Pearson & Fielding (1991, p. 847)

This preventive intervention strategy provides ways to scaffold students' cognitive processing. Students at risk are often confused, frequently lose track of what is going on, and sometimes do not grasp key concepts or directions when they are explained the first time. These students often cannot keep up with the sheer quantity of words they hear spoken and rarely are willing to ask for clarification. Creative and spontaneous lessons may be entertaining, but they are not educational for students at risk. These students need predictable routines that have been practised past perfection.

Background Knowledge

Psychologist George Miller (1956) advanced a theory of working memory stating that we can hold only about seven (plus or minus two) thoughts in our working memories (the desktops of our mind) at the same time before we start to get confused or forget some of them. Because struggling students often have little prior knowledge to which they can attach new information, they need to work with fewer concepts at one time until they form solid concept maps in their long-term memories. So to improve student learning and retention, reduce the cognitive load.

Our soft-wired brains have what cognitive scientists call *activity-dependent neuroplasticity*. This means that you have the power to alter certain parts of your students' brains by giving them multiple opportunities during a lesson to actively engage those brains (Thernstrom, 2006). Cognitive processing involves writing, talking with classmates, asking and answering questions, visualising and then drawing pictures, role playing or acting out a process, building a model or constructing a graphic organiser. In the very beginning of learning to read, cognitive processing is simply giving oral responses to questions and prompts from the teacher.

Research-Based Learning Principles for Intervention Groups

Following are two important learning principles that, when consistently applied during intervention instruction, will result in increased learning as well as improved retention for your students: (1) reduce the cognitive load, and (2) increase the opportunities for cognitive processing by students.

Reduce the Cognitive Load

Cognitive load refers to the total amount of mental activity imposed on working memory at a specific instance in time (for example, a classroom period or a lesson). The determinant of the "weight" of a cognitive load is the number of elements that need to be remembered. Students do not automatically remember what they hear or read in your classroom as if recording it on a brain-based CD or DVD. What students remember depends more on what they already know than on what you tell them. If the capacity of the working memory (about seven plus or minus two different elements) is exceeded during instruction, some, if not all, of the essential information you have presented to students will either be confused or forgotten. Consider modifying your instruction in these ways:

- Present only one important concept or idea at a time. For example, use a short presentation segment (for example, fifteen minutes) to introduce a new topic, and then structure a five- to ten-minute processing break in which students can connect the new information to something they already know, ask their classmates or teacher questions about the concept, or jot down a few key notes (see figure 2.1, and figure 2.2; see Intervention 31).

- Introduce only one letter at a time when first teaching letter-sound relationships. (See Intervention 7.)

- Write only one critical concept on the board or overhead at a time.

- Carefully design handouts so all of the information the student needs to understand or to complete an assignment is on one page.

- Pass out only one piece of paper at a time.

- Give only one direction at a time, chunk directions or processes into smaller sections, or provide visual cues that go with each step (see figure 28.3 and figure 32.3 for charts that provide visual clues to use during the teaching of inference and summarising).

- Give upper-year level students a summary of what they will be reading in a new story or content unit. (See Intervention 39.)

Increase Cognitive Processing

Cognitive processing takes place in the brain. As teachers, we cannot know for certain what is happening in the brains of our students. Often, a seemingly disengaged student who is staring into space will make a spectacular contribution to the discussion. However, more often than not, very little appears to be going on inside students' heads. The following activities are designed to motivate or even "force" your students to take some kind of cognitive action with new learning. Bransford (1979) calls these processing activities in which learners engage "acquisition activities", and he made the following observation:

Many people speak of their poor memories. What do they mean? Are they limited by inferior "storage capacity" because of the makeup of their brain? . . . It is the types of processing activities performed at acquisition that are important for learning and remembering. As these acquisition activities are changed, the ability to remember follows suit. (p. 52)

Think-Pair-Share is a cooperative learning acquisition activity that leads students to process new information and make connections between prior learning and experiences and new learning. Figure 2.1 shows a sample lesson for teaching the Think-Pair-Share routine in the context of learning new vocabulary.

Once you have explained and modelled the Think-Pair-Share routine using the sample lesson, students will be ready to process a new word, concept or skill in just minutes. If your mission is covering the content, you may be tempted to skip the prerequisite lessons on working with partners and brainstorming or even skip these important processing breaks. You do so, however, at the risk of leaving your struggling students (and quite a few others) behind.

Sample Lesson for the Think-Pair-Share Routine

The Think-Pair-Share routine can be adapted for any classroom activity or lesson in which you want students to cognitively process newly introduced material or concepts. The beauty of this routine is that, once mastered by your students, you can transition to implementing it with a quick reminder: "Today we're going to use the Think-Pair-Share routine as we continue reading the story we started in class yesterday."

Figure 2.1: Sample lesson for using the Think-Pair-Share routine to process new vocabulary.

Lesson Objective	Students will learn a routine to work with partners to process new information, specifically new vocabulary words.
Materials Needed for the Lesson	You'll need copies of figure 2.2 for students and an overhead transparency for the teacher.
Advance Organiser	**Teacher Says:** To remember new vocabulary words, you need practice in reading, writing and talking about the words. Today we are going to use a process called Think-Pair-Share. You will work with a partner to write and talk about a new vocabulary word. I am going to teach you the steps to the Think-Pair-Share process so you can use it with other words or in other lessons.
I Do It: Teacher Models	**Teacher Does:** Put up the overhead transparency or slide you have created with figure 2.2, Think-Pair-Share Thinksheet. Choose a familiar word that students know well. **Teacher Says:** I'm going to model for you how the Think-Pair-Share routine works using the Think-Pair-Share Thinksheet. Who would like to be my partner for the modelling? **Teacher Does:** Choose a student who comes forward to the overhead or computer. Think aloud with the volunteer as you complete the following steps. 1. *Think:* Take one minute to think about examples of the word in your life. As you think aloud, write your ideas as well as the volunteer student's ideas on the transparency. Set the timer for sixty seconds.

continued →

I Do It: Teacher Models *(continued)*	2. *Pair:* Work with a student volunteer for ninety seconds. Set a timer to keep the modelling moving. Together, think of new examples, and take turns writing them on the transparency. At the end of ninety seconds, choose your three most accurate or unique examples by writing 1, 2 and 3 next to your choices. 3. *Share:* Work with the student volunteer to choose your favourite example. Share it with the class. Have a third student act as the teacher and record the example on the board. Explain that when the whole class is playing the game, everyone will share an example and they will choose two or three examples to write at the bottom of their form.
We Do It: Teacher and Students Work Together	**Teacher Does:** Choose a new vocabulary word. Have pairs of students work with you to complete the game following the steps you described and demonstrated during modelling. [You may be tempted to skip the We Do It step, believing that your students already understand the process. However, this is where many of us lose our students. Don't assume that because they have watched you do it that they are ready to do it independently. They need the We Do It step so they can try out the process under your watchful eye. After students have worked together with you, they may be ready to "play the game" on their own. However, make sure they can do so before you release the responsibility of following directions to them.]

Source: McEwan & Bresnahan, 2008b.

Figure 2.2: Sample Think-Pair-Share Thinksheet.

Word of the Day

Think

Think about the word. Take one minute to write as many sentences as you can showing that you know the meaning of the word.

Pair

Take ninety seconds to talk with a partner about your examples. Write new examples here.

Share

Review the examples with your partner. Rank the three most accurate or unique examples with the numbers 1, 2 and 3. Choose a favourite idea to share with the class. Share your idea. Listen as your classmates share their ideas.

Close

Choose two or three good examples from other pairs. Record them here.

Source: McEwan & Bresnahan, 2008b.

INTERVENTION 3

Practising Beyond Perfection (Years P–6)

It is difficult to overstate the value of practice. For a new skill to become automatic or for new knowledge to become long-lasting, sustained practice, beyond the point of mastery, is necessary.

—Willingham (2004)

This preventive intervention shows you how to design and deliver instruction in a primary classroom using differentiated learning centres and teacher-taught intervention groups. The goal of this *preventive* intervention is to provide the amount and type of practice that readers at risk require to become skilled readers.

Background Knowledge

Perhaps you have never thought of *practice* as an intervention. However, as Willingham (2004) reminds us in the epigraph, we vastly underestimate the amount of practice that many of our students at risk need to become skilled readers. Unfortunately, core (basal) programs do not provide nearly enough practice (opportunities to learn) for reading disabled or ESL students or students at risk. Typically after a skill is introduced, the teacher's guide assumes mastery and moves on to new material. Often the new skill may not reappear in another lesson for a week or more.

The students targetted for the Practising Beyond Perfection intervention need more intensive and immediate practice when a new skill is introduced. For example, when teaching *main idea* as shown earlier in figure 1.5, provide students with at least three opportunities daily to answer main idea questions, write a summary of a story or an article, or choose a title for a short story they have read each day for about three weeks (Carnine, Silbert, & Kame'enui, 1997). In highly effective schools where all students attain year level by the end of year three (95–98 per cent), recursive teaching and practise to beyond perfection are built into every school day (Fielding, Kerr, & Rosier, 2004, 2007; McEwan, 2008).

Effective primary teachers have always recognised the importance of practice but too frequently have relied on parents to provide it. Students at risk, however, may or may not have available and knowledgeable parents. That doesn't mean you should give up on reaching out to parents with expectations, training and encouragement for them to work with students at home. However, these students are largely dependent on you for the kind of intensive, daily practice with skills like segmenting, blending and decoding that they need to become skilled readers. It takes a special kind of teacher to design differentiated centres that keep students engaged at their appropriate levels in meaningful practice, while at the same time conducting small intervention groups for those students who need a little boost to stay on track. It takes "someone who is on top of, tuned in to, aware of and in control of three critical facets of classroom life: (1) the management and organisation of the classroom, (2) the engagement of the students and (3) the management of time" (McEwan, 2002, p. 48). Such a teacher can preview, project and predict the challenges and contingencies of an upcoming school year and proactively design a set of experiences that will prepare students for the rigours of mastering the content-area or year-level outcomes (McEwan, 2006).

The time that these teachers invest in developing and teaching routines to their students during the first days and weeks of school will reap rich returns in student learning. These "with it" teachers maximise academic learning by making good use of class time, while simultaneously providing interactive learning time (direct instruction in a small, targetted group) that is tailored to students' specific needs (Saphier & Gower, 1997).

Providing Practice in Intervention Groups and Differentiated Centres

Candace Darling, Michelle Judware and Darlene Carino comprise the year one team at Barringer Road School. They do almost everything together at school—except teach. Each one teaches a heterogeneous group of year ones. Their class sizes average about twenty each year. I asked them to describe how they differentiate centres in their classroom to make every minute count for teaching them all to read. Note the variety of ways that students are grouped for instruction and practice in their classrooms.

> We call the block of time when our students work independently at various centres based on the Big Five (phonemic awareness, phonics, fluency, vocabulary and comprehension) workshop time. We believe that a strong foundation in the Big Five will strengthen our students' overall reading ability, as well as allow them to become more independent in applying the strategies they have learned in our classrooms. We set up six or seven centres that remain constant for the entire year. As the year progresses, the intensity and expectations within those centres increase to meet the needs and levels of our students.

> Before a new school year begins, we plan a schedule for the introduction and teaching of each new centre, as they are introduced one at a time. The students are then taught the "procedures" for that particular centre. We use the I Do It-We Do It-You Do It" lesson plan to introduce each individual centre. [Most of the sample lessons you will find in the book are based on this format.] We look ahead to anticipate possible problems that might arise within a centre. We then do little skits that model the various ways that students might handle potential problems on their own without disturbing the teacher who is working with other students.

> Once we feel confident that our students understand the objectives of a centre and will be able to find independent success within that centre, we move on to introduce the next one. Once we have introduced a few centres, we allow the students to begin rotating through the centres taught thus far. We carefully observe the students as they are working to ensure they are making the most of the materials and activities. Once the students have been carefully taught all of the rules and routines, the centres are essentially child-managed while we work with students who need additional teacher-directed instruction. The secret to creating totally child-managed centres lies in spending enough time to thoroughly teach the routines and the rules of each centre.

> Following are the centres in our classrooms and examples of the activities in which students are engaged.

- ***Word Play Centre (ABC)***—Becoming fluent with reading sight words (a list derived from Open Court's high-frequency word list, some of which are decodable and some of which are high-frequency exception words), becoming proficient with writing that same list of sight words, practising spelling words and phrase wall phrases, and creating sentences using verbs, nouns and adjectives

- ***Listening Centre***—Developing listening skills, reinforcing print awareness and tracking, modelling reading fluency and expression, identifying details from the story, comprehending story elements, listening for enjoyment and working cooperatively

- ***B.E.A.R (Be Excited About Reading) Centre***—Reading on students' independent levels, learning how to choose appropriately levelled books, developing comprehension strategies and story elements, and reading with a partner to build fluency and expression

- ***Fluency/Performance Centre***—Reading and rereading Reader's Theatre scripts and poems; working with new vocabulary, parts of speech and sight words; performing in front of an audience; gaining exposure to various text genres; building listening skills; and working cooperatively

- ***Writing Centre***—Building phonics and phonemic awareness through the use of alliterative sentences, writing lists, writing complete sentences, practising writing skills, building ownership (author/illustrator) and staying on topic

- ***Computer Centre***—Building phonemic awareness skills, integrating technology into reading, developing listening skills, following directions and sequencing

- ***Traveller/Group Centre***—Teacher-directed centre based on the individual needs of students within the group

If we find that a centre or a certain activity is not working as planned, we simply stop everything and teach a minilesson. If all goes well, after a few days of rotation, we introduce more centres. Workshop time in our classrooms is at least an hour a day. If our schedules allow, we try to fit in more time. During this time the students rotate through two thirty-minute centres. We chart everything out to be sure that the majority of our students visit each centre at least one time per week. This workshop time also includes "Group Centre", which is a chance for all students to work in a small, teacher-directed group that is based on the specific instructional needs (whether above, below or at benchmark) of the students in the group. We use various assessments and classroom observations when planning for these groups. This time is also when our intervention students are pulled out for smaller, more individualised groups with the reading teacher. Because some of our students are out of the classroom for a thirty-minute period each day, they have less time to explore the centres within our classrooms. Therefore, we make sure that they go to the centres that target their areas of greatest need.

Each centre is differentiated. Because we form heterogeneous student groups for moving through the centres—with the exception of the teacher-directed Group Centre—each activity can be adapted to meet the individual needs of each student that visits that centre. For example, the B.E.A.R Centre is set up as a Library Centre where students choose books to read and discuss based on their Library Card/Bookmarks. These cards are colour-coded to the independent reading level of the student. For example, the yellow basket contains books that have one word per page with a corresponding picture clue. One student may be able to read from the green baskets, and another can read from the blue, yet both students can share their book choice [read it aloud for someone in their group after they have read it on their own] with anyone they choose. This gives less proficient and more proficient readers opportunities to work together and learn from each other. We make sure that each of our centres can easily be adapted for any student level, so students are able to differentiate for themselves in many cases.

At the Computer Centre, the programs are based on each individual's mastery of the taught skills. The computer will not allow them to move on until they have completed/mastered a specific task. The skills are also scaffolded.

In the Writing Centre, our expectations for the amount and quality of writing are dependent on students' writing skills to that point. We always pair a more advanced writer with a less-advanced writer so they can help and learn from each other. This allows us (the teachers) to have two thirty-minute sessions of completely uninterrupted group time with small groups of students at various levels.

We use a wide variety of materials when planning for our centres. Some of our materials are purchased, but most activities are developed from ideas we have read about, adapted, or created, based on our professional development. Each summer, we sit down as a team and discuss what worked well during the past year and then decide what centres we need to change for the upcoming year. We bounce ideas off one another and incorporate things we have learned from our "summer reading". Then as a team, we begin the setup of our centres. We try to have all materials—pencils, crayons, and so on—at students' fingertips and ready to go so there is no wasted time.

We teach almost the entire core program to all of our students now. We have used *Open Court Reading* [Adams & Bereiter, 2002] in our school for seven years and have learned to incorporate more and more of the core program into our school day. We definitely see a difference in our students' progress to higher reading levels when we can keep coming back to an important skill several times during each day. We feel that our core program fits in nicely with the Big Five previously mentioned. As with any purchased program, we tweak our core program instruction to meet our own students' needs, as well as our own teaching styles. If we feel that the core program is not spending enough time on something, then we add to it. If our students have mastered something else, then we may not spend much time on it at all. We have taken the core program and made it our own. We are not teaching a program; we are teaching our students. We create an atmosphere that allows us to differentiate the lesson by using a variety of questioning techniques. After the core lesson has been taught to the whole group, we use the thirty-minute Group Centre to reteach, modify or extend to the next level for all of our students. We also try to fit in "booster moments" throughout the day where we may grab a student and read with him or her or do a five-minute minilesson with two to three other students.

© 2009 Hawker Brownlow Education • SOT4749

INTERVENTION 4

Teaching Task Engagement, Time Management and Self-Control (Years P–2)

Where there is harmony in the classroom environment,
there is order among the students.

Where there is order among the students,
there is learning in their minds.

—Chinese proverb (paraphrased by McEwan-Adkins)

This intervention is *preventive* in nature. It teaches primary students how to attend to and learn various instructional and organisational routines that are essential for maximising time for student learning. The sheer magnitude of teaching all students to read in P–2 classrooms requires that students pay close attention during instruction, use time wisely during child-managed periods of the Reading Block (for example, differentiated centres), and consistently follow classroom routines and rules.

Background Knowledge

Researchers who have investigated the relationship between reading failure and behavioural problems such as poor task engagement and lack of self-control have found that children with reading problems in year one were significantly more likely to display behaviour problems in year three. Conversely, students with attention difficulties in year one were more likely to have reading difficulties in year three (Morgan, Farkas, Tufis, & Sperling, 2008). The importance of teaching students rules, routines and rubrics *before* beginning to teach them to read cannot be overstated. A substantial body of research shows that the following beginning-of-the-year instructional practices are associated with increased student achievement (Emmer, Evertson, & Anderson, 1980):

- The teacher establishes clear routines and expectations.
- The teacher rehearses with the students the behaviours that match those expectations.
- The teacher ensures high levels of time on the task.

Sample Lessons for Teaching Classroom Routines

Teaching routines to primary students is essential to maximising their time on task and, ultimately, their learning. Just ahead you will find two examples for doing this: (1) an experienced and highly effective prep teacher's description of how she explicitly teaches her students how to attend and exercise self-control during reading instruction; and (2) a sample lesson for teaching a transition routine during the reading block in year two that is adaptable to any year level.

Getting Prep Students Ready to Learn

Paula Larson, a prep teacher in a high-poverty school in an urban area, believes that getting her students ready to learn how to read begins with high expectations, as described next.

> Teachers must believe that five-year-olds (or students of any age) can sit and wait for their turn, listen to others and keep their bodies still for a full twenty to thirty minutes. I keep my expectations extremely high to have the results I do. Teachers must remember that if students are not attending, they are not processing the information and skills being taught. It is impossible to talk and listen at the same time, so I am really tough on my students. I nail them the first time they start squirming. But I also shower them with praise when they get it right.
>
> I teach three nonnegotiable and consistently enforced rules to my students:
>
> 1. *When I am talking, you are not.* I ask my students to repeat that sentence with me often until they reach the point of automaticity. When I say, "When I am talking, you are . . . ", they answer, "Not."
>
> 2. *Sitting tall.* Most of my instruction takes place while students are sitting on the carpet. Rather than listing all of the things I want students to do while they're on the carpet, I teach them exactly what I mean by the phrase "sitting tall". It means: folded legs, hands in lap, mouths closed, eyes on me and leave your shoelaces alone. Once I have modelled, we practise and once they have mastered "sitting tall", all I need to say at the beginning of a lesson or as a reminder is, "Sitting tall".
>
> 3. *Quiet hands.* I explain to my students that they can only answer a question if I call on them, and that in order for me to call on them, I must see what I call *quiet hands*. Quiet hands are hands that are raised without students talking at the same time. I explain and model, and we practise how that works until they have it. I cannot and will not call on someone who does not have a quiet hand. In the beginning my students say what they want to say the minute they put their hands in the air. I stop them. I remind them. Then I call on a student who is doing the right thing. I make positive comments about that student doing the right thing. And then the very next person I always call on is the student who was talking out of turn earlier. I praise that student profusely for using a quiet hand.
>
> This process takes some time in the beginning of the year, but far less time than you might expect if you are consistent. I often say this during a question-and-answer time: "With a quiet hand, who can tell me what the setting of this story is?" Then I have communicated the expectation at the beginning, rather than taking time from the lesson.

Teaching Primary Students How to Transition Between Activities

Highly effective teachers maximise the amount of time they have for instruction by teaching their students a routine for moving from one area of the classroom to another. Once mastered, this routine saves time and minimises student disruptions. Figure 4.1 is a sample lesson for teaching year two students how they can return quickly and quietly to their desks after they have been in the computer centre or on the rug.

© 2009 Hawker Brownlow Education • SOT4749

Figure 4.1 Sample lesson for teaching a transition routine.

Lesson Objective	Students will be able to return to their desks when they leave the computer centre or rug with no noise and in less than five seconds.
Advance Organiser	**Teacher Says:** Boys and girls, today we're going to learn how year twos return to their desks when they leave the computer centre or the rug.
I Do It: Teacher Models—Part I	**Teacher Says:** What would happen if I weren't careful and ran to my desk? **Teacher Does:** Model the nonexample by showing students what it *doesn't* look like and then discuss some of the outcomes with students: It wouldn't be polite; it wouldn't be safe; someone could get hurt. **Teacher Says:** That's why it's important to learn a better way. Let me show you. **Teacher Does:** Stand up and without talking or touching anyone, go to sit at his or her desk. **Teacher Says:** Think about what you saw. **Teacher Does:** Go back and discuss with students what they observed: It was quiet. The teacher walked. Everyone was safe.
You Do It: One Student Models	**Teacher Says:** Andy, will you show everyone how you can stand up and, without talking or touching anyone, walk straight to your desk? **Teacher Does:** Compliment Andy as he models, and bring everyone's attention to the key points that have already been mentioned (and any others that are pertinent).
You Do It: More Students Model	**Teacher Says:** Brianna and Chris, will you show everyone how you can stand up and, without talking or touching anyone, walk straight to your desks from the rug? **Teacher Does:** Compliment them as they model and comment on the key points.
You Do It: Small Group Models	**Teacher Says:** Table Group 1, show us how you can stand up and, without talking or touching anyone, walk straight to your desks. **Teacher Does:** Again compliment them as they model and reinforce the important points.
You Do It: Whole Class Models	**Teacher Says:** You are doing a terrific job. Now let's see if the rest of you can do it as quietly as the others did. Stand up and, without talking or touching anyone, walk straight to your desks. **Teacher Does:** Practise it here, although the whole group would rarely leave the rug at once to avoid unnecessary traffic jams.
Feedback	**Teacher Does:** Provide specific feedback to teach and/or correct behaviour, and is enthusiastic and positive. If someone doesn't follow the procedure correctly, the teacher assumes that he needs more practice.
Practice	**Teacher Does:** Repeat the preceding steps (all or part) each time the routine is used until it is mastered. The teacher repeats the preceding steps occasionally throughout the year to review, for consistency, and when new students are in the class. The teacher also playfully practises the routine with a stopwatch to determine students' best time.
Reflections	**Teacher Does:** Choose an appropriate group time to reflect with students about the routine and remind them of the reason for the routine. **Teacher Says:** Who remembers why we need a routine for going to our desks from the rug? Is it working? **Teacher Does:** Discuss and listen for suggested improvements from students.

Source: Adapted from McEwan, 2004.

Part 2

Interventions for Building Phonemic Awareness

What the Research Says About Phonemic Awareness Instruction

The words *phonemic* and *phonological* are often used interchangeably, but technically, *phonological awareness* is a more encompassing concept that includes all levels of the speech sound system, including words, syllables, rhymes and phonemes (Moats, 2000). Think of phonological awareness as an umbrella and the various levels of the speech system as its spokes.

The U.S. National Institute of Child Health and Human Development (2000) reviewed multiple experimental and quasiexperimental studies of phonemic awareness instruction in skills such as blending and segmentation, and they reported positive effects on reading, spelling and phonological development, not only for students at risk but for average learners as well (Ball & Blachman, 1991; Byrne & Fielding-Barnsley, 1989; Cunningham, 1990; Lie, 1991; Lundberg, Frost, & Peterson, 1988; O'Connor, Jenkins, & Slocum, 1993; Torgesen, Wagner, & Rashotte, 1997; Vellutino & Scanlon, 1987).

In a comparison of studies conducted with P–2 students who were severely at risk, those programs with a literacy focus—that is, explicit instruction in phonemic awareness and decoding—yielded an estimated mean effect size between approximately three and a half to four times larger than those for studies that did not use a literacy-focused curriculum (National Early Literacy Panel, 2008).

Before you implement either of the two phonemic awareness strategies in Part 2, make sure that you have data from a reliable and valid assessment instrument to inform your decision. Such data can help you in targeting specific students as well as in making needed adjustments to the sample lessons that are provided. As you implement, informally assess the individual students in your group on specific skills as part of every lesson to adjust instruction for the next day. Also, give the regular curriculum-based progress-monitoring tests to collect more definitive data. If needed, schedule more instructional time or decrease the size of an intervention group.

INTERVENTION 5

Blending Sounds to Make Words (Years P–1)

> *Because auditory skills do not require knowledge of the letter-sound correspondences and do not require students to look at written letters (graphemes) or words, instruction on these skills can begin on the first day [of school], before any letter-sound correspondences have been introduced.*
>
> —Carnine, Silbert & Kame'enui
> (1997, p. 63)

This intervention strategy suggests alternative ways to give students more explicit and direct instruction, along with intensive practice in blending sounds into words than is generally found in most core programs. Mastering this skill is an important step toward building reading fluency. Once you and your students master the practice routines found in these lessons, you can readily return to them throughout the school day to provide short additional practice sessions for struggling students. Such short additional sessions can occur during periods of time spent waiting for special teachers, a call to an assembly on the intercom or a bathroom break. Two sample lessons are provided: one for blending individual sounds and one for blending continuous sounds. The sample lessons include teacher modelling, scaffolded practice and an opportunity for teachers to do immediate assessment on individual students.

Background Knowledge

Most reading programs teach segmenting and blending by having students pause between each of the segmented sounds. Bursuck and colleagues (2004) found that teaching students to pause between each of the sounds—a common instructional approach in most core programs—works well for the majority of students. However, Weisberg, Savard and Christopher (1993) found that some students at risk find blending the distinct sounds after a pause to be very difficult. Chard and Osborn (1999) recommend modifying your instruction to a stretching and connecting approach to blending. For example, if one or more students omit the initial consonant when blending together the sounds of a word—for example, saying "ad" instead of "sad"—they will benefit from an alternative instructional approach. This is variously called *continuous blending*, *stretching and connecting*, or *telescoping*. They are the same in that students do not pause between the sounds as they say them but stretch and connect the sounds—for example, stretching the word *sad* out as /sssaaaddd/ just before saying the word fast.

Sample Lessons for Blending Sounds

This section contains two sample lessons for use in small intervention groups. The focus skill is learning how to blend individual sounds so students can say (and eventually read) a word fast.

The first lesson found in figure 5.1 shows students how to blend the individual sounds in a word in preparation for saying the word fast. Use it with students who can blend and say words without dropping their initial consonants.

Some of your students may be unable to consistently say a whole word fast without dropping sounds. In that case, another approach is needed. Figure 5.2 contains a sample lesson for showing students how to stretch out and keep the sounds connected before saying the word fast.

Figure 5.1: Sample lesson for blending individual sounds.

Lesson Objective	After hearing the teacher say three separate sounds, students will blend them together to say the word fast.
Advance Organiser	**Teacher Says:** Today we're going to practise blending sounds together to make a word. We are going to use the I Do It-We Do It-You Do It routine for our practice session.
I Do It: Teacher Models	**Teacher Says:** Let me remind you about how the routine works. First I'll say each of the individual sounds in a word. Then I'll say the word fast: /m/-/ŏ/-/p/; mop. The word is *mop*.
We Do It: Teacher and Students Respond in Unison	**Teacher and Students Say:** Ready. /m/-/ŏ/-/p/. What word? *Mop*.
You Do It: Students Respond in Unison Without Teacher Support	**Teacher Says:** Now it's your turn to do it without any help from me. Ready. What word? **Students Say:** /m/-/ŏ/-/p/. *Mop*. **Teacher Says:** Yes, the word is *mop*. Good work.
Individual Students Respond	**Teacher Says:** Individual turns. Olive, what word? **Olive Says:** /m/-/ŏ/-/p/. *Mop*. **Teacher Does:** Keep calling on all of the students in the group. If they make errors, correct the errors and go back to the Together portion of the lesson. Once all students have tested out on the first word, return to the beginning of the I Do It step and model several more words, going through the sequence once more.

Note: This brief routine should be used for intensive practice until all of your students can continuously blend the sounds in a word and then say it fast. The number of times you model blending a word together depends on how much difficulty your students are having. Only when all students are responding correctly should you move from modelling to doing it together and subsequently to testing out individual students. Bursuck & Damer (2007) recommend that for students who are having trouble holding words in their short-term memory, eliminate the "What word?" prompt and go straight to saying it fast. The I Do It-We Do It-You Do It routine will enable you to fit small practice sessions in more frequently as students will have mastered the routine and know precisely what both you and they are supposed to do.

Adapted from Bursuck & Damer, 2007; Carnine et al., 2004.

Figure 5.2: Sample lesson for stretching and connecting sounds during blending.

Lesson Objective	Students will be able to blend three continuous sounds together and say a word fast.
Advance Organiser	**Teacher Says:** Today, we are going to do an activity called Stretchy Words. It's another way to blend sounds to make words. I have something in my hand that is going to help me stretch my words. **Teacher Does:** Show students a rubber band, one with lots of stretch so as not to endanger yourself or your students. **Teacher Says:** We are going to use the I Do It-We Do It-You Do It routine to stretch our words. We have used that routine before. First, I show you how to do it. Then we do it at the same time. Then, all of you do it on your own. **Teacher Says:** After you watch what I do with my rubber band, you can pretend to stretch your rubber band as you say each word.
I Do It: Teacher Models	**Teacher Says:** Let me show you how it works. First I'm going to say the word. *Mop.* Then I'm going to stretch out the sounds. /mmmoooppp/. **Teacher Does:** Stretch out a rubber band as you continuously sound out the word. **Teacher Says:** Then I'm going to say the word fast. *Mop.* **Teacher Does:** Quickly bring the rubber band back to its original size before the stretching.
We Do It: Teacher and Students Respond in Unison	**Teacher Says:** Together. Stretch *mop.* **Teacher and Students Say:** /mmmoooppp/. *Mop.* (Students should stretch out their pretend rubber bands as they continuously sound out the word. When the teacher gives the signal, they "retract" their rubber bands and say the word fast as the teacher models with the rubber band.)
You Do It: Students Respond in Unison Without Teacher Support	**Teacher Says:** Now do it on your own. Stretch *mop.* **Students Say:** /mmmoooppp/. *Mop.* (Students answer chorally without your support as they stretch out their imaginary rubber bands and then say the word *mop* fast as they bring their imaginary rubber bands back to their original positions.)
	Note: This brief routine should be used for intensive practice until all of your students can continuously blend the sounds in a word and then say it fast. The number of times you practise a word together depends on how much difficulty your students encounter with the process. Only when all students are responding correctly should you move on to testing out individual students.

Source: Adapted from Bursuck & Damer, 2007; Carnine et al., 2004.

INTERVENTION 6

Segmenting Words Into Sounds (Years P–1)

> *The most important insight of modern reading research has been the recognition that phonics instruction may not "take" with young readers unless they are aware of the segments of speech represented by the graphemes used to spell words in an alphabetic writing system.*
>
> —Moats (2006, p. 3)

This intervention strategy provides students with more intensive instruction and guided practice in *segmentation*: saying the individual sounds (phonemes) after hearing the word spoken at a normal rate. The sample lessons provide direct instruction and teacher modelling, along with scaffolded practice in breaking words apart into their separate sounds, beginning with the initial sound and then moving on to segmenting words containing up to four phonemes.

Background Knowledge

When the term *phonemic awareness* became part of the vocabulary of early reading instruction, teachers spent a great deal of time on phonemic skills like rhyming and sound substitution and deletion. After a decade of experience with phonemic awareness instruction, we now know that these activities do not provide the kind of instruction and intensive practice that students at risk need. Blending and segmentation are the most important skills for students to master.

Sample Lessons for Teaching Segmenting

Here are two sample lessons, one for segmenting the first sound of a word (figure 6.1) and one for segmenting the individual phonemes in a word (figure 6.2,). Figure 6.3 shows a sound-counting routine to give students another way to keep track of their sounds.

© 2009 Hawker Brownlow Education • SOT4749

Figure 6.1: Sample lesson for teaching initial sound segmentation.

Lesson Objective	Students will be able to say the initial sound in words they hear the teacher say.
Advance Organiser	**Teacher Says:** I have a mystery word written on the board. To read it, we need to know what the first sound is. To do that, we're going to use the I Do It-We Do It-You Do It routine. First I do it; then we do it together; and then all of you will have a turn on your own. When I want you to say the sound, I'll raise my pointer finger. Like this. **Teacher Does:** Show the signal.
I Do It: Teacher Models	**Teacher Says:** It's my turn. The first sound in *mop* is /m/.
We Do It: Teacher and Students Respond in Unison	**Teacher Says:** Together. The first sound in *mop*? **Teacher Does:** Signal to the students. **Teacher and Students Say:** /m/. **Teacher Says:** Yes.
You Do It: Students Respond in Unison Without Teacher Support	**Teacher Says:** Your turn. The first sound in *mop*? [Signal.] **Students Say:** /m/. **Teacher Says:** Yes, /m/.
Individual Students Respond	**Teacher Says:** Individual turns. The first sound in *mop*? Stacy? **Teacher Does:** Signal Stacy. **Stacy Says:** /m/. **Teacher Says:** Yes, /m/. The first sound in *mop*? Kim? **Teacher Does:** Signal Kim. **Keesha Says:** /m/. **Teacher Says:** Yes, /m/.

Note: Use this lesson for teaching initial sound segmentation to an intervention group that needs extra practice. Keep the pace brisk to maintain students' attention. Don't stop for extraneous teacher talk or comments other than brief words of praise and encouragement. To vary the lesson practice, use different words with the same initial sound and then move on to using words with different initial sounds.

Source: Adapted from Bursuck & Damer, 2007; Carnine et al., 2004.

Figure 6.2: Sample lesson for teaching whole word segmentation.

Lesson Objective	Students will be able to segment the sounds in three-letter words after hearing the teacher say the word.
Advance Organiser	**Teacher Says:** I have a mystery word written on the board. To read it, we need to know all of the sounds we hear in this word. To do that, we're going to use the I Do It-We Do It-You Do It routine. First I do it; then we do it together; and then all of you will have a turn on your own. When I want to begin saying the sounds in this word, I'll raise my pointer finger, like this. **Teacher Does:** Show the signal to the students. **Teacher Says:** As I say each sound, I'll raise another finger [show signal]. (See figure 6.3, for the counting routine.)
I Do It: Teacher Models	**Teacher Says:** It's my turn. Take apart *mop*. /m/ [raise pointer finger]; /o/ [raise middle finger]; /p/ [raise ring finger]. The sounds in *mop* are /m/-/o/-/p/.
We Do It: Teacher and Students Respond in Unison	**Teacher Says:** Together. Take apart *mop*. **Teacher Does:** Signal to students. **Teacher and Students Say:** /m/ [teacher and students raise their pointer fingers]; /o/ [teacher and students raise their middle fingers]; /p/ [teacher and students raise their ring fingers].
You Do It: Students Respond in Unison Without Teacher Support	**Teacher Says:** Your turn. Take apart *mop*. **Students Say:** /m/ [all students raise their pointer fingers.]; /o/ [all students raise their middle fingers]; /p/ [all students raise their ring fingers]
Individual Students Respond	**Teacher Says:** Individual turn. Take apart *mop*. Stacy? **Teacher Does:** Signal to Stacy. **Stacy Says:** /m/ [Stacy raises her pointer finger]; /o/ [Stacy raises her middle finger]; /p/ [Stacy raises her ring finger]. **Teacher Says:** Magnificent! I won't ask you to take apart magnificent. But I'll bet you can hear the first sound. /mmmm/.
Note: This brief routine should be used for intensive practice until all of your students can segment the sounds in a word. The number of times you do a word together depends on how much difficulty your students are having. In a small intervention group, test all students individually every day. If you have a few moments, pull aside those students who are having difficulty and practise with them during the day. Use figure 6.3 as a model for sound counting. The counting routine can also be used with any sound-counting games you may have your students play for extra practice.

Adapted from Bursuck & Damer, 2007; Carnine et al., 2004, 2007.

Figure 6.3: Sound-counting routine.

Sound #1	Sound #2	Sound #3
/s/	/a/	/t/

Source: Adapted from Bursuck & Damer, 2007.

To master the presentation techniques found in the sample lessons, practise them on your own or with year-level teammates who may also be learning the techniques until you feel relaxed and natural using them. They may seem awkward and too prescriptive, but research shows that the routine, the frequent opportunities for responses and the brisk pace achieve remarkable results with students at risk (Adams & Carnine, 2003). Once you and your students have fine tuned the routines, you will find that teaching and practising are much more relaxing than they were previously. Every student is on task and successful, and virtually no time is wasted.

When all of your students have responded correctly several times, with both your support and their peers' (watch and listen for errors), then call on individual students. If students have difficulty with individual responses, return immediately to the I Do It-We Do It-You Do It format to give students more supportive practice. When students make errors, immediately correct them using the error correcting routine found in figure 6.4. A routine differs from a lesson in that it teaches a specific procedure that is always executed in the same way. Your goal is to make it a habit for you and your students. Use this error-correcting routine immediately to eliminate the possibility of students mastering the wrong thing. The routine is only used when students make errors.

Figure 6.4: Error correcting routine for whole-word segmentation.

Individual Turn	**Teacher Says:** Take apart *mop*.
Student Response	Jonathan is confused and says /n/ instead of /m/.
I Do It: Teacher Models Again	**Teacher Says:** Listen. /m/ [teacher raises pointer finger]; /o/ [teacher raises middle finger]; /p/ [teacher raises ring finger].
We Do It: Teacher and Student Respond	**Teacher and Jonathan Say:** /m/ [teacher and Jonathan raise pointer fingers]; /o/ [teacher and Jonathan raise middle fingers]; /p/ [teacher and Jonathan raise ring fingers]. **Teacher Says:** Yes. /m/-/o/-/p/. Now take apart *mop*.
You Do It: Individual Student	**Jonathan Says:** /m/-/o/-/p/.

Sources: Adapted from Bursuck & Damer, 2007; Carnine et al., 1997.

Part 3

Interventions for Building Word Identification Skills

What the Research Says About Word Identification Instruction

Becoming a skilled reader with a large repertoire of *sight words* (words that have been decoded a sufficient number of times to become words that are recognised in under one second by the reader) requires knowledge of phonemic segmentation, letter-sound correspondences and spelling patterns (Ehri, 1980, 1995, 1998; Rack, Hulme, Snowling, & Wightman, 1994; Reitsma, 1983; Share, 1999). The belief that children can become fluent readers only if they learn to skip words, sampling the visual information in text to support their hypotheses about its meaning, is erroneous. According to this belief, teachers are supposed to encourage guessing about words to help children become free from their so-called bondage to print. With skilled guessing, students can make it to about year four before their guessing catches up with them.

In fact, the understanding of skilled reading that emerges from the past twenty years of scientific research is, again, just the *opposite* of the view of skilled readers as word skippers. Two important facts about the way that skilled readers process text are relevant to this new understanding. The first is that skilled readers fixate on, or look directly at, almost every word in the text as they read (Rayner & Pollatsek, 1989). Skilled readers read rapidly, not because they selectively sample words and letters as they construct the meaning of text but because they read the individual words rapidly and with little effort. They have solid visual representations of how words are spelled stored in their long-term memories. Researchers call them orthographic images or mental orthographic images (MOIs) to emphasise the fact that each letter of a word is fixed in the brain. We will use the term *mental orthographic image* throughout the book to refer to the visualisation of correctly spelled words that students have fixed in their long-term memories.

A key piece of knowledge here, and the second important fact relevant to our understanding of skilled reading, is that good readers use information about *all* the letters in the words, even when they recognise them at a single glance (Just & Carpenter, 1987; Patterson & Coltheart, 1987). Because many words are differentiated from one another by only one or two letters, a global, or gestalt, image of a word is not sufficient to help recognise it reliably. Instead, the mental orthographic images used in reading words by sight must include information about all, or almost all, of the letters in a word. Even when reading very rapidly, the good reader extracts information about all of the letters in a word as part of the recognition process.

The best way to bring students at risk to the point of fluent year-level reading is not a debatable topic. They must initially have differentiated, explicit, systematic, supportive instruction in how to identify (that is, read) words—regular words, irregular words and more advanced multisyllabic words. They must have access to texts at their independent level and be able to enjoy a variety of interesting texts on a daily basis—texts they have selected, as well as scaffolded reading in instructional texts their teachers have chosen—to give them the opportunity to learn from a broad range of genres and content areas.

Before you implement any of the word identification intervention strategies in part 3, "Interventions for Building Word Identification Skills", make sure that you have data from a reliable and valid assessment instrument to inform your decision. Such data can help you in targeting specific students as well as in making needed adjustments to the sample lessons that are provided. As you implement, informally assess the individual students in your group on specific skills as part of every lesson to adjust instruction for the next day. Also, give the regular curriculum-based progress-monitoring tests to collect more definitive data. If needed, be open to scheduling more time or decreasing the size of an intervention group to bring students to mastery.

INTERVENTION 7

Mastering Letter-Sound Correspondences (Years P–1)

Teachers working with struggling readers must know and be able to pronounce the sounds that are most commonly associated with letters and combinations of letters.

—Cooper, Chard, & Kiger (2006, p. 56)

This intervention provides several sample lessons for directly teaching, reviewing and practising the letter-sound correspondences that students must master to read "regular" words. Regular words are those that can easily be decoded using the letter-sound correspondences. They follow all of the rules, and once students have mastered the most common one-to-one letter-sound correspondences, the more quickly they can begin to engage in real reading on their own.

Background Knowledge

The term *letter-sound correspondence* means how a particular sound is represented either by a single letter or by a cluster of two or more letters. The word *relationship* is sometimes used in place of the word *correspondence,* but the meaning is the same. Learning to read is a mapping process in which students recognise a letter, map a sound they have learned to that letter, and then produce the sound, orally at first and silently later on. In the beginning, it is a multistep process. Once students have decoded a word several times, all of this information is stored in long-term memory to be retrieved instantly whenever the student encounters the word again. The goal of teaching letter-sound correspondences is to enable students to independently decode words and eventually be able to identify words in under one second.

In the field of reading instruction, you will also encounter the term *sound-letter correspondence*. When the words *sound* and *letter* are reversed, the meaning changes—from reading to spelling. Knowing what letter or combination of letters correspond to one of the forty-four phonemes or sounds of the English language enables students to do just the opposite of reading: spelling. *Decoding* is the process used to read words. *Encoding* is the process used to spell words. Spelling and reading sound pretty simple when you think in terms of just twenty-six letters and forty-four sounds.

If you are curious as to the precise identity of those forty-four sounds, figure 7.1 displays the twenty-five consonant sound–spelling correspondences, and figures 7.2–7.5 show the nineteen vowel sound–spelling correspondences in four different categories (long vowels, short vowels, diphthongs and long and short /oo/, and *r*-controlled vowels). Note that the sounds represented by the letters are found in the first column, the letters (spellings) in the second column and some sample words in the third column. Most of the major published reading series and many phonics programs begin instruction with the most common letter–sound relationships: a few consonants and a couple of the easiest vowels.

© 2009 Hawker Brownlow Education • SOT4749

Figure 7.1: Consonant sound–spelling correspondences.

Sound	Spelling	Sample Words	Sound	Spelling	Sample Words
/s/*	[s]	sat, sit	/k/**	[k]	kid, key
	[c]	cent, city		[c]	cup, cake
/m/*	[m]	mat, miss him, hum	/v/*	[v]	vet, vim
/t/**	[t]	tonne, tin hat, cat	/w/*	[w]	wit, will
/f/*	[f]	fit, fat	/z/*	[z]	zoo, zebra quiz, whiz
	[ph]	phone, phonics			
/b/*	[b]	bat, bit cab, fib	/y/*	[y]	yell, yes
/r/*	[r]	rat, run far, sir	/ch/	[ch]	chip, church
/n/*	[n]	not, net can, tan	/sh/	[sh]	sheep, shine
/p/**	[p]	pit, pet cap, cup	/si/ /su/	[zh]	adhesion, Asia, casual
/d/**	[d]	dog, dot rid, had	/th/	[th]	the
/h/**	[h]	hand, hit	/th/	[th]	thing
/g/**	[g]	girl, got	/wh/	[hw]	wheat, where
/j/**	[j]	jet, jam	/ng/	[ng]	ring
	[g]	giraffe, gem			
/l/*	[l]	let, loan pail, soul			

Note: The consonants c, q and x can be represented by two phonemes and are not included in this chart.

*Continuous sounds are indicated with a single asterisk. **Stop sounds are indicated with two asterisks.

Source: Chall & Popp, 1996; McEwan, Nielsen & Edison, 2008; Spalding & North, 2003.

Figure 7.2: Long vowel sound–spelling correspondences.

Sound	Spelling	Sample Words	Sound	Spelling	Sample Words
/ā/	[a]	make, made, gate	/ō/	[o]	yoke, pole, cone
/ē/	[e]	need, these, Pete	/ū/	[u]	music, you
/ī/	[i]	nice, bike, line			

Source: Chall & Popp, 1996; McEwan, Nielsen, et al., 2008; Spalding & North, 2003.

Figure 7.3: Short vowel sound–spelling correspondences.

Sound	Spelling	Sample Words	Sound	Spelling	Sample Words
/ă/	[a]	at, apple cat, can	/ŏ/	[o]	on, ox hot, hog
/ĭ/	[i]	it, in, hit	/ŭ/	[u]	up, us cup, bug
/ĕ/	[e]	egg, end leg, met			

Source: Chall & Popp, 1996; McEwan, Nielsen, et al., 2008; Spalding & North, 2003.

Figure 7.4: Sound-spelling correspondences of diphthongs and long and short /oo/.

Sound	Spelling	Sample Words	Sound	Spelling	Sample Words
Three Dipthongs			Long and Short /ōŏ/ Sounds		
/au/	[au] [aw]	Paul crawl	/ōō/	[ōō]	moon
/ou/	[ou] [ow]	house cow	/ŏŏ/	[ŏŏ]	book
/oi/	[oi] [oy]	noise toy	A diphthong is a combination of two vowels, each with two different spellings.		

Source: Chall & Popp, 1996.

Figure 7.5: Sound-spelling correspondences of *r*-controlled vowels.

Sound	Spelling	Sample Words	Sound	Spelling	Sample Words
/ər/*	[er] [ir] [ur] [yr]	her, fern, germ bird, first, sir hurt, burst, nurse martyr	/är/	[ar]	ark, car, hard, part
			/or/	[or]	cork, cord, fort
*The schwa *r* sound is spelled four ways.			/air/	[air]	fair, chair, hair

Source: Chall & Popp, 1996.

Your initial goal as a reading educator is to bring your students to an understanding of the alphabetic principle: the concept that letters, either singly or in combination, represent various sounds. Without an understanding of the alphabetic principle, automatic and accurate word identification is impossible.

Although comprehension is our ultimate goal, before students can comprehend text, they must come to understand that different letters may represent the same sound or that one letter may represent different sounds. In order to accomplish this goal, teachers need a system or a method. Therein lies the secret to meeting the needs of students at risk: teaching students to read must involve a systematic approach.

© 2009 Hawker Brownlow Education • SOT4749

The intervention strategies in this section assume that your core program began with introducing students to the one-to-one *letter-sound correspondences,* focusing on the most common sounds and spellings first. If you have not approached your beginning reading instruction with an organised and systematic plan, that might very well be the reason your students at risk are failing to learn. Before you use this intervention, determine whether the instructional sequence of your core or phonics program might account for any of the difficulties your student(s) are having with mastering the letter-sound relationships (Carnine et al., 1997). If you answer *no* to any of the following questions, your struggling students may simply be confused by the lack of explicit, systematic and supportive instruction that provides ample amounts of practice and cumulative review.

- Have *you* mastered the sound-spelling correspondence you are teaching your students? If you have not tested your own sound-spelling knowledge with an expert, your lack of solid knowledge, hesitations or mispronunciations when you model the sounds for students may be confusing them. Sit down with the speech pathologist for a session on how to say the sounds.

- Have you intentionally planned instruction so as not to confuse students? Did you introduce the most useful letters before the less useful letters? Did you introduce the lowercase (small) letters before uppercase (capital) letters? Students at risk are easily confused when letters with similar sounds or visual appearances are introduced at the same time.

- Did you introduce only the most common sounds (such as the sounds heard in three-letter words like *sit* and *met*) when you began your instruction? If you are teaching the sounds without giving any consideration to which ones are most difficult to learn, you are placing an undue cognitive burden on your students at risk. Begin with the sounds that are the easiest to learn—for example, the continuous sounds like /s/ and /m/ and the two short vowels /a/ and /e/.

- Have you taught at least four or five continuous sounds before teaching any of the stop sounds? In figure 7.1, the consonants with continuous sounds are indicated with one asterisk. Continuous sounds, such as /m/ and /s/, can be sustained for a few seconds without changing to a different sound, and they are much easier to produce and learn. Stop sounds like /b/ and /d/ cannot be held and are thus more difficult to learn. Consonants with stop sounds are indicated with two asterisks in figure 7.1.

- Are you teaching the letter-sound correspondences one at a time in an explicit and direct way? Teaching sound-spelling correspondences in the context of literature may work for your average or above-average students. Students at risk, however, need to master individual letters with multiple opportunities for review and practice before going on to other letters. Of course, you should read stories aloud and do oral comprehension activities, but don't mix those activities with letter-sound instruction. Once students are reading sentences and passages, you will always focus on meaning.

- Does your instructional pace give students at risk an opportunity to master one letter before you introduce several more? Another potential source of difficulty for students at risk is the rate at which new letters are introduced. If you use the same instructional pace as that for average and above-average students, students at risk will likely get discouraged, sense your frustration and just give up.

- Have you introduced only one vowel at a time and provided extra practice time for the students at risk to master before moving on? A new vowel may be introduced if your students are having trouble with one or two consonants, but introducing a new vowel while students are still struggling with a vowel or vowels will only confuse and frustrate students at risk. Vowel sounds are the most difficult to learn because they sound so similar.

- Do you correct students' errors when they say a sound for another letter or distort the sound when they say it? Listening to students' oral responses and monitoring them for confusion or pronunciation errors are critical aspects of letter-sound instruction. If you immediately correct errors as you go along, your students will not waste time practising an incorrect sound. If your students are having difficulties with pairs of letters that either look alike (for example, *m* and *n*) or sound alike (for example, /f/ and /v/), concentrate on one until it is mastered, spending two or three days on other letters that have nothing in common with the similar letters. Then, slip in the second confusing letter or sound and work on it. If a student shows signs of total confusion, work on just one letter at a time until the student has correctly identified the letter for three consecutive days.

- Do your students at risk have several opportunities each day to orally practise a new sound and review previously taught sounds with your support? The kind of practice you provide in the context of letter-sound instruction should be oral, and students' responses should be in unison until they have solidly mastered a sound. Avoid any practice activities that involve worksheets, colouring or cutting during letter-sound instruction. Your goal is to have students say the sound perfectly. Some students at risk may need up to fifteen repetitions before they can produce a sound correctly on the first day. You must be a positive cheerleader for students during this process, giving them praise and encouragement at every step.

Sample Lessons for Teaching Letter-Sound Correspondences

This section contains two sample lessons: one for introducing a single letter-sound correspondence to students for the first time, and a second lesson for giving students opportunities to practise discriminating between various letter-sound correspondences that you have previously taught.

Before you begin instruction, choose and practise which signal you will use to cue students to begin saying the sound during the We Do It and You Do It steps of the lesson. Various signals are shown in figure 1.2. You can simply put your pointer finger under the letter when you want students to begin making the sound. If the sound is a continuous one like *a* or *m*, for example, tap lightly under the letter for two seconds while saying the sound. If the sound is a stop, like *p* or *t,* touch the letter and then take your finger off the letter immediately after saying the sound. You can use any type of signal as long as it communicates when students should start making the sound and when they should stop.

The sample lesson in figure 7.6 can be used for teaching any new letter-sound correspondence. It introduces the short vowel *a*. In preparation for introducing a new letter-sound correspondence, write the letter on the board, poster paper or overhead. Face your students so you can observe their mouths as they make a new sound in unison or hear the sounds as you check students individually. Ideally, if students are seated at a kidney-shaped table, you can point to the letter on a table chart and still be "knee-to-knee" and "eye-to-eye" with your students. Figure

7.3 displays the short vowels. Most experts recommend teaching short vowels first because they are the most frequently encountered in English text. The short vowels *a* and *i* should be the first vowels you teach.

Figure 7.6: Sample lesson for introducing a letter sound for the first time.

Lesson Objective	Students will be able to see a letter and say the sound it represents in under three seconds.
Advance Organiser	**Teacher Says:** Today we're going to learn a new sound. Our new sound goes with the letter *s*. We'll use the I Do It-We Do It-You Do It routine so after I make the sound for you, you will have many turns to practise the sound. When you know the sounds that go with the letters, you will be able to read words and books. Listen to what I say, and watch my lips.
I Do It: Teacher Models	**Teacher Says:** Here's our new sound for today. **Teacher Does:** Point to the *s* on the board. **Teacher Says:** This letter says /s/.
We Do It: Teacher and Students Respond in Unison	**Teacher Does:** Point to the letter. **Teacher Says:** Together. What sound? **Teacher and Students Say:** /s/. Yes, /s/. **Teacher Does:** Repeat this segment several times, watching students' eyes and mouths to see if any students are having difficulty.
You Do It: Students Respond in Unison Without Teacher Support	**Teacher Does:** Point to the letter. **Teacher Says:** Your turn. What sound? **Teacher Does:** Point to the letter. Tap your finger under the letter to indicate students must sustain the sound for two seconds. If the letter is a stop, tap only once to indicate that they say the sound and stop immediately. **Students Say:** /s/. **Teacher Does:** Try to determine if all students are correctly making the sound and responding confidently (if you are working with a small intervention group). If not, do two or three We Do It sequences for additional practice. Once the You Do It response is strong, do an individual checkout with each child.
Individual Students Respond	**Teacher Says:** Individual turns. What sound? **Teacher Does:** Point to the letter. Pause to give every student a chance to think of the sound before you call a student's name. **Teacher Says:** Angelica? **Angelica Says:** /s/. **Teacher Says:** Yes, /s/. **Teacher Does:** If a student makes an error, use the error-correcting routine found in figure 6.1 and then return to the I Do It-We Do It steps in the lesson.

Source: Bursuck & Damer, 2007; Carnine et al., 2004.

Teach two letters per week, monitoring the students' progress and success. Once you have introduced and practised several letters, try the sample lesson in figure 7.7. This lesson serves as a review of all of the previous letter-sound correspondences you have introduced, *and* it requires that students carefully note the new correspondence and differentiate it from previous ones. Discrimination practice is very important for both you and your students to feel confident that they have mastered the various correspondences.

Figure 7.7: Sample lesson for discriminating between various letter-sound correspondences.

Lesson Objective	Students will be able to say the sounds that individual letters represent in under three seconds when presented with previously mastered letter-sound correspondences.
Advance Organiser	**Teacher Does:** Write several letters that have already been taught, along with several repetitions of the new letter on the board or overhead. Leave lots of space between the letters, and stagger them in placement. a f s m o s l f s f **Teacher Says:** Today we're going to learn a new letter and review some of the letters we have already learned. Our new letter says the sound /s/. I have written all of the other letters we have learned so far along with our new letter. I have written some of them more than once. You will have to look and listen carefully to tell the differences. We'll use the I Do It-We Do It-You Do It routine so after I make the sound for you, you will have lots of turns to practise the sound. You will have to use your ears to listen to the sound and your eyes to watch my lips while they are making the sound. Then you will be able to make the sound exactly the way I do.
I Do It: Teacher Models	**Teacher Says:** Here's our new sound for today. **Teacher Does:** Point to the *f* on the board. **Teacher Says:** This letter says /f/. Again, this letter says /f/.
We Do It: Teacher and Students Respond in Unison	**Teacher Does:** Point to the letter. **Teacher Says:** Together. What sound? **Teacher and Students Say:** /f/. Yes, /f/. **Teacher Does:** Repeat this segment several times, watching students' eyes and mouths to see if anyone is having difficulty with the new sound.
You Do It: Teacher Tests the Group on All of the Letters, Including the New One	**Teacher Does:** Point to the letter. **Teacher Says:** Your turn. What sound? **Teacher Does:** Point to the letter. Tap your finger under the letter to indicate students must sustain the sound for two seconds. If the letter is a stop, tap only once to indicate that they say the sound and stop immediately. Follow an alternating pattern in which you gradually increase the length of time between testing a previously learned letter and the new letter. **Teacher Does:** Test all of the students on the letters introduced to that point (if you are working with a small intervention group), ensuring they are correctly making the sound and responding assertively. If not, do two or three We Do It sequences for additional practice. Give extra practice time to those students who are still having difficulty.

Source: Adapted from Bursuck & Damer, 2007; Carnine et al., 2004.

INTERVENTION 8

Reading Regular Words (Years P–2)

It has been proven beyond any shade of doubt that skillful readers process virtually each and every word and letter of text as they read. This is extremely counterintuitive. For sure, skillful readers neither look nor feel as if that's what they do. But that's because they do it so quickly and effortlessly. Almost automatically; with almost no conscious attention whatsoever, skillful readers recognise words by drawing on deep and ready knowledge of spellings and their connections to speech and meaning.

—Adams (1991, p. 207)

This intervention guides you and your students through the three steps to automatically recognising regular words:

1. Sounding out the words orally
2. Sounding out the words subvocally by moving the mouth but not making any sounds
3. Saying the word quickly (the fast way)

Average and above-average students may not need to move through all of these steps, but they are critical for students at risk. A sample lesson is provided for each step.

Background Knowledge

Regular words can be phonemically decoded because all of their letters match up to the expected sounds. Although learning to read regular words might seem like a relatively simple undertaking, students at risk cannot do it in one step. Using the three steps to reading regular words will give students the scaffolding they need to gain confidence and speed. Take your time, and give your students the opportunity to master each of these steps.

Sample Lessons for Reading Regular Words

Each of the three steps in learning to read regular words presents unique challenges for both students at risk and their teachers. During the first step—the oral sounding out of regular words—the most challenging aspect for some teachers is taking care not to add the schwa sound—/uh/—to the stop sounds—*b, p, t* and so on. The schwa sound is the vowel sound in the unstressed syllables in words with more than one syllable—for example, the *a* in *adept* and the *y* in *syringe*. The sound is symbolised by an upside-down rotated e in phonetic respellings: /ə/. When you began teaching initial consonants, you might have automatically added that sound to initial stop sounds. This creates two extra phonemes, which can be confusing to students. For example, the word *bat* might become /b/-/uh/-/a/-/t/-/uh/. The schwa sound should not be heard when segmenting the sounds.

A second challenge you may encounter in teaching the first step is providing students with enough practice to become confident readers. Core reading programs seldom allow for enough practice time for students at risk. The focus is generally on reading or covering one story per week. Set aside as much time as possible for extra daily practice, especially when the words are difficult. Don't rush through modelling in the My Turn section of the lesson. Also, give your students many opportunities to blend words in unison before you expect them to sound out words independently.

As you transition your students from step 1, orally sounding out the words, to step 2, "sounding out" the words in their heads while silently moving their lips, carefully watch your students to see that their eyes are on the page as they sound out a word in their heads and then say it the fast way.

Step 3 teaches reading regular words quickly. In the beginning, give students enough think time to do their "in the head" sounding out. Gradually reduce their think time as they become more fluent in the sounding-out process. To reach the ultimate goal of this three-step process—the construction of solid mental orthographic images of new words—students need to be cognitively processing the words themselves, first as a group and then as individuals. Figures 8.1, 8.2 and 8.3 contain sample lessons for each of the three steps to reading regular words.

Figure 8.1: Sample lesson for orally sounding out regular words.

Lesson Objective	Students will orally sound out new regular (decodable words) before saying the word fast. Write the new words on the board in rows of four. (See information on serial processing in Intervention 19.)
Advance Organiser	**Teacher Says:** We have eight new words to learn today. We'll use the I Do It-We Do It-You Do It routine to learn and practise our new words. [Give brief student-friendly definition and/or sentence for each new word. Do not assume your students will automatically know the meanings of new words, even if they are one-syllable words. Depending on the number of new words and the difficulty of those words, you might spend anywhere from five minutes (prep) to twenty minutes (year one) learning and practising the new words.]
I Do It: Teacher Models	**Teacher Says:** My turn sounding out this word: /t/-/ă/-/n/. What word? *Tan*. [Students do not respond during teacher modelling. Their job is to listen and watch. Model the new word at least three times, pointing to the letters on the overhead as you make the sounds.]
We Do It: Teacher and Students Respond in Unison	**Teacher Says:** Together, sound out this word. What word? **Teacher and Students Say:** /t/-/ă/-/n/. **Teacher Says:** Yes, *tan*. **Teacher Does:** Practise reading the word together at least three times, pointing to the letters as you articulate the sounds and running your hand under the word when you say it fast.
You Do It: Students Respond in Unison Without Teacher Support	**Teacher Says:** Your turn to sound out the word. What word? **Students Say:** /t/-/ă/-/n/. *Tan*. **Teacher Says:** Yes, *tan*. **Teacher Does:** Repeat this step for every word in the row.
Individual Students Respond	**Teacher Does:** Point to a word. **Teacher Says:** Sound out this word. Samantha? **Samantha:** /t/-/ă/-/n/. *Tan*. **Teacher Does:** Perform an individual assessment of each student. When every student is accurate on a word, move to the second row of words, using the You Do It step. If a student makes an error, go back to the I Do It-We Do It-You Do It routine, making sure that each student correctly sounds out the word and says it fast.

Source: Adapted from Bursuck & Damer, 2007; Carnine et al., 2004.

Figure 8.2: Sample lesson for sounding out regular words subvocally.

Lesson Objective	Students will subvocally sound out (silently mouth the letter sounds) new regular (decodable) words before saying the word. Write the new words on the board in rows of four. (See information on serial processing in Intervention 19.)
Advance Organiser	**Teacher Says:** Today we are going to sound out our new words in our head before saying them out loud. **Teacher Does:** Give brief student-friendly definition and/or sentence for each new word. Do not assume your students will automatically know the meanings of new words, even if they are one-syllable words. **Teacher Says:** We'll use the I Do It-We Do It-You Do It routine to learn and practise our new words. [Depending on the number of new words and the difficulty of those words, you might spend anywhere from five minutes (prep) to twenty minutes (year one) introducing and practising new words. Readers at risk need ample amounts of practice to master an ever-increasing list of words.]
I Do It: Teacher Models	**Teacher Says:** My turn sounding out this word in my head, [silently mouthing the letter sounds] /t/-/ă/-/n/, as I move my finger from letter to letter. What word? *Tan.* **Teacher Does:** Model the new word at least three times, pointing to the letters on the overhead. Students do not respond during teacher modelling.
We Do It: Teacher and Students Respond in Unison	**Teacher Says:** Together, sound out this word in your head [silently mouthing the letters], /t/-/ă/-/n/. What word? **Teacher and Students Do:** Silently mouth the letters. /t/-/ă/-/n/. **Teacher Says:** Yes, *tan*. **Teacher Does:** Practise reading each word in the row with the students at least three times, pointing to the letters as you silently move your mouth while pointing to each letter and then moving your hand under the whole word when you say it out loud fast.
You Do It: Students Respond in Unison Without Teacher Support	**Teacher Says:** Your turn to sound out the word in your head. What word? **All Students:** [Silently mouthing the letter sounds together] /t/-/ă/-/n/. *Tan.* **Teacher Says:** Yes, *tan*. **Teacher Does:** Repeat this step for every word in the row.
Individual Students Respond	**Teacher Says:** Sound out this word in your head. Samantha? **Teacher Does:** Point to the word. **Samantha Says:** [Silently mouthing the letter sounds] /t/-/ă/-/n/. *Tan.* **Teacher Does:** Perform an individual assessment of each student. When every student is accurate on a word, move to the second row of words, using the You Do It step. If a student makes an error, go back to the I Do It-We Do It-You Do It routine, making sure that each student correctly sounds out the word and says it fast.

Sources: Adapted from Bursuck & Damer, 2007; Carnine et al., 2004.

Figure 8.3: Sample lesson for orally reading regular words the fast way.

Lesson Objective	Students will orally read regular words the fast way.
Advance Organiser	**Teacher Says:** Today we are going to sound out our new words the fast way. **Teacher Does:** Give a brief, student-friendly definition and/or sentence for each new word. Do not assume your students will automatically know the meanings of new words, even if they are one-syllable words. If you think students will have trouble reading some of the words the fast way, use the sounding-out lesson in figure 8.1 the first time the word is introduced. **Teacher Says:** We'll use the I Do It-We Do It-You Do It routine to learn and practise our new words. [Depending on the number of new words and the difficulty of those words, you might spend anywhere from five minutes (prep) to twenty minutes (year one) introducing and practising new words.]
I Do It: Teacher Models	**Teacher Says:** My turn to read this word the fast way: *tan*. **Teacher Does:** Model the new word at least three times, pointing to the letters on the overhead as you orally read each word fast. Students do not respond during teacher modelling.
We Do It: Teacher and Students Respond in Unison	**Teacher Says:** Let's read the rest of the words together. What word? **Teacher Does:** Point to the word and run your hand quickly underneath the word from left to right. **Teacher Says:** *Tan.* **All Students Say:** *Tan.* **Teacher Says:** Yes, *tan*. What word? **All Students Say:** *Tan.* **Teacher Says:** Yes, *tan*. **Teacher Does:** Repeat this step for every word in the row. If students are accurately responding in unison with you, skip to individual student responses.
Individual Students Respond	**Teacher Says:** What word? Samantha? **Teacher Does:** Point to the word. **Samantha Says:** *Tan.* **Teacher Says:** Yes, *tan*. What word? George? **George Says:** *Tan.* **Teacher Does:** Perform an individual assessment of each student. When every student is accurate on a word, move to the second row of words, using the You Do It step. If a student makes an error, go back to the I Do It-We Do It-You Do It routine, making sure that each student correctly sounds out the word and says it fast.

Source: Adapted from Bursuck & Damer, 2007; Carnine et al., 2004.

INTERVENTION 9

Reading Irregular (Exception) Words (Years P–3)

> *Sight words are words that readers have read accurately on earlier occasions. They read the words by remembering how they read them previously. The term* sight *indicates that sight of the word activates that word in memory, including information about its spelling, pronunciation, typical role in sentences, and meaning.*
>
> —Ehri (p. 12, 1998)

This intervention strategy gives teachers an alternative approach to teaching exception words as sight words when flash cards, drills, practice at home and practice at school have failed to help students create the essential mental orthographic images that are needed for the accurate and automatic recognition of an exception (irregular) word as a sight word (Ehri, 1980). The strategy leads the student through a visualisation process that requires the student to attend to each individual letter in a word.

Background Knowledge

The term *sight word* has two different meanings in the reading literature and classrooms, which can create confusion. In this book, a sight word is a word that is recognised by a reader in under one second, as defined in the epigraph by Linnea Ehri. In some texts, the term *sight word* refers to phonically irregular words or exception words (such as *Wednesday*, *was* and *the*) that must be memorised as whole words. Make sure that you know which way the term is being used in your core program or supplementary phonics programs that you are using in your classroom. The most efficient way to acquire sight words is through phonemic decoding: mapping sounds to the letters in words.

The challenge for primary-year teachers lies in helping beginning readers acquire as quickly as possible a set of high-frequency irregular (exception) words as sight words. Lists like Dolch's or Fry's, or more commonly, a set of words suggested by the core program, contain two kinds of words: (1) words that can be phonemically decoded, some of which may already have been mastered by students, and (2) words with irregular spelling patterns that cannot be decoded. The latter group requires whole-word memorisation. The words that seem to be the most difficult for students are *was*, *of* and *said*. Students with strong visual memories can "memorise" these words rather quickly, but some students just can't seem to remember irregular words from one day to the next despite intense practice. Their parents become frustrated, their teachers grow weary and the students themselves begin to despair of ever learning to read. They can read the decodable words just fine because they have mastered the appropriate letter-sound correspondences. What they need is explicit instruction regarding how to develop mental images of the words that defy decoding—the same kind of mental images that students develop when they decode a word several times and then eventually retain it in their long-term memories.

© 2009 Hawker Brownlow Education • SOT4749

As you read through the sample lesson in preparation for using it, you may wonder about the directions that tell the students to say (name) the letters of the word in reverse order. Understand that you are not asking students to visualise the word actually spelled backwards or to write the word spelled backwards. The task is to look at a word spelled correctly on a word card and visualise it spelled correctly when the spelled word is removed. Then, while your students are visualising the correctly spelled word, you will ask them to name the letters starting at the end of the word and going back to the beginning. Asking students to orally name the letters in a word in reverse order while visualising it spelled correctly is supported theoretically by the work of Linnea Ehri (1980) and is further developed in the work of Wasowicz, Apel, Masterson and Whitney (2004).

This exercise creates the need for students to hold orthographic information (for example, the configuration of each separate letter) as an image (mental picture) in order to perform the task. The reverse letter-naming activity works against the use of a partial-cueing strategy in which students only process a few letters in a word and then make a guess about a word based on an incomplete orthographic image. The detrimental effects of such a strategy on reading and spelling are well documented in the literature (Adams, 1998).

Sample Lesson for Teaching Exception Words

Figure 9.1 is a sample lesson to help students develop mental orthographic images (MOIs) of irregular words. If you skimmed through the earlier section describing the research regarding word identification, you might want to re-view the comprehensive description of MOIs and their importance in fluent reading found there. The information is directly applicable to this intervention strategy. This lesson requires a picture of a familiar scene (for example, a family at the beach or park, or a group of children on a playground) to use as a model in the visualisation process. The sample lesson is designed to be taught to one student, but it can readily be adapted to a group of three to five students if they are seated at a kidney-shaped table where the teacher can directly observe students' eyes during the lesson.

Figure 9.1: Sample lesson for teaching exception words.

Lesson Objective	Student will be able to acquire exception words as sight words after visualising, spelling and writing them.
Materials Needed for Lesson	Prepare a set of index cards with selected irregular words that the student has been unable to acquire as sight words—for example, *was*, *of*. Select one or two photos of familiar scenes (for example, a park or playground; a campground).
Advance Organiser	**Teacher Says:** There are several words in our Word List [could be the Dolch list or a set of words that accompany the core reading program] that are very hard for you to remember. Today we're going to learn how to use the "camera in your mind" to "take pictures" of words that just don't follow the rules.

continued →

Reading Irregular (Exception) Words

I Do It: Teacher Models Visualising	**Teacher Does:** Show the student a photograph and talk about what you see in it. (You could use a personal family photo, a picture taken at school or a photo from a software program. A colour photo is preferable. The following script is based on the sample photo.) **Teacher Says:** When I look at this photo, I see a dad and his two sons playing with toys in the sand. The dad is in the middle of the picture, and the older boy is on the dad's right-hand side. The younger boy is over here on the left-hand side of the dad. The older boy is playing with a dump truck right here. The younger boy has his hat on backward. [Point to each part of the photo as you talk about them.] **Teacher Does:** Turn the picture over and describe the scene, "pointing" to the important parts of the imaginary picture. **Teacher Says:** I see the dad right about here. I see the dump truck right about here.
We Do It: Teacher and Student Visualise Together	**Teacher Does:** Turn the photo over. **Teacher Says:** Look at this photo, and use the camera in your mind to take a picture of it. I'm going to turn it over, and I want you to tell me about the different things you see. **Teacher Does:** "Point" to the various parts of the imaginary picture, asking the student to tell you what he or she sees. **Teacher Does:** Next, tell the student to visualise a familiar place (for example, the student's kitchen or bedroom). Then, instruct the student to describe that place aloud, "pointing" to significant parts of the imaginary kitchen. Repeat the previous steps until the student demonstrates an understanding of the concept of visualisation. **Teacher Says:** Now we are going to use visualisation to learn some of the irregular words on your list.
I Do It: Teacher Models Identifying Each Letter and Noting Its Characteristics	**Teacher Does:** Show one word card to the student, read aloud the card's word and use the word in a sentence that clearly communicates the meaning of the word. **Teacher Says:** The word is *of*. This is one of my favourite books. **Teacher Does:** Hold the word card in the air and point to each of the letters as you read them aloud from left to right, raising your voice for letters that rise above the midline and lowering your voice for letters that fall below the bottom line. When you have finished, talk about the number of consonants and vowels in the word. **Teacher Says:** O [say in a normal tone of voice]. F [say in a louder tone of voice because this letter falls above the midline]. I see one vowel letter at the beginning of the word and one consonant letter at the end of the word.
We Do It: Teacher and Student Work Together to Identify Each Letter and Note Its Characteristics	**Teacher Does:** Direct the student to name the letters aloud from left to right and talk about the number of consonants and vowels in the word. Direct the student to name the letters aloud as you point to each of them moving from right to left. **Teacher Does:** Turn over the word card and relate how you can still "see" the written word, pointing to each letter in the visualised word as you spell it forward. Point out to the student that he can also name or identify the letters in the word by starting at the end of the word and going back to the beginning of the word. **Student Does:** Point to each letter in the visualised word as the student spells it forward. **Teacher Does:** Ask the student, while he is still "looking" at his visualisation of the word to name each letter in the word starting at the end of the word and moving back to its beginning. **Teacher Does:** Instruct the student to write the word on his writing paper. Ask the student to flip over the word card, verify the correct spelling of the word, and then use the word in a spoken sentence. If time and student attention are sufficient, show a new word card and repeat the previous steps.

Source: Adapted by permission from SPELL—Links to Reading and Writing: A Word Study Curriculum. Wasowicz et al., 2004. Evanston, IL: Learning by Design.

© 2009 Hawker Brownlow Education • SOT4749

INTERVENTION 10

Facilitating Advanced Word Reading (Years 2–6)

> *Spelling instruction that is carefully and intentionally integrated into a beginning reading program can help students improve both spelling and reading skills.*
>
> —Santoro, Coyne & Simmons (2006, p. 122)

Students who are at risk of reading failure need explicit and direct instruction beyond the one-to-one letter-sound correspondences taught in prep and year one. This intervention suggests ways to intervene with students who are having a difficult time learning to read multisyllabic words, especially words with prefixes, suffixes and inflected endings.

Background Knowledge

To make a smooth and successful transition from learning to read in the primary year levels to reading to learn in the upper year levels students need to acquire and integrate five different kinds of linguistic knowledge into their word reading:

1. The ability to think about, talk about and manipulate speech sounds

2. A set of orthographic skills needed to translate language from spoken to written form (spelling) or from written to spoken form (reading)

3. Knowledge of the *morphographs* (root words, nonword Latin and Greek roots, prefixes, suffixes and inflectional endings) and their meanings, which are necessary to master advanced word reading (see figures 10.2 and 10.3 for lists of the twenty most common prefixes and the twenty most common suffixes)

4. Knowledge about the effect spelling has on word meaning and usage

5. Clear mental images of words or morphemes (word parts) stored in long-term memory (Apel, 2007)

Instruction in prep and year one focuses largely on the first two kinds of knowledge: phonological and orthographic. Advanced word reading instruction requires that you pull together morphographic knowledge from several different content areas: spelling, reading and English. Very few reading (or even spelling) programs provide a complete package that teaches students skills and concepts from all five of the linguistic knowledge bases described earlier.

© 2009 Hawker Brownlow Education • SOT4749

Instructional Activities for Advanced Word Reading

Absent a comprehensive, research-based reading or spelling program from which to draw advanced word reading lessons, one way to help your students is to pinpoint the precise pieces of advanced word reading that they are missing and then to meet their needs by using the various instructional activities in this section.

Teaching Big-Word Reading

Teach your students one of these two sets of steps that lead students through reading multisyllabic words: 1) Cooper, Chard and Kiger's Big Word Strategy, and 2) Anita Archer's Six Steps to Reading Big Words. If you see difficult multisyllabic words in the text that the students will be reading, model the process for your students *before* reading the story. If any students haven't first used the steps on their own, send them back to try. Only after they have made their way through the steps should they ask a peer or teacher. Remember, however, that these approaches to decoding big words are useful only if students recognise the word they have decoded as one they already know. If students do not know the meaning of a decoded word, it's time to look it up in the dictionary as noted in #5 of the following strategy for reading big words.

Cooper, Chard and Kiger's Big Word Strategy

Cooper et al. (2006) suggest the following steps for students to follow when they encounter a big word they can't read:

1. Have the students try to pronounce the difficult word using phonics.

2. If the students figure it out, have them try reading the text aloud. Does it make sense to them? If not, go to #3.

3. Have them look for parts they don't know: prefixes, suffixes, base words and root words. Have the students think about their meanings.

4. Have them read to the end of the sentence or paragraph, trying out the meaning of the hard word. Does it make sense to them?

5. If they still don't know the word, have them ask someone or look it up.

Anita Archer's Six Steps to Reading Big Words

An adaptation of Archer, Gleason and Vachon's (2005) Big Word Reading Strategy can be found in figure 10.1. As your students learn to follow these steps whenever they encounter unfamiliar multisyllabic words, you can gradually begin to eliminate the circling and saying and expect them to go through the steps without the oral and written prompts. Please note that to use these steps, students must be familiar with, and on their way to mastery of, short and long vowel sounds, common prefixes and suffixes, and auditorily blending the parts of a word (Bursuck & Damer, 2007).

Teaching your students how to follow one of these two sets of steps for reading big words presupposes that they will recognise a word and know its meaning once they have decoded it. If that is not the case, teaching the meanings of big words *before* reading a story is essential.

Figure 10.1: Steps to reading big words.

1.	Circle the prefixes at the beginning of the word.
2.	Circle the suffixes at the end of the word.
3.	Underline the letters that represent vowel sounds in the rest of the word.
4.	Say the syllables of the word.
5.	Say the syllables fast.
6.	Figure out if there is a word you know that sounds very similar to the one you said, and then correct your pronunciation to match the word you already know.

Source: Adapted from Archer et al. (2005).

Teaching Orthographic Knowledge (Advanced Letter-Sound Correspondences)

Students who have had explicit, systematic phonemic awareness and phonics instruction in prep and year one have likely mastered all of the one-to-one sound correspondences. However, it is not unusual to find upper-year level students who have major gaps in their letter-sound knowledge. These students need word work with the following three categories of advanced letter-sound correspondences:

1. Blends in two or more consonants that make their common sounds so each sound can be heard (for example, /bl/, /br/, /cl/, /cr/ or /shr/)

2. Letter combinations that include consonant digraphs (for example, /ch/, /sh/), vowel digraphs (/ai/, /ee/, /ea/ or /oa/), diphthongs and *r*-controlled vowels (/ar/, /er/ or /ir/)

3. Vowel-consonant-silent *e* patterns (for example, ade, ide, ake and so on.)

These advanced letter-sound correspondences are rarely taught systematically in reading and spelling programs, leaving many students with major gaps in their orthographic knowledge.

Teaching Morphological Awareness (Prefixes and Suffixes)

Morphological awareness includes knowledge about *morphographs*—word parts that change the meanings of words. Morphographs include real words or root words such as *man* and *can*; nonword Latin and Greek roots, such as *aqua*, meaning "water" (Latin) and *auto*, meaning "self" (Greek); and the twenty most common prefixes and suffixes. Knowledge of these morphographs can help students read, spell and understand a vast number of words. However, they must be intentionally and directly taught to students at risk. Figures 10.2 and 10.3 list the twenty most common prefixes and suffixes (including inflectional endings such as –*s* and –*ed*) with meanings and examples. Figure 10.4 contains a sample lesson for teaching these word parts.

Figure 10.2: Twenty most common prefixes.

Prefix	Definition	Examples
anti-	against	anticlimax
de-	opposite	devalue

continued →

Prefix	Definition	Examples
dis-	not opposite of	discover
en-, em-	cause to	enact empower
fore-	before front of	foreshadow forearm
in-, im-	in	income impulse
in-, im-, il-, ir-	not	indirect immoral illiterate irreverent
inter-	between among	interrupt
mid-	middle	midway
mis-	wrongly	misspell
non-	not	nonviolent
over-	over too much	overeat
pre-	before	preview
re-	again	rewrite
semi-	half partly not fully	semifinal
sub-	under	subway
super-	above beyond	superhuman
trans-	across	transmit
un-	not opposite of	unusual
under-	under too little	underestimate

Source: McEwan, Nielsen, & Edison, 2008.

Figure 10.3: Twenty most common suffixes.

Suffix	Definition	Examples
-able -ible	is can be	affordable sensible
-al -ial	having characteristics of	universal facial

continued →

Suffix	Definition	Examples
-ed	past-tense verbs and/or adjectives	the dog walked the walked dog
-en	made of	golden
-er -or	one with whom the person connected	teacher professor
-er	more	taller
-est	the most	tallest
-ful	full of	helpful
-ic	having characteristics of	poetic
-ing	gerunds (an *-ing* word that functions as an adjective, such as *sleeping baby* or an *-ing* word that functions as a verb, such as "The baby was sleeping")	sleeping
-ion -tion -ation -ition	act or process	submission motion relation edition
-ity -ty	state of	activity society
-ive -ative -itive	adjective form of noun	active comparative sensitive
-less	without	hopeless
-ly	how something is	lovely
-ment	state of being; act of	contentment
-ness	state of; condition of	openness
-ous -eous -ious	having qualities of	riotous courageous gracious
-s -es	more than one	trains trenches
-y	characterised by	gloomy

Source: McEwan, Nielsen, & Edison, 2008.

The following sample lesson provides a format for teaching prefixes and suffixes—or, as they are alternately called, word parts.

Teaching Mental Orthographic Images (MOIs)

This source of linguistic knowledge is essential for both reading and spelling. To identify words automatically and spell them accurately, students need solid mental orthographic images "cemented" into their long-term memories (Ehri, 1980). See the lesson for teaching students how to develop MOIs of irregular words in Intervention 9 and a second lesson in Intervention 12 for teaching keywords for analogous reading using MOIs.

Figure 10.4: Sample lesson for teaching word parts (prefixes and suffixes).

Lesson Objective	Students will be able to identify word parts and new words using those correspondences and word parts (roots, root words, prefixes and suffixes).
Practise Using the Correspondence or Word Part	**Teacher Does:** Write the new advanced letter-sound correspondence or word part on the board along with others you have already taught. Use the sample lesson in figure 7.6 to introduce and practise the new letter-sound correspondence or word part. Alternate practising the new correspondence or word part with others that have previously been taught. Practise for several days until students are able to discriminate the new word parts from those previously taught.
Words Containing the New Correspondence or Word Part	**Teacher Does:** Write four or five words containing the new word part on the board. For example, if you are teaching the prefix *over-*, write overeat, overwork and overtime on the board. Remind students that the meaning of *over-* is "too much". Have students read the individual parts of the word first before pronouncing the whole word. Read the list, pronouncing the whole words two times. Practise reading the list for several days before moving on to *discrimination practice*, in which you mix words using the word part just taught with words using the previously taught word part.
Words With the New Word Part Along With Words Containing Previously Taught Word Parts	**Teacher Does:** Put a list of regular words with previously taught word parts on the board. Mix in the new words, presenting them more than once in the list. Introduce a new word part only when students are able to read this discrimination list without error on the first try for two consecutive days.

Source: Carnine et al., 2004; McEwan, Nielsen, et al., 2008.

INTERVENTION 11

Reading Decodable Books (Years P–1)

The average child needs between four and fourteen exposures to automatize the recognition of a new word. Therefore, in learning to read it is vital that children read a large amount of text at their independent reading level (95 per cent accuracy) and that the text format provides specific practice in the skills being learned.

—Lyon (1998, p. 6)

This intervention strategy provides a sample lesson for scaffolding your students' transition from identifying single words to reading simple decodable books. This transition is almost as exciting for students as taking the training wheels off their first bicycle. Students will need to practise holding the book open as they rest it on top of the table, following the text with the pointer finger of their dominant hand and keeping their eyes focused on the page. This intervention also offers guidelines for selecting decodable text.

Background Knowledge

Select your students' first decodable book with care. Cooper et al. (2006) offer these guidelines:

- Ensure that the phonic elements, high-frequency words and irregular words in the text have been mastered by students.

- Prior to the first reading, isolate phonic elements and words that may be barriers to the students' initial success, and have students read them ahead of time so that they have a better chance of recognising them in continuous text.

- Provide students with ample opportunity to read and reread both stories and expository texts to build confidence and fluency.

- Systematically increase the difficulty of texts as students master more phonic elements and words. (p. 70)

Sample Lesson for Teaching Decodable Books

In preparation for teaching students how to independently read decodable books, you must decide whether you will read the story aloud to students—as is often suggested by the core program's teacher's guide—or expect the students to read it themselves. If you are working with a small intervention group and its members have mastered the sound-spelling correspondences that are found in most of the words in a decodable book, it is not necessary to read the story aloud to them first. If your students have been individually assessed on their abilities to read regular (decodable) words as well as the list you have provided to them of irregular (exception) words, you should give them a chance to show what they know. Give each child the opportunity to do a "cold read" in your small group. This cold read is not the typical round-robin reading where the group contains a range of students at multiple reading levels with varying degrees of engagement with the text. In that kind of setting, struggling readers tend to avoid the teacher's eyes, hoping they won't be called upon to read, and the high-level readers read ahead or read a library book. The following sample lesson for reading decodable text with your intervention group assumes a homogenous skill-based group.

Expect your intervention group students to follow along in the text with their pointer fingers. This simple technique enables them to focus on the text and in the beginning keeps them from losing their places. Call on students randomly, and have them read one to three sentences of the story or book. Call on students quickly, and avoid unnecessary tangential teacher talk by focusing comprehension questions on key ideas, vocabulary and supporting details. Write any words that students miss on the board. At the end of the story, have students sound out each missed decodable word and read it. If the missed word is an exception word, tell the student the word. If you have the time to build orthographic images of high-frequency irregular words, use the sample lesson in Intervention 9. Note any obvious error patterns in certain kinds of words or in the group as a whole to determine if a short reteaching lesson is needed. Explain to your students that their goal is 97 per cent accuracy. After the first reading, read the story once more together before having students pair up and orally read the story to each other. Monitor for accuracy during these readings. Figure 11.1 is a sample lesson for teaching the first oral reading of decodable books.

Figure 11.1: Sample lesson for introducing decodable book reading.

Lesson Objective	Students will orally read a decodable book or passage for the first time with 97 per cent accuracy.
Advance Organiser	**Teacher Says:** Today is a very important day. You are going to read a book out loud. I'll call on different students to read. When it's your turn to read, please use your biggest voice so everyone can hear you. Pause when you come to a period. If I don't call on another student, read the next sentence. If it's not your turn to read, point to the words that are being read. Look at your book very carefully. Who can read the title? Who do you think the main character of this book is? Good thinking. The main character's picture is often on the front cover of a book. Who is the author?
I Do It: Teacher Models	**Teacher Says:** Let me show you how I want you to read. **Teacher Does:** Read the first sentence with expression. **Teacher Says:** I'm going to read that sentence again, and I want each one of you to use your pointer finger to follow along as I read. When I say the word, your finger should be right underneath the word. Let's try that. **Teacher Does:** Read the first sentence again and watch students use their pointer fingers. **Teacher Says:** Excellent work, everybody. Let me show you exactly what I mean about using your pointer finger. John, would you read that first sentence for us? **Students Do:** Move their pointer fingers under the first word and move along their fingers as John reads each word. **Teacher Says:** I will be doing the same thing and watching to see how you are doing. **Teacher Does:** Repeat this step until all of the students are following along according to the directions.

continued →

You Do It: Individual Students Read 1–3 Sentences	**Teacher Says:** Let's begin. John, would you please read that first sentence for us, and keep reading until I tell you to stop. **Teacher Does:** Call on a new student every one to three sentences. Call on students in an unpredictable order. Pick one, two or three sentences in an unpredictable order. Watch students to make sure they are following along when their classmates are reading. Keep the pace brisk. Call on the next student as the one who is reading finishes the last word in the sentence. Keep extraneous teacher talk to a minimum.

Note: If the reading is going smoothly and students are not having difficulties, ask comprehension questions during the first reading. If the students are reading quite slowly, read the story a second time and then ask comprehension questions at appropriate intervals. When a student makes an error, let the student read several more words, and then say, "Stop". Always give students a chance to self-correct. For misread words, say the correct word and ask the student to repeat it. Ask the student to go back and read the sentence from the beginning so as not to lose the meaning of the sentence. Say as little as possible during the correction process to avoid interrupting the flow of the reading and students' ability to comprehend the text.

Source: Adapted from Bursuck & Damer, 2007; Carnine et al., 2004.

INTERVENTION 12

Building Mental Orthographic Images for Keywords or Frequently Misread Words (Years 2–6)

> *Consistent use of proper decoding strategies—combined with encoding that requires more detailed attention to the individual letters of words than required for reading—establishes clear and complete mental orthographic images of words in long-term memory.*
>
> —Wasowicz (2007, p. 5)

This intervention strategy is designed for students with more serious reading disabilities who seem unable to master phonemic decoding, and who often have difficulty even acquiring a basic sight vocabulary of keywords for reading by analogy. Keywords, when taught in the context of an analogy-based approach to phonics instruction, are words with common phonograms and word parts (for example, *date, fine, bone* and *fish*). However, when students seem unable to even acquire the common phonograms, continually misread or misspell seemingly easy words, or appear to know a word one day and forget it the next, they likely do not have accurate mental orthographic images of the words stored in their long-term memories. This intervention strategy is based on the work of Linnea Ehri (1980) and Wasowicz et al. (2004), and teaches students how to systematically analyse words letter by letter, noting their size relative to each other, whether they are vowels or consonants. The strategy then requires testing the strength of the orthographic image by asking students to close their eyes and visualise the word, and from that visualisation to name the letters moving both right to left and left to right.

Background Knowledge

We know that good readers use their knowledge of rimes (the vowel-consonant-vowel patterns) in words they know how to read in order to decode unknown words in a fairly automatic way (Perfetti, 1985). Struggling readers do not figure these relationships out on their own and need explicit instruction in how to apply what is known about a familiar word to an unknown one. There are other cases when older students have cobbled together their own unique approach to reading that combines some phonemic decoding skills, an overabundance of guessing at words based on context, and quasi-complete decoding by analogy that uses keywords acquired from their primary classroom word walls. These students have frequently been taught to read using every method from a variety of different teachers and progams. This eclectic method usually begins to interfere with reading comprehension in year-level text at the beginning of year four as students encounter more and more words for which they can't even make a guess.

The word identification program at the Benchmark School for students with serious learning and reading disabilities is called Word Detectives (Gaskins, 2005). Irene Gaskins and her staff developed the program, which teaches word identification by analogy. While the program was highly successful for about 85 per cent of Benchmark students, staff soon realised that by middle school, about 15 per cent of students who had been taught to decode by analogy using keywords were slow readers and inaccurate spellers in the upper year levels. With the help of researcher Linnea Ehri, the educators at Benchmark discovered that while in primary school, this group of students was totally dependent on the word wall, where keywords could be found written on cutout shapes of the words (Gaskins, Ehri, Cress, O'Hara, & Donnelly, 1996/1997). These students had never developed mental orthographic images for these words, preferring to use the various shapes of the objects or animals pictured on the word cards as a clue to the word. Once they discovered this problem, lower-year level teachers began to more intentionally teach their students how to acquire orthographic images of keywords rather than encouraging students' dependence on the word wall. They developed a process called "Talk to Yourself", in which students are taught to closely examine the spelling pattern and the letters in the word, similar to this intervention strategy.

Sample Lesson for Teaching Keywords or Frequently Misread Words

Figure 12.1 is a sample lesson to teach students how to develop a mental orthographic image for words they continually misread and misspell, or are unable to automatically retrieve as keywords to figure out new words they encounter in reading.

Figure 12.1: Sample lesson for teaching keywords or frequently misread words.

Lesson Objective	Students will acquire mental orthographic images of words with uncommon spellings that are very difficult for them to read and spell.
Materials Needed for Lesson	Each student will need a set of cards containing the frequently misread words from a story or fluency passage.
Advance Organiser	**Teacher Says:** Today I'm going to teach you a way to remember difficult words. For the past week, I've been collecting words from our story that we seem to have trouble reading every time we come to them: *ghost, canyon, guide, who, whole, one, once.*
Step 1: Explain the Purpose of the Activity	**Teacher Does:** Give a card for the first word to each student. **Teacher Says:** Sometimes you might find it difficult to correctly read or spell one or more parts of a word unless you have a clear picture of the word in your mind. I'm going to show you one way to create those clear word pictures.
Step 2: Discuss the Characteristics of the Word	**Teacher Says:** Let's look at the first word, *ghost*. Take a close look at the word. Now look at each of the letters. **Teacher Does:** Point to the word on the overhead transparency.
Step 3: Spell the Word With the Printed Form Present	**Teacher Says:** Now let's spell the word together. **Teacher Does:** Along with the students, slowly spell the word while looking at the printed form of the word. **Students Do:** Point to each letter in the word and say it aloud.

continued →

Step 4: Visualise the Word	**Teacher Says:** Now, take one more careful look at the letters in the word, because in a moment I am going to ask you to turn over your word card and close your eyes. Then I will ask you some questions about the letters in this word. I want you to close your eyes now and picture this word inside your head. Do you see the word? With your eyes still closed, as we say the letter together, stand up on your tiptoes if the letter is a tall one. Stay in a normal position if the letter is a short one, and crouch down if the letter goes below the line. **Teacher Does:** If students have difficulty with changing their positions for the various letters, model for them how to go up on tiptoes for tall letters (for example, *h* and *t*), stay in a normal position for short letters (for example, *o* and *s*) and crouch down for letters that go below the line (for example, *g*). **Students Do:** Crouch down for the letter *g*, stand up on tiptoes for the letter *h*, remain in the normal position for the letters *o* and *s*, and stand up on tiptoes for the letter *t*.
Step 5: Spell the Word Without the Printed Word Present	**Teacher Does:** Turn off the overhead projector so that students cannot see the word. **Teacher Says:** Open your eyes now. Do you still have a picture of the word in your mind? Look up at the blank overhead screen. **Students Do:** Look up at the blank overhead screen. **Teacher Says:** Do you see the word floating there? Look at each of the letters in the word and count the number of vowels. From left to right, what are they? **Students Do:** Count one vowel and identify it by name (*o*). **Teacher Says:** Now count the number of consonants. How many? **Students Do:** Count four consonants and identify them by name (*g*, *h*, *s* and *t*). **Teacher Says:** Can you still see the word in your head? Can you see any words inside the word? What are they? Now, while you are looking at the word floating there, name each of the letters in the word starting at the end of the word and going from right to left. Now, say the word, use it in a sentence that shows you understand its meaning and write the sentence in your notebook. [Attaching word meaning to the MOI is very important.] [If students have difficulty answering any of the questions, their MOI is not firmly fixed in their memory. Go back to Step 4 and visualise the word once again. Continue to work with the chosen words for the day. At the end of the lesson, students can retain their cards and use them for fluency practice throughout the day.]

Source: Masterson, Apel, & Wasowicz, 2002, p. 44; personal communication with J. Wasowicz, August 2008–January 2009.

Part 4

Interventions for Building Fluency

What the Research Says About Fluency Instruction

Since the release of the *Report of the National Reading Panel* (National Institute of Child Health and Human Development, 2000), *fluency* has become the new buzzword. Repeated oral reading of text has become the intervention strategy of choice for struggling readers. What the panel's summary failed to point out, however, was *what kind* of text students should be repeatedly reading.

Seventy-four per cent of the fluency studies reviewed by the U.S. National Reading Panel used texts with *controlled vocabularies* (for example, books with a carefully selected and limited number of words that are frequently repeated in the story so as to give students several practices at reading a word). Four of these studies used literature for repeated reading. Only one of the four literature-based studies reported any improvement in students' fluency, and in that study, treatment and comparison groups did not differ significantly. What is crucial for practitioners to know is that *the effect size for fluency reported by the National Reading Panel came from the studies that used texts with controlled vocabulary* (Hiebert & Fisher, 2005). The implication of this research for practitioners is this: if you want to facilitate the development of fluency in your students, provide them with passages and books that contain limited and controlled vocabularies that ensure multiple encounters with words, rather than choosing literature that contains an abundance of rare and multisyllabic words that are only used once in the text.

Fluency encompasses at least five different components (Torgesen, Rashotte & Alexander, 2001):

- The proportion of words that are recognised as orthographic units—that is, sight words that can be immediately retrieved from long-term memory

- The variation in speed with which sight words are processed, either because they have not yet been fully fixed in the reader's long-term memory or because the reader has some difficulties with processing speed

- The speed of the processes that are used to identify novel words that have never been encountered previously by the reader (such as phonemic decoding, analogy to known words, or guessing from the context or meaning of the passage)

- Use of context to speed word identification, which is largely dependent on extensive vocabulary knowledge

- Speed with which word meanings are identified

Of these five aspects of reading fluency, one stands out as the biggest roadblock: problems identifying individual words fluently. If your students have deep deficits in word identification, consider whether the intervention strategies in part 3, "Interventions for Building Word Identification Skills", might be more relevant to their needs. Students who can identify words but do so slowly and without fluency are more likely to benefit from fluency interventions. Students who cannot read regular words at all need intensive word identification instruction.

Before you implement any of the five fluency intervention strategies in part 4, "Interventions for Building Fluency", make sure that you have data from a reliable and valid assessment instrument to inform your decision. Such data can help you in targetting specific students as well as in making needed adjustments to the sample lessons that are provided. As you implement, informally assess the individual students in your group on specific skills as part of every lesson to adjust instruction for the next day. Also, give the regular curriculum-based progress-monitoring tests to collect more definitive data. If needed, be open to scheduling more time or decreasing the size of an intervention group.

INTERVENTION 13

Crossing the Fluency Bridge (Years 1–3)

> *Helping students become more fluent readers should be a very high priority if they are very dysfluent, but it is likely that many "moderately dysfluent" readers would do much better on comprehension assessment if they had better vocabularies and approached text more thoughtfully.*
>
> —Torgesen (2009, p. 27)

This intervention strategy is focused on getting students from the decoding side of the "fluency bridge" to the comprehension side by increasing their ability to read words in connected text with accuracy, automaticity and prosody (the linguistic term for the features of oral language that give expression to the words on the printed page) at increasing levels of difficulty, gradually moving from scaffolded oral reading to independent silent reading. It intervenes early and focuses on the "big picture" of fluency to include wide reading in a variety of texts along with personalised accountability.

Essential Program Components for Building Fluency by the End of Year Two

Fluency is the bridge between decoding and comprehension (Pikulski & Chard, 2005), and beginning readers will never move from painstaking decoding to comprehension and a love of reading unless they come across that fluency bridge with automaticity, accuracy and prosody tucked away in their reading toolkit. Some students are scarcely aware that they crossed a bridge, the transition is so effortless for them. Others experience delays and detours that make the comprehension destination nearly impossible to reach.

There are dozens of books and programs on the market showing you how to build fluency with repeated oral reading in years 2–6. They contain activities like echo reading, partner reading, assisted reading and Reader's Theatre, to name a few. I have described these and many other approaches in several books (McEwan, 2009; McEwan, Dobberteen, & Pearce, 2008a, 2008b). In this book, I offer some alterative ways to look at fluency building.

Repeated oral reading represents the now almost conventional wisdom for struggling readers who fail to reach the benchmark on any reading fluency probe. Do not allow your quest for speed to overshadow the main idea of reading: comprehension. If students are not focused on meaning while they are racing through their fluency passages, their focus on speed may become their primary goal in reading—something we want to avoid at all costs.

The following intervention strategy is a schoolwide endeavour that begins in prep. This preventive "intervention" is based on the most current research, my personal experiences in raising student achievement in a low-performing school, and my ethnographic research in high-performing primary schools regarding what it takes to teach them all to read (McEwan, 2008, 2009):

1. Explicit, systematic, supportive instruction in accessible text for all students

2. Daily oral independent reading in accessible text for at least forty-five minutes with a focus on comprehension

3. An emphasis on comprehension, endurance and accountability, along with speed and accuracy in oral reading

4. An at-home reading component of thirty minutes per day

Explicit, Systematic, Supportive Instruction in Accessible Text for All Students

The challenge of teaching all students to read using a core or basal program cannot be underestimated. The research is clear regarding the importance of providing accessible text to develop fluent, independent readers (Hiebert, 2008). Yet educators persist in trying to teach a year-level basal program to all of the students in the class, regardless of their instructional needs. It is well known that basal programs are designed to meet the needs of a narrow band of students from slightly below average to slightly above average. This, however, leaves the poor "average" classroom teacher to cope with students at risk, students with reading disabilities and gifted students in some type of differentiated group. Skill-based reading groups are unpopular in many circles, but if you use skill-based reading groups from the beginning with intensive, explicit, systematic instruction, you will both eliminate the need for specialised and intensive interventions and reduce your special education referrals (McEwan, 2009).

The first step to facilitating fluency is building fluent sight-reading of words in a serial processing format (see figure 19.6). Students learn to first orally sound out words, then sound out words silently to themselves, and then blend the word fast and say it out loud. The goal of a first reading of words in lists or text at a students' instructional level is word identification within three seconds (Bursuck & Damer, 2007). Be aware that students can readily memorise words in a list, so you should present the words in a different order each time a list is repeated. After students are skilled at sight-reading words serially, transition to passage reading. Students are introduced to the idea of passage sight-reading and then practise sight-reading a story in unison. Once again, pay attention to any errors students make, correcting them immediately. As you orally practise sight-reading passages with your students, listen carefully for the following kinds of errors:

- Letter-sound correspondence errors (saying "hat" for "hit", or "ten" for "tin")

- Word-type errors (leaving off the final consonant in a *CVCC* word [a word that has a consonant/vowel/consonant/consonant spelling pattern]—saying "lam" for "lamp")

- Random-guessing errors (errors that follow no specific pattern and indicate the student is not paying attention to all of the letters in words)

- Fluency errors (student reads much more slowly than the rest of the group)

These types of errors indicate the need for more intense practice to build up automaticity. Figure 6.4 shows a routine for correcting errors.

Daily Oral Reading in Accessible Text

As noted later in Intervention 39, there is no substitute for students engaging in as much reading of text at their independent reading level as possible. Some call it *wide reading*. Others call it *voluminous reading*. I recommend at least forty-five minutes per day at school for beginning readers—and more if you can squeeze it in. This time period can be divided into shorter segments that feature different activities or configurations of partner reading, choral reading or echo reading. In the beginning, real reading must be monitored to make sure that students are individually processing the text with understanding. Silent reading comes later, when you are certain a student has crossed the fluency bridge from decoding to comprehension.

Comprehension, Endurance and Accountability

Constantly remind your students to focus on the meaning of the text. Research has shown that certain fundamental comprehension processes become automatic with practice, and these automatic processes can help students perform much better in all situations in which they are reading for meaning. Encourage your students to read with expression (prosody), and periodically listen to each student reading aloud to determine if his or her expression shows an understanding of the text.

In one school, educators have forsaken the one-minute readings as a way of building fluency in favour of a longer three-minute read. Their goal is to build *endurance*, a reading pace that is brisk enough to leave working memory free to comprehend but not so fast and furious as to make comprehension impossible (personal communication, A. Boden, January, 2009). One-minute timed readings are done only during benchmark testing. During their three-minute reads, students read short, nonfiction, controlled-vocabulary books at their independent reading levels, marking where they left off in their oral reading after three minutes. They must then choose one of four ways to demonstrate their comprehension:

1. Writing a sentence about the main idea
2. Choosing a word they did not understand and finding a definition for it
3. Writing a question they would like to ask the author about the text
4. Writing down a connection they made from this text to something else they have read or experienced

Students who are unable to complete one of the four squares are required to reread the same passage.

At-Home Reading Component of Thirty Minutes per Day

As part of this intervention, students are expected to read orally at home for at least thirty minutes per day—reading aloud accessible texts to parents, siblings, neighbours, pets and anyone else who will listen. Training is provided for parents.

Much is expected of students, teachers and parents from this model. Teachers will need support from paraprofessionals, the librarian, the principal and parents. Students will need to be encouraged and motivated by the principal and their parents. Parents will need training at all-school Literacy Nights and continued encouragement from teachers and administrators to urge their students across the fluency bridge by the end of year two. This is a journey that requires commitment and effort from all of the stakeholders. However, with a program like this, only a handful of students should fail to readily respond because you have held high expectations coupled with providing multiple opportunities to learn.

INTERVENTION 14

Facilitating Fluency in Your Reading Groups (Years 1–2)

> *We do not want students to simply "read fast". We want them to read fluently while they are extracting and constructing meaning from what they have read.*
>
> —Torgesen (2009, p. 31)

This intervention strategy describes several ways to approach reading a story during whole-group instruction or in skill-based intervention groups with the goal of building fluency. Used with the whole class, these approaches are not interventions in the strictest sense of the word. However, used as a preventive intervention, embedded oral reading can catch students before they fall through the cracks into the abyss of reading failure and often results in higher achievement for average and above-average students as well.

Background Knowledge

Students who score well on high-stakes assessments can actually have widely varying reading rates. Helping students become more fluent readers should be a high priority if they are very dysfluent, but according to Torgesen (2009), it is likely that many "moderately dysfluent readers would do much better on comprehension assessments if they had more extensive vocabularies, had been instructed in the application of cognitive strategies whenever and whatever they read, and approached all reading tasks with mindfulness" (p. 27).

Sample Lessons for Facilitating Fluency

Figure 14.1 summarises three distinct approaches for use either with the whole class or with teacher-directed intervention groups. Figure 14.2 describes a "cold reading" approach that is impossible to use with a heterogeneous group of students, many of whom are unable to access the text without substantial amounts of scaffolding. However, if your goal is to prepare students for fluent reading of year-level textbooks in years 3 and beyond, or taking a high-stakes reading comprehension test, the best way to differentiate reading instruction is in skill-based groups rather than heterogenous groups (Bursuck et al., 2004). You will have the time to teach the essential skills, build in generous amounts of massed practice and cumulative review, and provide daily opportunities for students to read widely and independently with confidence.

Figure 14.1: Fluency lesson formats.

Format	Description	Background Knowledge
Fluency Development Lesson	A combination of reading aloud, choral reading, listening to students read and reading performance is implemented over a period of several days. Students first listen to the teacher read a poem or other text to the class. Then they read the text chorally, then pair and practice reading the text with a classmate, and finally perform for an audience—either another class at their year level or a class of younger or older students.	Developed by Rasinski, Padak, Linke and Sturdevant (1994), this format works well with short selections or poetry from the literature anthology. It will also work as a cooperative centre activity in which a confident reader is paired with a struggling reader.
SAFER	Successful Anxiety-Free, Engaged Reading is a lesson format that builds reading fluency in a different way: by having students independently decode passages at their instructional level using the phonemic decoding skills they have acquired in prior lessons. This method only works when students are grouped by skill so all students in the group are on nearly the same level.	SAFER was developed by Bill Bursuck and Mary Damer in conjunction with research conducted in low-performing schools. Project PRIDE (Preventing and Remediating Reading Problems Through Early Identification and Direct Teaching of Early Literacy Skills), a Model Demonstration Project for Children with Disabilities funded through OSEP (Office of Special Education Programs) is a multitiered model for years P–3 that offers extra support for students at the first sign of reading difficulty (Bursuck et al., 2004).
Fluency Oriented Reading Instruction	FORI is a five-day lesson format. On Day 1, the teacher reads the core program selection to the students and leads a comprehension and vocabulary discussion. Depending on the time available, the teacher might have students echo read with her or have student pairs orally practise parts of the story. On subsequent days of the week, students use a variety of oral reading configurations. There is also a wide reading component at school (fifteen minutes per day) and an extensive reading at home component for thirty minutes.	This format was originally developed for year two classrooms (Stahl & Heubach, 2005). The idea of this format is appealing with one exception: students are never expected to tackle text at their instructional level on their own to practise and refine their phonemic decoding skills. The teacher first reads the story aloud, and students are never expected to do a cold read without first having heard all of the words in the story. In some cases, students are off on their own repeatedly, reading the story, having had no error correction or reteaching when needed.

© 2009 Hawker Brownlow Education and Elaine McEwan-Adkins.

Figure 14.2: Sample lesson for a cold read.

Steps to SAFER Reading	Some Things to Think About
1. Call on individual students randomly, and have them read one to three sentences in the story.	Although Step 1 may appear to be round-robin reading, it is not. What makes SAFER reading different is that all of the students in the SAFER group have the skills needed to read the text independently. Students will not be embarrassed or intimidated. They will be tuned in to the text, knowing that they will be called on and feeling confident that they are ready. In the typical round-robin reading session, the students are at multiple reading levels with varying degrees of engagement with the text. High-level readers are skipping ahead. Struggling readers are avoiding the eyes of the teacher, hoping they won't be called upon to read.
2. Expect students to follow along in the text with their pointer fingers.	This simple technique enables students to focus on the text and keeps them from losing their places.
3. Call on students quickly, and avoid unnecessary tangential teacher talk by focusing comprehension questions to key ideas, vocabulary and supporting details.	Make this aspect of your SAFER reading as "perky" and "brisk" as you can. Resist the temptation to engage in teacher talk (meandering side trips that create mindless reading).
4. Write missed words on the board. At the end of the story, have students sound out each missed decodable word and read it. If the missed word is an exception word, tell the student the word.	In addition to telling students missed exception words, encourage them to visualise the word with their eyes closed and then orally spell it using the visualisation method described in figure 12.1. The error correction aspect of SAFER reading is critical because when immediate and corrective feedback is provided, accurate word reading and comprehension significantly improve (Pany & McCoy, 1988).
5. Note any obvious error patterns to determine if reteaching is needed.	
6. Explain to students that their goal is 97 per cent accuracy. Reread the story once more before having students pair up and read the story to each other. Monitor for accuracy as students read.	At this point, students should engage in a variety of repeated oral readings until the fluency goal of 97 per cent accuracy is achieved. The FORI lesson plan offers a variety of ways to structure the remaining days of the week.

Source: The steps to SAFER reading have been adapted from Bursuck & Damer, 2007. SAFER is based on procedures for instructing group oral reading originally developed by Carnine et al. (2004). "Some Things to Think About" are the author's.

INTERVENTION 15

Structuring Repeated Oral Reading Activities Using Prosody as a Motivator or Indicator of Text Comprehension (Years 3–6)

If speed and accuracy are the primary components that are assessed, students will soon figure this out. They will then concentrate on saying the words correctly as fast as they can and pay less attention to the process of understanding and enjoying what they read.

—Caldwell & Leslie (2009, p. 111)

This intervention strategy is designed for two different types of students: (1) dysfluent students who have difficulties with comprehension because of their painfully slow reading and (2) fluent readers who have excellent listening comprehension but have developed careless and mindless oral reading habits that often result in poor comprehension. This strategy consists of repeated oral reading performance activities to improve fluency and comprehension. The activities can be used as interventions, extra practice or for take-home programs in which students read aloud to their parents.

Background Knowledge

Fluency consists of three key elements: (1) accurate reading of connected text, (2) at a conversational rate, (3) with appropriate prosody (Hudson, Mercer, & Lane, 2000). If fluency was the forgotten piece of the reading puzzle for many years, it can now be said that, until recently, prosody was the forgotten piece of the fluency puzzle. In most measures, no mention is made of *prosody*—reading with expression and intonation appropriate to the meaning of the text.

Lack of prosody in oral reading can be observed in two kinds of readers:

1. Fluent readers who are unable to read with appropriate expression and intonation because they do not comprehend the text

2. Skilled readers who are able to comprehend the text but are so focused on reading speed that they fail to attend to meaning and thus are unable to read with expression

Using fluency-building exercises for students in the first category who are unable to understand the text is not a productive use of instructional time. Those students need diagnostic testing to determine the source of their comprehension difficulties (such as inadequate word identification skills, or lack of background knowledge, vocabulary and cognitive strategies).

© 2009 Hawker Brownlow Education • SOT4749

However, skilled readers who *could* comprehend the text if they attended to what they were reading and were held accountable for doing so is a problem that *can* be remediated. Torgesen (2009) advises that the most productive and research-based approach to the prosody-comprehension connection is for teachers to always expect students to read with prosody and to model prosody regularly for students when reading aloud to them. This kind of accountability during oral reading for fluency building, or even during the test, probes students to focus on, think about and pay closer attention to the text in order to determine what kind of expression and intonation to use in their oral reading. Mindless reading—both oral and silent—is well documented. It is not evidence of a lack of ability to comprehend text per se, but evidence of periodic disengagement with the text (Schooler, Reichle, & Halpern, 2004). In this case, prosody functions like any number of strategies that teachers employ to motivate their students to concentrate on what they are reading.

Repeated Oral Reading Performance Activities to Improve Comprehension

Figure 15.1 contains descriptions and brief directions for five different repeated oral reading performance activities.

Figure 15.1: Repeated oral reading performance activities as a motivator and an indicator of comprehension.

Activity	Description of the Activity	Directions
Reader's Theatre	Reader's Theatre helps text come alive as students take on roles in short plays. This method of repeated reading enables students to participate in the reading of a play without the props, scenery and endless rehearsals. Students do not memorise lines or wear costumes. They just repeatedly read their parts orally in preparation for the performance (Opitz & Rasinski, 1998).	Follow these steps: (1) Select a script. (2) Assign parts to students. (3) Gather the play group together, and give everyone a chance to review their parts. Provide definitions if there are any unknown words. (4) Go through the script together, pointing out different places where people can mark their scripts for expression because of certain words or because of punctuation marks (? !). (5) Assign people to practise their parts by reading each line three times with the appropriate expression. Use the echo reading technique below to model prosody for students.
Echo reading	To echo read, the teacher orally reads the first line of the text in a poem or play, and the student then reads the same line, modelling the teacher's example. The purpose of echo reading in this context is to model intonation and phrasing for students who have difficulties with prosody.	Blevins (2001) suggests that one way to teach intonation is to have students recite the alphabet as a conversation, using punctuation to cue inflection (for example, ABCD? EFGHI! JKL. MN? OPQ. RST! UVWXYZ!). Another way to help students pay attention to punctuation cues for their intonation is to recite the same sentence using different punctuation. Still another way to practise inflection is to use a sentence in which the meaning changes depending on the word that is stressed. *I* am tired. I *am* tired. I am *tired*.

continued →

Activity	Description of the Activity	Directions
Radio reading	In radio reading, students are assigned selected portions of a text that will be used for shared reading, a read-aloud activity or a lesson in the content area (Searfoss, 1975).	This read-aloud activity is far more motivating and productive than round-robin reading. (1) Have small groups of students work together. Prepare sections of a chapter to be read either chorally or individually. (2) Ask students to read their portion as many times as needed to develop expression and fluency. (3) More proficient students might read parts of the chapter solo. (4) Ask one student to be the announcer and read the opening and closing parts of the story or chapter.
Read around	Reading around provides an easy method for motivating students to read a passage of their own choosing until it is polished for a quick performance (Tompkins, 1998).	Ask students to choose a favourite poem, narrative text or song with lyrics. Have students rehearse the passage until they can read it fluently. Students then read the passage aloud to a peer, a small group or the entire class.
Talking for two	Short plays for two students provide motivating practice that takes less time than preparing for a complete Reader's Theatre.	Follow these steps: (1) Find (McEwan et al., 2008a) or write your own talking for two scripts. (2) Assign each student a part in the play. (3) Have students repeatedly practise their parts to improve their prosody. (4) Invite students to perform their play for the rest of the class.

© 2009 Hawker Brownlow Education and Elaine McEwan-Adkins.

Remediating the Robotic Reader With or Without Comprehension

In almost every workshop I give, a participant asks me about an intermediate-year level student who reads like a robot—automatic and accurate with a speed of 130 words correct per minute but with very poor comprehension. Here are some ways to assess and help a robotic reader:

- Make him aware of his inexpressive reading by having him listen to a tape of his reading.

- Tape a short session of echo reading with the student, as described in figure 15.1.

- Assess the student's reading comprehension during a short period of scaffolded silent reading. Choose a selection on the student's independent reading level that he has not previously read. Direct him to read the first two or three sentences silently and to make a slash mark after the third sentence when he is finished. Observe him closely while he is reading to see if he seems to be paying attention to and processing the text. Interrupt his reading and ask him one or two questions about what he has read. If he answers the questions satisfactorily, ask him to read until you tell him to stop. Ask him to make a slash mark after the word he was reading when you told him to stop. Ask one or two additional questions. If he answers the questions satisfactorily, ask him to read the remainder of the selection silently and answer the five multiple-choice questions at the end. If the student has serious comprehension problems, he will be unable to answer any of your questions correctly, and he will need scaffolded comprehension instruction. However, if the student's comprehension is satisfactory, you can conclude that he is a perfect example of the adage "what gets measured, gets done". You communicated to the student that the critical attributes of oral reading were speed and accuracy. He gave you what you measured. Now, you need to communicate to him the importance of attending to meaning and changing some of his bad habits through performance reading.

INTERVENTION 16

Choosing Books for Independent Reading (Years 3–6)

> *Too often, even participating in a supplemental intervention program does little to optimize matching struggling readers with appropriate texts. . . . Many schools seem to be enamored with providing too-hard texts for students, especially struggling readers.*
>
> —Allington (2006, p. 101)

In this intervention, students learn how to evaluate text for its accessibility. Students will choose books that match their independent reading levels. Teachers will understand the importance of having a wide variety of accessible texts available and of using accessible texts for intervention instruction.

Background Knowledge

The three levels of text that students encounter in school are (1) frustration, (2) instructional and (3) independent. These levels are described in detail in figure 16.1.

Struggling year one readers are frequently caught in a catch-22. To develop fluency, they must engage in wide reading in accessible text—text at their independent reading level. However, it can be hard to convince both teachers and struggling readers of the importance of reading easier materials. Reluctant readers are embarrassed to be seen with "easy" books, so they use the "pretending to read" technique. Teachers often do not have a lot of experience with matching students with accessible text, or may not have an available supply of books that are accessible to students (Allington, 2006; Swanson & Hoskyn, 1998). This is a problem to be tackled by the librarian, the principal, the reading specialist and the classroom teacher jointly. Administrators cannot expect teachers to completely stock a classroom library without monetary support.

Figure 16.1: Levels of text.

Frustration	Never give students text at their frustration level. When expected to read text at this level, students tune out, talk to their classmates, distract the teacher and find excuses to move about the room.
Instructional	Choose text at students' instructional level when the goals are building word and world knowledge, and when scaffolding comprehension strategies that have previously been taught. When text is at their instructional level, students need teacher support to read the text with understanding. Instructional text is text that students can read "cold" with at least 90 per cent accuracy. No more than one in ten words should be too difficult for students to read on their own.
Independent	Choose text at your students' independent reading level for repeated oral reading to build fluency, for oral reading to increase comprehension of text or for independent reading at home. When text is at students' independent levels, they can generally read the text with ease and fluency. Texts at this level can be read with at least 95 per cent accuracy on a first or "cold" read. No more than one in twenty words should be too difficult for the student to recognise through analytic means (phonemic decoding, analogy, context). Many words should already be sight words, instantly retrievable in a second or less.

Source: Armbruster, Lehr, & Osborn, 2001; Bursuck & Damer, 2007; Harris & Sipay, 1985.

Sample Lesson for Teaching Book Selection

Figure 16.2 is a lesson for teaching students how to differentiate among the three levels of text. Figure 16.3 displays the readability of three samples of teacher text, and figure 16.4 displays the readability of three samples of student text.

Figure 16.2: Sample lesson for teaching how to choose the right kind of books.

Lesson Objective	Students will be able to name the three levels of text difficulty and evaluate books they are choosing for independent reading to determine if the books are at their independent reading level.
Materials Needed for the Lesson	You'll need overhead transparencies of different levels of text to model for students regarding your personal reading level (see figure 16.3). You'll also need a second set of three levels of text for students to choose the best kind of text to build fluency (see figure 16.4).
Advance Organiser	**Teacher Says:** Today we're going to learn about the best kinds of books for you to read if you want to become a better reader. But first, I want to show you how I find the best books for myself.

continued →

I Do It: Teacher Models	**Teacher Says:** I have samples of three different kinds of books that I might pick to read while I'm on holiday. I'm going to the beach, so I need something that I will enjoy reading.
Teacher Does: Put up three examples of personal text: one sample each of frustration-level, instructional-level and independent-level text. Cover all but the frustration-level text (figure 16.3).
Teacher Says: As I think about reading this and trying to understand it, I get a little nervous. It looks really hard. There are a lot of words, and even though I can figure out how to pronounce them, I don't know what they mean. I think this book is at my frustration level. Do you know what I mean? If I had to read this and answer questions about it, I would not be at all happy. In fact, I would be upset. I might even not do the assignment, not because I don't want to, but because I can't.
Teacher Does: Next, display personal text at the instructional reading level.
Teacher Says: This text looks a little easier. I do know something about this subject, and I think if I looked up the words I don't know in the dictionary and maybe asked one of my friends to explain a few things to me, I could read this and understand it. I might have to read some parts of it two or three times to understand it well. This text is at my instructional level. I need help, but not a lot.
Teacher Does: Display the personal text at your independent reading level.
Teacher Says: Now this text looks like something I could read on an aeroplane or when I'm at the beach. I could read it quickly, and I'd understand everything I read. My reading wouldn't have to stop and start and stop and start while I tried to figure out what I was reading about. This is text at my independent reading level.
We Do It: Teacher and Students Work Together	**Teacher Says:** I'm going to put up samples of three different reading assignments that you might be given in class (figure 16.4).
Teacher Does: Put the overhead on the screen, covering all but the first sample frustration-level text.
Teacher Says: Does this text have a lot of difficult words? [Students shake their heads.] Do you think you could write a summary of it? When the assignments you are given don't make sense, we say that the text is at your frustration level.
Teacher Does: Show the next reading level: instructional.
Teacher Says: What about this assignment? Does it look a little easier to read? [Students nod their heads.] What makes it easier to read? [Possible answers might include bigger print, easier words, knowing something about the topic, being able to read most of the words.] Reading like this is at your instructional level. That means you'll be able to read it if we talk about it ahead of time, or I tell you the meanings of the hard words, or I give you some background knowledge to help you understand what's going on.
Teacher Does: Display the final reading assignment: students' independent reading level.
Teacher Says: What about this assignment? Does it look easier to read? [Students nod their heads yes with more enthusiasm this time.] What makes this one so much easier to read? [Answers might include knowing all of the words, knowing something about the subject, bigger print or pictures to give clues.] Let's make a list of things that make text easier to read. [Drawing on all of the former answers, make a list together.]
Teacher Says: I have a collection of what I call *QuickReads* [Hiebert, 2003]. These are books at your independent reading level that will help you learn new things and become better readers.
Teacher Says: Look through the books and choose one that looks interesting to you. Make sure that you pick a book that is near or on your independent level so you can develop reading fluency. Tomorrow we're going to talk about the best way to read words.

© 2009 Hawker Brownlow Education and Elaine McEwan-Adkins.

Figure 16.3: Three levels of teacher text.

Difficulty of Text	Reading Sample
Frustration Level	According to the classical doctrine—generally adopted by physicists until the beginning of the twentieth century—one associates with physical systems whose evolution one wishes to describe a certain number of quantities or dynamical variables; each of these variables possesses at each instant a well-defined value, and the specification of this set of values defines the dynamical state of the system at that instant. One further postulates that the evolution in time of the physical system is entirely determined if one knows its state at a given initial instant. (Messiah, 1999, p. 3) 12.0 Year Level
Instructional Level	In sum, this study took a multilevel and multivariate latent variable modelling perspective to investigate different potential sources of influences at the classroom level. This approach had several advantages over univariate regression. First, it shifted the focus of research from simplistic prediction to understanding the structure of literacy. Second, a multivariate approach allowed us to empirically evaluate competing but theoretically specified models of literacy in a confirmatory fashion. Third, the multilevel approach made a conceptual and empirical distinction between the construct of literacy at the levels of individual students and classrooms. (Mehta, Foorman, Branum-Martin & Taylor, 2005, p. 90) 12.0 Year Level
Independent Level	He stood at the kitchen window and watched her coming through the hedge. What was she lugging this time? It appeared to be a bowl and jug. Or was it a stack of books topped by a vase? The rector took off his glasses, fogged them, and wiped them with his handkerchief. It was a bowl and jug, all right. How the little yellow house next door had contained all the stuff they'd recently muscled into the rectory was beyond him. (Karon, 1996, p. 1) 2.2 Year Level

© 2009 Hawker Brownlow Education and Elaine McEwan-Adkins.

Figure 16.4: Three levels of student text.

Difficulty of Text	Reading Sample
Frustration Level	High in the Swiss Alps, an imposing tenth-century monastery stands at a treacherous mountain pass. Led by a man who would be known to the world as St Bernard, monks built the monastery and included a hospice where travellers could get help on the difficult journey across the mountain. Even in the summer, the narrow trails were tricky to navigate. But in the harsh winter, they were nearly impossible. The snow and ice-covered terrain were extremely hazardous. Blizzards with gale-force winds and avalanches could turn it into a death trap where victims could be buried in an instant or freeze to death in blinding snowstorms. (107 words) Readability Microsoft Word 9.3
Instructional Level	The unicorn is an animal of myth. People of the Middle Ages said it was as white as new-fallen snow. It looked like a beautiful horse with a long curly mane and tail. Sometimes it had a small white beard at the tip of its chin. The unicorn was a magical animal. Its magic was in a spiral horn in the middle of its forehead. Baby unicorns were born with a tiny star where the horn would grow. The horn made dirty water fresh again. It was also a cure for poison. That is why people hunted unicorns. The unicorn was shy. (103 words) Readability Microsoft Word 4.3

continued →

Choosing Books for Independent Reading

Difficulty of Text	Reading Sample
Independent Level	Some spiders build webs, and some do not. The trapdoor spider does not build a web. It digs a burrow. Under its fangs it has spines. The spider uses its spines to scrape a hole in the ground. It lines its burrow with spider silk. The silk is made in the spider's body. It comes out through a hole in the underside of the spider. The trapdoor spider makes a special lid of earth and leaves or grass. Some spiders build in escape routes or false doors. The burrow protects the spider from rain. The spider stays in its burrow during the day. (103 words) Readability Microsoft Word 2.4

Source: Reading sample passages are adapted from McEwan et al., 2008b. Year level readability scores obtained using Microsoft Word 2.4.

INTERVENTION 17

Teaching the Fastest Way to Read Words (Years 3–6)

> *If words are not identified accurately in sufficient numbers of repetitions, then accurate orthographic representations are not formed, and words must be recognised through analytic means (phonemic analysis, analogy, context) that take more time than recognition on the basis of a unitized orthographic representation. One of the principle characteristics of most children with reading disabilities after the initial phase in learning to read is a severe limitation in the number of words that can be recognised instantly.*
>
> —Torgesen, Rashotte & Alexander
> (2001, p. 348)

This intervention strategy is designed to help struggling upper-years students understand the four ways to read words and how to become skilled at reading the fastest way—that is, the most efficient and effective way—thereby eliminating guessing as the strategy of choice. Struggling students in years 4–6 often have gaps in almost every area of reading. This is not evidence that they have never been taught, but simply that they have not put together all of the pieces of the reading puzzle. They lack complete letter-sound knowledge as evidenced by their inability to fluently decode some nonsense words. They lack complete letter-sound blending knowledge as evidenced by their inability to quickly blend sounds they have decoded to make a familiar word. Lacking these skills, they have failed to develop an adequate lexicon of sight words. Thus, they fall back on the least effective and most error-prone way to read words, *contextual guessing*, which results in dysfluent reading and poor comprehension.

Background Knowledge

Many upper-years students have a serious case of what I call the "guessing syndrome". Perhaps you will recognise the symptoms:

- Students seem to know a word one day but forget it the next.

- Students miss details and even main ideas in text for which their listening comprehension is excellent.

- Students frequently misread multisyllabic words and sometimes stumble over the simplest words.

- Students have serious problems with spelling.

For these struggling readers, guessing is the strategy of choice. They look at the pictures (if there are any), they look at the first letter in the word, and then they make their best guess. Using context *is* an excellent strategy for determining word meaning (see Intervention 20 for a lesson plan to teach this strategy to students). However, guessing to identify words leads to bad habits that are difficult to break. Furthermore, the guessing strategy actually inhibits the development of sight words.

The guessing syndrome seems to have had its genesis in an approach called the three-cueing system, in which students are taught to figure out hard words by taking their best guess and then asking the following questions about their guess: Does it make sense? Does it sound right? Does it look right? No one seems to know where the three-cueing system came from, but noted reading expert Marilyn Adams (1998) hypothesises that it might have had its roots in the practice of using predictable books for repeated reading or reading practice by readers at risk, books in which context provides multiple word identification cues. However, Adams (1990) warns, "Where context is strong enough to allow quick and confident identification of the unfamiliar word, there is little incentive to pore over its spelling. And without studying the word's spelling, there is no opportunity for increasing its visual familiarity" (p. 217).

Sample Lesson for Teaching the Fastest Way to Read Words

Many upper-years struggling readers look at reading as a great mystery, even after all of the remediation they have endured. They feel a great sense of helplessness and discouragement and do not really believe they are capable of reading. Before you enrol them or send them to one more intervention, help them to understand what the intervention is intended to accomplish, why it will work (because it's research-based) and what they must do to make it work (effort). Prior to using a fluency-building program, also deliver the lesson about the three reading levels found in figure 16.1.

Just ahead is figure 17.1, a lesson for teaching students these four ways. Once you have taught this lesson, you will explore which way is the most efficient and explain how to acquire these mental orthographic images (mental visualisations of how the word is spelled) that are so essential for fluent reading. This sample lesson can help your students understand the reasons behind their intervention group lessons. Figure 17.2 contains the text for the lesson. Use one of the steps to reading big words found in Intervention 10 to help students divide the word *Punxsutawney* into syllables.

Figure 17.1: Sample lesson for teaching the fastest way to read words.

Lesson Objective	Students will understand the four ways to read words and be able to identify those ways in their own reading experiences.
Materials Needed for the Lesson	Write the four ways to read words on your whiteboard: contextual guessing, phonemic decoding, analogising and sight. Prepare an overhead transparency or PowerPoint slide using the text found in figure 17.2.
Advance Organiser	Teacher Says: Today we're going to learn about four different ways to read words. I've listed them on the whiteboard. Maybe you're surprised that there are only four, or maybe you haven't even thought about it. Once you understand these four ways, you will have a better idea of the fastest way to read words and want to learn more about how you can use this way to read words all the time.

continued →

I Do It: Teacher Models Contextual Guessing	**Teacher Does:** Put up the overhead transparency or slide you have created with the text in figure 17.2. **Teacher Says:** I'm going to model for you what the four ways to read words look like. I'm going to take them in the order they are listed on the whiteboard, starting with *contextual guessing*. Have you ever heard teachers say, "Take a good guess," when you haven't been able to figure out a word? What they mean is look around and see if there are any clues you can use to identify a word. The word I want to identify is the first one in the paragraph. That is a tongue twister. If I skip the first word and read the rest of the words in the first sentence, I find out that this unknown word is the name of a city. I think I can make an intelligent guess here. There are two cities I know of that begin with the letter *p*: Perth and Philadelphia. It's probably one of those. What do you think? Let's see if contextual guessing works for us here. How many vote for Perth? Wrong, it's not Perth. How many vote for Philadelphia? Wrong, it's not Philadelphia, either. How many knew it wasn't either of those cities? How did you know? [Some students give answers about decoding.] My question for you is this: is guessing a good way to read a word? [Students answer no.]
I Do It: Teacher Models Phonemic Decoding	**Teacher Says:** Let me show you another way to read words: *phonemic decoding* (sounding out the word). I know that you know how to sound out some words, but how about the word we're working on right now, the first word in the paragraph up on the screen? To decode, we have to use a big word strategy and divide it into syllables. [See figure 10.2] I know that each syllable will have a vowel in it, so here's what I come up with: *punx-su-taw-ney*. Well, it looks a little more manageable now. But I'm not quite sure what to do with that *x*. I don't know what sound the letter *x* would make in this word. Let's look at the third way to read words and see if that way can help us out with this big word.
I Do It: Teacher Models Analogising	**Teacher Says:** The third way to read a word is by *analogising*. Using this method helps me come up with a keyword that is spelled and pronounced like one of the syllables or parts of the word I'm trying to figure out. I do know a keyword that would help me with that *x*. *Box* is my keyword, and the sound *x* makes in *box* is /ks/. I also know a keyword for the word part *taw*. That would be *saw*. It rhymes with *taw*. I think that might give me the right pronunciation. But again, this is taking too long. I'll never get my assignment read if I have to spend a minute or more on every word. I have to be able to read a word in under a second to be a fluent reader.
I Do It: Teacher Models Retrieving Sight Words (MOIs) From Long-Term Memory	**Teacher Says:** The last and fastest way to read words is to have what is called a mental orthographic image (MOI) of this word fixed in my brain. When that happens, the word is called a *sight word*. That means the minute I see the word, I can say it correctly in a split second. The best way to create an MOI is to decode the word correctly several times. Here goes: *Punxsutawney, Punxsutawney, Punxsutawney*. Sometimes I only need to say a word orally or read it silently four times to get it fixed in my brain. But this word is impossible. There is one more way to get really hard words like this one or words that you can't possibly sound out because they don't follow any spelling rules: you can visualise them in your mind. It's like using your "mental camera" to take a picture of the word. If you do that, you can read the word and spell it. I'm going to visualise this word a few times, spelling it out loud and writing the letters at the same time: *p-u-n-x-s-u-t-a-w-n-e-y*. Now I'm going to close my eyes and visualise the word, saying the name of each letter starting at the end of the word and moving left to the beginning. Now I can read this story from start to finish without stopping to figure out the meaning. Of course, you knew all the time that the whole point of reading is meaning. That's why the more automatically and accurately you can read words, the better your comprehension will be. [See figure 12.1, for a lesson to teach mental orthographic images.]
We Do It: Teacher and Students Read in Unison	**Teacher Says:** Let's read this paragraph together. **Teacher Does:** Teacher and students chorally read the paragraph with the teacher, setting a brisk reading pace. If you hear students saying *Punsatawney* and leaving out the /ks/ sound, stop them immediately and say the word correctly for them. Then ask them to say the word correctly. Finally, begin reading the paragraph again. **Teacher Says:** Excellent reading. Now let's try it one more time. [If time permits, have students work in pairs to read the paragraph together.]

© 2009 Hawker Brownlow Education and Elaine McEwan-Adkins.

Figure 17.2: Text for the lesson in figure 17.1.

How Long Will Winter Last?

Punxsutawney is a city in America. It is known for its annual observance of Groundhog Day, 2 February. Every year a groundhog who is always named Punxsutawney Phil comes out of his burrow. The people in Punxsutawney say that if Phil sees his shadow, their winter will last for six more weeks. There is no scientific basis for this belief, but the residents of Punxsutawney have created an annual event that has made their city famous for at least one day every year.

© 2009 Hawker Brownlow Education and Elaine McEwan-Adkins.

Part 5

Interventions for Building Vocabulary

What the Research Says About Vocabulary Instruction

Language development is inextricably linked to reading success (Biemiller, 1999), and vocabulary knowledge is an important predictor of reading comprehension. When Becker (1977) first posed the idea that the school failure of disadvantaged children was due to lack of vocabulary knowledge, it was a new idea that stimulated vigorous discussion and research regarding how many words students should be learning and how many they learn from direct instruction and incidentally at school (Cunningham & Stanovich, 1998; Nagy & Anderson, 1984).

Although the idea of "linguistically poor" students is no longer a new one, solutions to the problem continue to frustrate educators. While we may be able to teach discrete reading skills, we are depressingly familiar with what often happens to linguistically poor students once they leave the cocoon of the primary year levels. If these students are not consistently, directly and intensively taught word knowledge from the moment they enter school, their hard-won achievement gains from the primary year levels will begin to fade as they struggle to handle the demands of more difficult upper-year texts. Low-SES students, racial and ethnic minority students, and students whose first language is not English are especially hard-hit by what Moats (2001) calls "linguistic poverty" (p. 8).

Linguistic poverty includes partial knowledge of word meanings, confusion regarding words that sound similar but that contrast in one or two phonemes, and limited knowledge of how and when words are typically used. The gap in vocabulary knowledge between economically disadvantaged and economically advantaged children that begins in preschool persists through the school years and is a depressing correlate of poor school performance (Coyne, Simmons, & Kame'enui, 2004).

Simply giving students definitions of new words is not enough to improve their comprehension when they encounter those words in future reading (Stahl & Fairbanks, 1986). However, if students are provided with *both* definitional and contextual information about a new word, their comprehension improves significantly (Stahl, 1999).

Teaching definitional information includes teaching antonyms and synonyms for new words, rewriting or restating definitions in students' own words, providing examples and nonexamples of the word, and comparing and contrasting the word and related words. *Providing contextual information* includes giving students several sentences that illustrate the word being used in different contexts, creating a short story or scenario in which the word plays a role, or acting out the word or drawing a picture for younger students. Students are then asked to create their own sentences using the featured word as well as sentences using more than one of the new words, which helps them see relationships between the words.

Ehri and Rosenthal (2007) investigated whether experience with the written spellings of the new words would help students (lower-SES year two and fives) learn the pronunciations and meanings of those words (which were nouns). The two year levels were each taught two sets of words. The words were defined, depicted and embedded in sentences. During study periods, the students were shown the written forms of only one set of words. Spellings were not presented for the other set of words.

Presenting the spellings of the words enhanced students' memory for the pronunciations and meanings compared to the words for which students did not have spellings presented. In both groups, students who were initially better spellers and readers did increasingly better than students who were poorer spellers and readers.

Before you implement any of the eight vocabulary interventions in part 5, "Interventions for Building Vocabulary", make sure that you have data from a reliable and valid assessment instrument to inform your decision. Such data can help you in targetting specific students as well as in making needed adjustments to the sample lessons that are provided. As you implement, informally assess the individual students in your group on specific skills as part of every lesson to adjust instruction for the next day. Also, give the regular curriculum-based progress-monitoring tests to collect more definitive data. If needed, be open to scheduling more time or decreasing the size of an intervention group.

INTERVENTION 18

Using Context to Infer Word Meanings (Years 2–6)

> *In order for any word learning to occur from reading, two conditions need to be met: First, students must read widely enough to encounter a substantial number of unfamiliar words. . . . Second, students must have the skills to infer word meaning from the contexts they read. The problem is that many students in need of vocabulary development do not engage in wide reading, especially of the kinds of books that contain unfamiliar vocabulary, and these students are less able to derive meaningful information from the context.*
>
> —Beck, McKeown & Kucan (2002, p. 4)

This intervention strategy teaches students a systematic method for using context to determine the meaning of unknown words they encounter in their reading. Students with extensive vocabularies and good phonemic decoding skills will often discover they already know a word and its meaning after they have decoded it and said it the "fast way". Using context to infer the meaning of a word is about being a word detective and using as many context clues as possible to solve the mystery of what the author is trying to convey to the reader by using this particular word.

Background Knowledge

Researchers agree that you cannot rely on context alone to give students all of the word and world knowledge they need to become successful readers (Feldman & Kinsella, 2002; Santa, Havens, & Valdes, 2004). Being able to use context to infer meaning is just one tool in the skilled reader's toolkit. On the other hand, when students encounter an unfamiliar word in the context of a high-stakes test, they need to have had multiple experiences with frequent teacher modelling of how to use context to infer a word's meaning.

Beck et al. (2002) give the following advice to teachers who would like to become more skilled at supporting their students' abilities to infer meaning from context:

- Anticipate that at first students will tend to engage in inappropriate meaning-deriving characteristics: limited use of context, attributing the meaning of a word to the meaning of the entire context, and creating a scenario for a word's possible meaning.

- Keep in mind that natural contexts do not act in logical and systematic ways and vary widely in the amount of information they provide about a given word.

- Because of the unreliability of natural contexts, in-struction needs to be presented as a process of figuring out meaning within individual contexts, rather than focusing on the product: a word's meaning.

- When implementing instruction, always start with ask-ing students to explain what is going on in the portion of text being read, and then what the word might mean. (pp. 114–115)

Sample Lesson for Teaching How to Use Context to Infer Word Meaning

Using context to determine a word's meaning may not be the most effective way to learn all there is to know about a word, but as an aid to reading comprehension, it is an essential strategy for students to have in their toolkits. Most readers don't stop and look up every new word they encounter, but the smartest readers recognise that some words are essential to extracting meaning from the text, and if they want to understand what they are reading, they must figure out the meaning of the word in any way they can.

Figure 18.1 contains a sample lesson for teaching primary students how to use context to determine a word's meaning. The lesson plan is easily adaptable to upper-years students. Choose text that is appropriate for those year levels, and prepare a simple poster containing these steps:

1. Underline the familiar word.
2. Read the sentences *before and after* the sentence containing the word.
3. Describe what you know so far.
4. Summarise what the story is about to this point.
5. Use what you know about the story and the sentence containing the word to infer what the word might mean.
6. Read the sentence again and substitute your idea of the word.
7. Decide if the word makes sense.

Keep in mind that teaching students how to use context to infer word meaning is of little value if you are not also teaching new words daily, getting excited about new words and featuring words prominently in all of your instruction.

Figure 18.1: Lesson plan for teaching primary students to use context to infer a word's meaning.

Lesson Objective	Students will be able to use context clues to infer word meanings.
Materials Needed for the Lesson	Prepare a poster containing the suggested guidelines, and prepare transparencies of various literature excerpts.
Advance Organiser	**Teacher Says:** Sometimes when you are reading, you will come to a word that you do not know. You may be able to use the words and sentences around that word to figure out what it means. The words and sentences around a word are called *context*. When you use the other words and sentences around a word to figure out its meaning, you are using context clues. You need to use context clues because they will help you understand what you are reading. Clues don't tell you the meaning. You have to become a detective and make a very good guess. First, I'm going to show you how to use context to figure out what a word means. Then we'll do it together. You can help me. Then, we'll work in pairs.

continued →

Using Context to Infer Word Meanings

I Do It: Teacher Models	**Teacher Says:** The example I have on the overhead is from the story "Marvin Redpost: Is He a Girl?" (Sachar, 1993). Follow along as I read it aloud. "He dreamed he was hanging from the monkey bars by his knees. A warm breeze blew in his face. Birds were singing." [p. 39]
	I can read the word *breeze*, but I do not understand what it means. I do not understand what is blowing in his face. I will underline *breeze*. That is Step 1.
	Teacher Does: Point to the poster.
	Teacher Says: Now I have to read the sentences before and after that word and think about what they mean. "He dreamed he was hanging from the monkey bars by his knees. Birds were singing." [p. 39] I have completed Step 2.
	Teacher Does: Point to the poster.
	Teacher Says: The next step is to summarise what the story is about up to this point. To summarise the story is to explain it in my own words. Here's my summary about the story to this point: The main character is worried that he might be turning into a girl. He is dreaming about "girl things" while hanging from the monkey bars. I have completed Step 4.
	Teacher Does: Point to the poster.
	Teacher Says: I am thinking about what Marvin is doing and where he is. When I am outside on the playground, the only thing that blows in my face is the wind. That is my guess about what the word breeze means. That takes care of Step 5.
	Teacher Does: Point to the poster.
	Teacher Says: Now let's try Step 6 and put the word *wind* in the sentence instead of *breeze*. "A warm light wind blew in my face." That makes perfect sense. A breeze must be a "light wind". That's Step 7, and we're done.
	Teacher Does: Point to the poster.
We Do It: Teacher and Students Work Together	**Teacher Says:** Let's try a word together. This one is from the story we started reading on Monday. It's from a part of the story we'll read today. Read aloud with me.
	Teacher Does: Place text from "Grandfather's Journey" (Say, 1993) on the overhead.
	Teacher Says: "The endless farm fields reminded him of the ocean he had crossed. Huge cities of factories and tall buildings bewildered and yet excited him. He marveled at the towering mountains and rivers as clear as the sky" (pp. 10–11). The word I have underlined is *bewildered*. Let's work together on using the clues in the context to figure out what the word means here.
	Let's read the sentences before and after the sentence with our mystery word: *bewildered*. [Teacher and students chorally read the two sentences.]
	Step 3 on our poster says: describe what you know so far. Tell me some things that we know so far in our story. I'll write them on the board.
	Andrew, tell me one thing about the story so far.
	Andrew Says: A man from Japan is on a trip to a new country. It's a long time ago because his clothes are different. They're old-fashioned.
	Teacher Says: Excellent. You used a picture clue to help you answer that question. That's a good detail to remember. Anna, can you tell me another thing you know so far about the story?
	Anna Says: The new country is different from his country.
	Teacher Says: Another good detail. Does anyone else have something we know about this story?
	Sasha Says: We know how he feels.

continued →

We Do It: Teacher and Students Work Together *(continued)*	**Teacher Says:** You know quite a bit about the story already. Let me see if I can summarise all of the things we know about the story so far. A summary means thinking about all of those details and putting them into a short sentence in our own words. Remember now, we haven't finished reading the story, so this is a summary of what we know so far. Grandfather, our main character, is having many different feelings about what he is seeing in his new country. Now, let's use what we know about the story as well as the sentence the word is actually in to guess what the word might mean. You guess in your heads while I guess out loud. I think that our mystery word might be one way Grandfather feels about what he is seeing. It says that the buildings excited him. So I'm guessing that *bewildered* could be another way he feels. I know what *excited* means. That's a good feeling. I think if *bewildered* meant about the same thing as *excited*, the author would have said the buildings bewildered and excited him. But he didn't. The author said, "bewildered and yet excited". Let's see if we can figure out what that word *yet* means in this sentence. I'm going to use the word *yet* in another sentence and see if that helps me: "I'm worried about whether I'll ever get to sleep again, and yet I'm excited about my new baby brother." *Yet* is a little word that adds a lot of meaning. Sometimes it means "so far" and sometimes, it means "in spite of everything". I can see that *yet* tells me that I have two different feelings at the same time. So being bewildered is different from being excited. I can think of an experience I had in traveling to a brand-new country. I was standing in an airport in Frankfurt, Germany, airport. I was confused because there were hundreds of ticket counters, and I couldn't read German, and yet I was excited. Now, I think I know how Grandfather felt. He was confused by all of the tall buildings, yet he was excited. Let's put that meaning in the sentence: "Huge cities of factories and tall buildings confused and yet excited him." Does that make sense? Yes. Thank you for helping me to figure out what *bewildered* means. I am no longer bewildered by the meaning of that word. I am bewildered by why we haven't heard the lunch bell ring when it is lunchtime! I am also bewildered by the fact that I didn't get homework from two people this morning. Perhaps you can clear up my bewilderment by stopping at my desk before you go to lunch.

© 2009 Hawker Brownlow Education and Elaine McEwan-Adkins.

INTERVENTION 19

Teaching More Vocabulary Every Day (Years 2–6)

It is true that not all of the words that appear in students' environments will be learned. But, then again, if students do not encounter new words, there is no possibility of learning them.

—Beck et al. (2002, p. 118)

This intervention directly teaches thirty words from the core program's weekly reading selection. Typically, the teacher's manual in a core program identifies only five or six words from a selection to be taught per week. These words usually do not provide sufficient background knowledge for struggling students to fully comprehend the story. The five-day lesson plan provides daily practice in reading and spelling the words as well as learning their meanings.

Background Knowledge

Word knowledge consists of vocabulary and background knowledge that students require to understand text. However, given the limited word and world knowledge that the majority of students at risk have when they enrol in school, this intervention must be viewed as a long-term investment in increased reading achievement as students learn the meanings of an increasing number of new words.

Students do not learn a word after hearing the word and a definition only once. McKeown, Beck, Omanson and Pople (1985) suggest that even as many as four "teaching" encounters with a word do not give learners enough knowledge to improve their reading comprehension in text that contains that word. It may take as many as twelve experiences. Word and world knowledge is acquired incrementally, in bits and pieces here and there (Nagy & Scott, 2000), so teachers must recursively teach words to help students make the connections that will affix them and their associated world knowledge into long-term memory. Walsh (2003) found that none of the widely used core programs provide the amount and the depth of vocabulary instruction needed to result in comprehension.

Sample Lessons for Teaching Vocabulary

Depending on the number of students in your class who lack sufficient vocabulary and background knowledge to fully comprehend year-level core program stories, consider using this intervention with the whole class. Classes with large numbers of English language learners or students at risk will benefit from whole-class instruction, with some small-group intervention activities added to provide further practice.

This intervention requires an initial investment of time, but if the workload is shared among a team of teachers, the payoff will be realised in your students' increased comprehension and enjoyment of the weekly story. Begin by selecting twenty to twenty-five words from the story to add to the list of recommended words. Then use the following sample lessons and routines to teach and practise the words with students during a five-day lesson cycle. As our model for this intervention, we use "Grandfather's Journey" (Say, 1993), in Unit 1, Book 1 of the *Macmillan McGraw-Hill Reading Program* (Flood et al., 2001). The teacher's manual selects the following new words to be taught for this story: *scattered, journey, surrounded, enormous, towering* and *astonish*.

Our goal is to teach the words in the most efficient way possible so as to make the best use of instructional time. Note that some of the selected words can be taught very quickly with pictures or gestures, thereby eliminating the need for extensive discussions and giving ESL students an opportunity to acquire new vocabulary quickly. Although the six chosen words are important, they do not provide the background knowledge that year three readers need to understand "Grandfather's Journey". Furthermore, at the rate of 6 words per week, students would be directly taught only 216 words in a school year.

As you page through a story, think in terms of the background knowledge students need to comprehend the story. Adding an additional 24 words or phrases to the words selected increases the yearly total of words taught from 216 words to 1188 words. You will teach the word meanings in three ways: (1) photos or cartoon illustrations, (2) gestures or short dramatic scenarios presented by either the teacher or the students or (3) student-friendly definitions with deeper discussions of word meanings as needed. Figure 19.1 shows a sample five-day lesson plan. At first glance, it may appear to be complicated, but once you have introduced your students to the various routines, the daily vocabulary lesson should take only about fifteen minutes. You might prefer to do some things with the whole group and other activities with a smaller group. The five-day plan is adaptable to your class. For example, you could preteach the new words to a smaller group of students in advance of reading the story. Then, when you introduce the words to the whole group, your group at risk would be hearing the words a second time. Choose from the menu of various approaches, tailoring your weekly plan to your students, the content and the characteristics of the words you have chosen. The pace of each day's lesson should be brisk, with no extraneous teacher talk. Review the proven presentation techniques in figure 1.3.

Figure 19.1: Five-day plan for teaching vocabulary.

Monday Day 1	Tuesday Day 2	Wednesday Day 3	Thursday Day 4	Friday Day 5
Whole-Group Instruction Introduce the ten Day 1 words from column 1 of figure 19.2. Explain the Day 1 words, showing pictures of the words in column 1 of figure 19.3, making gestures for the Day 1 words in column 2, and directly teaching the meanings of Day 1 concept words using the routine in figure 19.4. Place the words in a vocabulary chart or on the word wall after instruction. Introduce the serial processing sheet (figure 19.5), and practise the first four rows using the routine in figure 19.6. Use the overhead for this activity, showing only the words that have been introduced thus far.	*Whole-Group Instruction* Use the routine (figure 19.7) to read/spell/read Day 1 words. Introduce the ten words for Day 2 as in Day 1. Place the words in the vocabulary chart and/or place on the word wall as in Day 1. Use the routine in figure 19.6 for the first eight rows of figure 19.5.	*Whole-Group Instruction* Use the routine in figure 19.7 to read/spell/read the Day 1 and 2 words. Introduce the ten words for Day 3. Place the words in the vocabulary chart and/or place on the word wall as in Days 1 and 2. Use the routine in figure 19.6 for all of the words in figure 19.5.	*Whole-Group Instruction* Use the routine in figure 19.7 to read/spell/read all of the new words. Read the entire serial processing sheet (figure 19.5) two times using the routine in figure 19.6.	*Whole-Group Instruction* Read the entire serial processing sheet two times using the routine in figure 19.6. Use the overhead. Review all concept words and other words you identified as needing more work using the routine in figure 19.8. Expect more individual student responses during this last review session.
Independent or Small Group Students make vocabulary cards for concept words. They write the vocabulary word on one side and the student-friendly definition on the back. The students then hole-punch the cards and place them on a ring.	*Independent or Small Group* Students continue to make vocabulary cards for concept words. Vocabulary word on one side and student-friendly definition on the back.	*Independent or Small Group* Write a "7-Up" sentence, seven words or more, for each concept word in the vocabulary log.	*Independent or Small Group* Practise reading the serial processing sheet three times.	*Independent or Small Group* Practise reading the serial processing sheet three times with a partner. Complete a graphic organiser of your choice.

© 2009 Hawker Brownlow Education and Elaine McEwan-Adkins.

Let's walk through each of the activities in the five-day plan and look at examples of each one. On Monday, introduce ten new words from the part of the story you will be reading together. Figure 19.2 shows you the words from our sample story. If some of the words are multisyllabic, teach your students to use either of the sets of steps to read big words found in Intervention 10.

Figure 19.2: Words from a sample story.

Day 1	Day 2	Day 3
journey	North America	village in Japan
surrounded	deserts	daughter
enormous	sculptures	married
astonished	amazed	grandson
towering	endless farm fields	grandparents
scattered	tall buildings	family
grandfather	bewildered	homeland
Japan	marvelled	explored
Pacific Ocean	longed	travelled
steamship	California	

Source: Say, 1993.

Figure 19.3 categorises the word list found in figure 19.2 for instruction. Column 1 contains words that can be taught with pictures, photos or artefacts. Column 2 contains gesture words that can be taught with a facial expression or body movement or that one or two students can act out in a short scenario. Column 3 contains the more difficult concept words that can be taught using the lesson in figure 19.4. Use your own judgment about the placement of words in categories. For example, the meaning of *astonish* could be either illustrated with a picture or cartoon illustration of a person who looks astonished, or acted out by the teacher or students. Remember to write student-friendly definitions for the new words. Dictionary definitions are often confusing.

The next activity suggested for Day 1 to Day 3 is placing each word in an appropriate category on a word wall, either immediately after the word is introduced or when all of the words for the day have been introduced. The purpose of the wall is to help students build word and world knowledge schemas (concept maps) in their long-term memories. Words can be categorised in several ways, depending on the year level of your students and how you intend to use the wall for instruction. Some teachers divide their walls into two categories—for example, fiction and nonfiction, using subsections like character traits, setting and so forth on the fiction side of the wall and curricular content areas like science and social studies on the nonfiction side. If your wall space is limited, have students transfer the words to a vocabulary notebook.

Figure 19.3: Words in meaning categories for Days 1–3.

Picture Words	Gesture Words	Concept Words
married	amazed	towering
tall buildings	enormous	journey
grandfather	bewildered	homeland
sculptures	scattered	longed
North America	marvelled	explored
endless farm fields	astonished	travelled
daughter	surrounded	
grandson		
Japan		
grandparents		
Pacific Ocean		
California		
deserts		
family		
village in Japan		
steamship		

Source: Say, 1993.

Figure 19.4: Sample routine for teaching the meanings of concept words.

Teacher	Word 1 is *towering*. What word? [Teacher gives signal by dropping hand, snapping finger or clapping hands.]
Students	*Towering.*
Teacher	The meaning of *towering* is very tall. What is the meaning of *towering*? [Give signal.]
Students	Very tall.
Teacher	In this story, we will read that there are some very tall mountains. Watch for that word as we read, and imagine what very tall mountains would look like.
Teacher	Word 2 is *journey*. What word? [Give signal.]
Students	*Journey.*
Teacher	The meaning of *journey* is a very long trip. What is the meaning of *journey*? [Give signal.]
Students	A very long trip.
Teacher	If I went to the shops, that would not be a journey. In the story we will read, someone will go on a journey, a very long trip.
Teacher	Word 3 is *homeland*. What word? [Give signal.]
Students	*Homeland.*
Teacher	The meaning of *homeland* is the country in which a person is born. What is the meaning of *homeland*? [Give signal.]
Students	The country in which a person is born.

© 2009 Hawker Brownlow Education and Elaine McEwan-Adkins.

A *serial processing activity* is the final step on Day 1 (Nelson, Cooper, & Gonzalez, 2004). This fluency-building activity gives students daily practice in reading the words serially—that is, left to right and top to bottom, as compared to the way students generally read a list of words (top to bottom). Serial processing reinforces the left to right, top to bottom habit in students as they practise. Figure 19.5 shows a sample serial processing list (for student and teacher use). The I Do It-You Do It routine for reading the serial processing list with students is found in figure 19.6. During serial processing, listen closely for any errors students may make. If you hear one or more students mispronouncing a word, stop reading and say, "I'll do it" and then pronounce the word correctly. Then say, "You do it." Students will then pronounce the word correctly. Then say, "Go back two." The students jump back two words and then begin to chorally read the serial list once more. By slightly delaying the practice reading of the mispronounced word, you are more likely to ensure that students will read the word correctly when they encounter it in the course of the story. Also, students are more likely to focus their working memories on understanding the meaning of a word rather than on simply decoding it. Note that students have multiple opportunities to see the word as they are hearing it. They have a copy of the serial processing list, the list appears on the screen, and the teacher has the words written on cards that are either moved to the vocabulary chart or word wall after instruction of the word.

Figure 19.5: Serial processing list.

journey	surrounded	enormous
astonished	towering	scattered
grandfather	Japan	Pacific Ocean
steamship		
North America	deserts	sculptures
amazed	endless farm fields	tall buildings
bewildered	marvelled	longed
California		
village in Japan	daughter	married
grandson	grandparents	family
homeland	explored	homesick
travelled		

© 2009 Hawker Brownlow Education and Elaine McEwan-Adkins.

Figure 19.6: I Do It-You Do It routine for serial processing.

Teacher	I do it. Journey, surrounded, enormous. You do it. [Signal.]
Students	Journey, surrounded, enormous.
Teacher	I do it. Astonished, towering, scattered. You do it. [Signal.]
Students	Astonished, towering, scattered.
Teacher	I do it. Grandfather, Japan, Pacific Ocean. You do it. [Signal.]
Students	Grandfather, Japan, Pacific Ocean.
Note: Continue using this routine until all of the words introduced to that point have been practised as many times as indicated in the five-day plan.	

© 2009 Hawker Brownlow Education and Elaine McEwan-Adkins.

Figure 19.7 is a quick review routine to be used on Tuesday, Wednesday and Thursday to review the pronunciations and spellings of any previously taught words that students find difficult to learn. Figure 19.8 is a lesson for reviewing the pronunciations, spellings *and* meanings of concept or other words that need more intensive practice on Friday. This lesson would not likely be used for all of the words given the fifteen-minute time limitation.

Figure 19.7: Quick review routine for Days 2, 3 or 4.

Teacher	Word 1 is *journey*. What word? [Teacher gives signal by dropping hand, snapping fingers or clapping hands.]
Students	*Journey.*
Teacher	Spell *journey*. Get ready. [Signal.]
Students	J-o-u-r-n-e-y.
Teacher	The word is *journey*. What word? [Signal.]
Students	*Journey.*
Teacher	Word 2 is *surrounded*. What word? [Teacher gives signal by dropping hand, snapping fingers or clapping hands.]
Students	*Surrounded.*
Note: Continue in the I Do It-You Do It format until all of the words for that day have been read/spelled/read as indicated in the five-day plan.	

© 2009 Hawker Brownlow Education and Elaine McEwan-Adkins.

Figure 19.8: Sample routine for teaching pronunciation, spelling and meanings of concept words for Day 5.

Teacher	Word 1 is *journey*. What word? [Teacher gives signal by dropping hand, snapping fingers or clapping hands.]
Students	*Journey.*
Teacher	Spell *journey*. Get ready. [Give signal and tap for each letter in journey.]
Students	J-o-u-r-n-e-y.
Teacher	The meaning of *journey* is a very long trip away from home. What is the meaning of *journey*? [Give signal.]
Students	A very long trip away from home.
Teacher	I went to the shops to pick up some milk and bread. Would that be a journey? Why?
Student: Emily	No. The trip was too short to be considered a journey.
Teacher	My husband and I took a trip across Australia. Would that be a journey?
Student: Sam	Yes. You took a very long trip and were gone a long time from home.
Teacher	I went to the next suburb to visit my friend. Would that be a journey?
Students	No.
Note: Read, spell and review meanings for as many words as time permits. This routine can also be used to check out individual students in the class regarding their mastery of the pronunciations, spellings and meanings of the words. Use contextual statements and questions to deepen students' understanding of the words.	

Source: This routine was informed by the work of Beck et al., 2002; Bursuck & Damer, 2007; Carnine et al., 2004.

Teaching vocabulary is an ongoing endeavour. Each new piece of text that students encounter, whether during instruction or in their recreational reading, presents its own unique challenges in terms of background knowledge and vocabulary. Effective teachers build connections and help students to construct word schemas in their long-term memories on a daily basis.

INTERVENTION 20

Using Read-Alouds to Teach New Words (Years P–2)

Vocabulary instruction is not just one of several important aspects of reading; it is a gift of words, a gift that one gives generously to others.

—Stahl (2005, p. 113)

This intervention uses read-alouds that are connected in some way to the classroom curriculum to bring new words to life in primary classrooms. Choosing the stories and words and preparing the posters that go with each story takes time. But when these tasks are shared among several teachers, the stories can be used for as long as the reading series is being used.

Background Knowledge

In the three-tier vocabulary model proposed by Beck et al. (2002), Tier 1 words are familiar words that most students would know. They require little if any instruction. Tier 3 words are low-frequency words limited to very specific knowledge domains. Tier 2 words have the following attributes:

1. They are characteristic of mature language users and appear frequently across a variety of contexts.

2. They can be taught in various ways to help students build in-depth knowledge and make connections to other words and concepts.

3. They provide precision and specificity in describing a concept for which the students already have a general understanding. (pp. 8–9)

Choose Tier 2 words from your daily read-alouds to teach vocabulary.

Use a Daily Read-Aloud With a Classroom Connection to Teach New Words

The morning routine in the year one classrooms of Candace Darling, Michelle Judware and Darlene Carino includes a read-aloud (both fiction and nonfiction titles are used) that is related to the current theme in their reading series, a recent holiday or a topic from another curricular area. After choosing the read-alouds for each day, teachers identify three vocabulary words, describe how they are used in the text and write a child-friendly definition of each word. Once the story has been read and the words have been discussed, a wizard for the day is chosen. Wizards become human "word walls" for the day, wearing their word cards with definitions on a necklace and carrying a sign indicating they would like to be asked about the words they are wearing. Wizards must provide definitions of their words to anyone who asks. Once worn, the words are hung on the vocabulary wall, and points are awarded to students who are "caught" being a word wizard (using the word in writing or conversation in the classroom). Figure 20.1 contains a sample set of words and definitions from a Dr Seuss (1990) story, *Oh, the Places You'll Go!*

Figure 20.1: Oh, the Places You'll Go! Word Wizard poster.

Oh, the Places You'll Go!
By Dr Seuss

"And will you succeed?"
to do well or to get what you want — succeed

"On you will go though your enemies prowl . . ."
someone who wants to hurt or harm you — enemies

"And the chances are, then, that you'll be in a slump."
a sad, depressed state — slump

Source: Adapted and reprinted with permission of Darlene Carino, Candace Darling and Michelle Judware. Copyright ©2006. Corwin Press, Inc. All rights reserved. Reprinted from *How to Survive and Thrive in the First Three Weeks of School* by E. K. McEwan.

Use Nonfiction Read-Alouds to Teach Word and World Knowledge

Linda Gibb, a reading coach, undertook a project to encourage primary-years reading teachers to directly teach more vocabulary to students after learning about the research of Beck and her colleagues.

Teachers use read-aloud trade books that enrich a basal story theme and prepare a poster using some appropriate clip art. Teachers write the routine on the back of the poster so they can be ready with (1) the pronunciation of the word, (2) a student-friendly definition, (3) a sentence from the story that uses the word and (4) a sentence starter for students to use during the first few weeks or until they are able to start sentences on their own.

When students bring in evidence of hearing, seeing or using the target words outside the classroom, the teacher writes their names on a sticky note she then places next to the word on the book poster. The posters hang in the classrooms all year as a resource for students and teachers to use whenever they have opportunities in their daily language and written work.

INTERVENTION 21

Organising Vocabulary for Understanding and Retention (Years 4–6)

> *What is the trick behind our ability to fill one another's heads with so many different ideas?.... The first trick, the word, is based on a memorised arbitrary pairing between a sound and a meaning.*
>
> —Pinker (1999, pp. 1–2)

This intervention teaches students how to construct three different graphic organisers that enable them to investigate and learn about important words (concepts and big ideas in your classroom) in three dimensions: the semantic word map, the Frayer Model and the word structure map. The short-term goal is for students to understand the text they read; the long-term goal is for students to become more skilled readers and writers using *visualising–organising*, a cognitive strategy in which readers construct a mental image or graphic organiser for the purpose of extracting and constructing meaning from text.

Background Knowledge

Students learn important concepts or acquire the specialised vocabulary found in content texts in three ways (Novak, 1998; Novak & Gowin, 1984):

1. Hearing words explained and used in conversation and context at least three to five times

2. Seeing words brought to life with pictures, models and diagrams

3. Constructing graphic organisers that show relationships between words—the focus of this intervention

Graphic organisers are visual representations that provide a framework for remembering important information about a word, which is pertinent when the word is a critical content concept or a big idea. When students construct graphic organisers (either alone or with a partner), they can organise and compact large amounts of information into a limited space, thus making the understanding and retention of complex concepts much easier. Teach any one or all of these graphic organisers, one at a time, giving your students enough time to become comfortable with the format. As they work with the organisers, remind them to think about which one is a favourite or is especially effective in helping them learn new words and make connections.

Sample Lesson for Teaching a Graphic Organiser

Figure 21.1 is a sample lesson for teaching any one of the featured organisers (or other organisers you may wish to add to this intervention). Teach each organiser as a separate lesson. Always model the construction of at least one or two organisers in each category before working on one with your students.

Figure 21.1: Sample lesson for teaching a graphic organiser.

Lesson Objective	Students will be able to construct a vocabulary graphic organiser independently.
Advance Organiser	**Teacher Does:** Show students several models of the specific organiser you want to teach (two well-constructed samples and two poorly done nonexamples). Explain the purpose of constructing the organiser and how it can be used to understand and remember the meanings of words. Define and explain each of the labels on your blank organiser.
I Do It: Teacher Models	**Teacher Does:** Introduce a keyword or concept from an upcoming unit, and tell students you are going to model for them and think aloud while you construct a sample organiser. Put a blank graphic organiser on the overhead, and think aloud about how you come up with the words to put in the various parts of the organiser.
We Do It: Teacher and Students Work Together	**Teacher Does:** Move to the We Do It portion of the lesson (once the sample organiser is complete) in which you and your students work together to construct the organiser. Choose another concept (an easy one with which students are already familiar from a prior unit). Activate students' background knowledge about the word by asking them to think of as many related words as they can. Then ask them to suggest categories and possible words for you to write in the appropriate boxes on the organiser you have placed on the overhead.
You Do It: Students Work in Pairs or Individually	**Teacher Does:** Work with students to construct another organiser together with you before you assign them to work with a partner. This step in the lesson can be held over for another day. Then choose a third concept from an upcoming lesson and ask students to first activate prior knowledge (brainstorm a list of related words) as a whole class and then complete the organiser in pairs.

© 2009 Hawker Brownlow Education and Elaine McEwan-Adkins.

Teaching Students to Construct a Semantic Word Map

The semantic word map is a graphic organiser that provides a structure for breaking down a concept into various categories. The organiser enables students to extend their learning about a word into related categories, ideas, characteristics or examples. In the beginning, provide the category labels for your students. As students become more skilled, work with the group to choose the categories together. Eventually, students can choose their own category labels. Use the sample lesson shown in figure 21.1 to teach not only the semantic word map but other types of graphic organisers as well. Figure 21.2 is a completed semantic word map. Many teachers' guides provide completed graphic organisers, but students only reap the benefits of visually organising a concept or word when they construct their own organisers. There are no "right" answers per se. The process is just as important as the product when you are graphically organising a word or concept.

Teaching Students to Construct a Word Structure Map

The construction of a word structure map involves answering four questions about a word or concept: What is it? What is it like? What is it *not* like? What are some examples? Figure 21.3 is a sample word structure map.

Figure 21.2: Sample semantic word map.

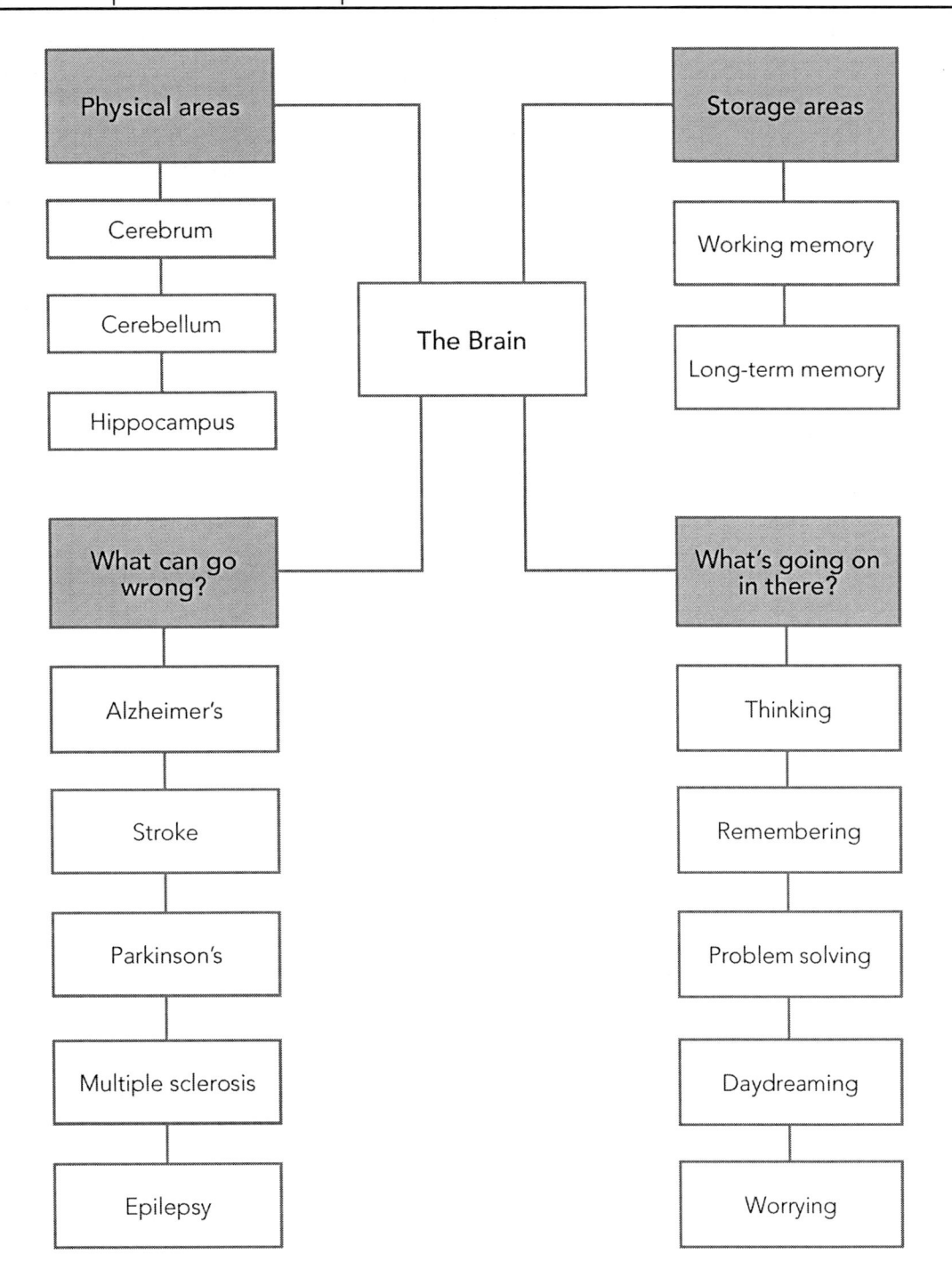

```
                    ┌─────────────────┐                    ┌─────────────────┐
                    │ Physical areas  │                    │  Storage areas  │
                    └────────┬────────┘                    └────────┬────────┘
                    ┌────────┴────────┐                    ┌────────┴────────┐
                    │    Cerebrum     │                    │ Working memory  │
                    └────────┬────────┘    ┌───────────┐   └────────┬────────┘
                    ┌────────┴────────┐    │ The Brain │   ┌────────┴────────┐
                    │   Cerebellum    │    └───────────┘   │ Long-term memory│
                    └────────┬────────┘                    └─────────────────┘
                    ┌────────┴────────┐
                    │   Hippocampus   │
                    └─────────────────┘

                    ┌─────────────────┐                    ┌─────────────────┐
                    │  What can go    │                    │ What's going on │
                    │     wrong?      │                    │    in there?    │
                    └────────┬────────┘                    └────────┬────────┘
                    ┌────────┴────────┐                    ┌────────┴────────┐
                    │   Alzheimer's   │                    │    Thinking     │
                    └────────┬────────┘                    └────────┬────────┘
                    ┌────────┴────────┐                    ┌────────┴────────┐
                    │     Stroke      │                    │   Remembering   │
                    └────────┬────────┘                    └────────┬────────┘
                    ┌────────┴────────┐                    ┌────────┴────────┐
                    │   Parkinson's   │                    │ Problem solving │
                    └────────┬────────┘                    └────────┬────────┘
                    ┌────────┴────────┐                    ┌────────┴────────┐
                    │Multiple sclerosis│                   │   Daydreaming   │
                    └────────┬────────┘                    └────────┬────────┘
                    ┌────────┴────────┐                    ┌────────┴────────┐
                    │    Epilepsy     │                    │    Worrying     │
                    └─────────────────┘                    └─────────────────┘
```

Copyright © 2007, Corwin Press, Inc. All rights reserved. Reprinted from 40 Ways to Support Struggling Readers in Content Classrooms, Grades 6–12 by E.K. McEwan.

Figure 21.3: Sample word structure map.

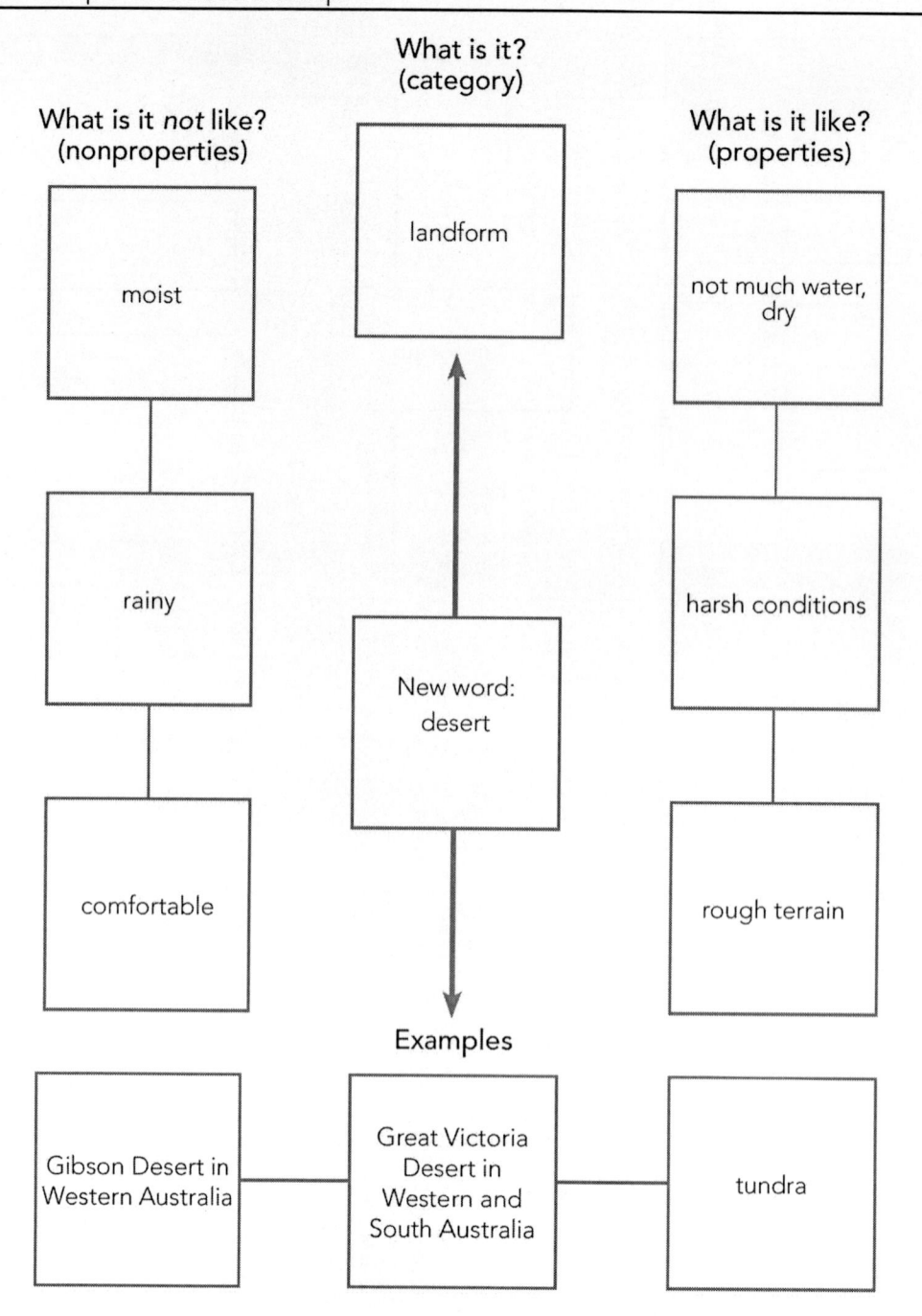

What is it not like?
(nonproperties)

- moist
- rainy
- comfortable

What is it?
(category)

landform

New word: desert

Examples

What is it like?
(properties)

- not much water, dry
- harsh conditions
- rough terrain

- Gibson Desert in Western Australia
- Great Victoria Desert in Western and South Australia
- tundra

Source: McEwan & Bresnahan, 2008.

Teaching Students to Construct a Frayer Model

The Frayer Model is a graphic organiser designed by Dorothy Frayer and colleagues a (Frayer, Frederick, & Klausmeier, 1969). This model uses a four-square format to distinguish the essential characteristics from those that are only marginally associated with a word. This variation from the traditional model prompts students to think about words in terms of examples, essential characteristics, nonexamples and nonessential characteristics.

For students to construct a Frayer Model in pairs or independently, they will need a lesson on the meaning of the words *essential, example* and *nonexample*. Essential characteristics are relevant properties, but that definition needs to be boiled down to a student-friendly definition—possibly *important characteristics*. Your students will not understand your modelling if they do not know the meanings of the words used to label the various parts of the organiser. Figure 21.4 shows a sample of a Frayer Model.

Figure 21.4: Sample Frayer Model.

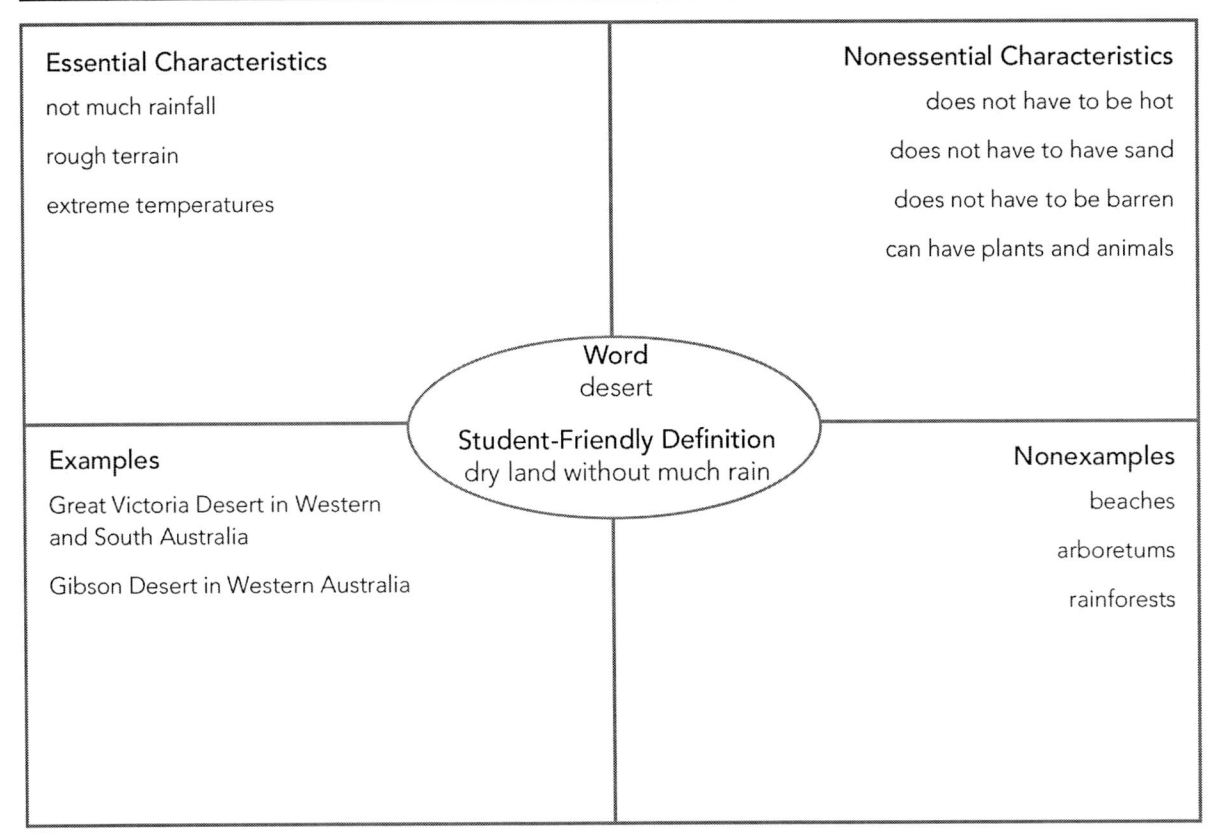

Essential Characteristics	Nonessential Characteristics
not much rainfall	does not have to be hot
rough terrain	does not have to have sand
extreme temperatures	does not have to be barren
	can have plants and animals
Examples	**Nonexamples**
Great Victoria Desert in Western and South Australia	beaches
Gibson Desert in Western Australia	arboretums
	rainforests

Word: desert
Student-Friendly Definition: dry land without much rain

Source: McEwan & Bresnahan, 2008b.

INTERVENTION 22

Writing Sentences to Show You Know (Years 4–6)

> *The nuances, subtleties, and characteristics of a word's role in the language can only be understood through repeated exposures to the word in a variety of contexts.*
>
> —Beck et al. (2002, p. 100)

The Show You Know intervention teaches students how to write sen-tences that show they understand a certain word or term. One typical classroom activity is using the vocabulary word in a sentence. However, many students, especially learners at risk, create sentences that tell very little about a new word. They frequently write short sentences such as *It is scary*. When asked to tell more, they often do not know what to do. Students need specific strategies to create meaningful sentences that expand their understanding of a new word. This intervention is a multistep strategy for helping students write sentences that show they understand a word's meaning and how to use it.

Background Knowledge

Effective teachers teach vocabulary in multiple ways. This particular intervention provides two ways to extend your students' linguistic knowledge. First, it shows them how language works as you demonstrate and explain the conventions of grammar and writing during your modelling. Second, your sentences provide a model for students to emulate—a critical scaffold for struggling students.

Sample Lesson for Teaching Show You Know Sentences

Figure 22.1 is a sample lesson for teaching this multistep strategy for building sentences. Figure 22.2 is the Show You Know scaffolding form for students to fill in prior to constructing their sentences for new words. Once you have modelled how to construct a Show You Know sentence and worked with the class to build one or two additional sentences, have students work in pairs to create a sentence. Monitor their progress to determine if they are ready to work individually. One way to provide additional support is to walk the students through each of the sentences they have constructed to determine if any words need to be rearranged or added. Model this important step in writing daily so students gain confidence about their sentence writing.

Figure 22.1: Sample lesson for Show You Know.

Lesson Objective	Students will be able to write a Show You Know sentence independently using the graphic organiser (figure 22.2).
Materials Needed for the Lesson	You'll need copies of the Show You Know organiser (figure 22.2) for students and an overhead transparency for the teacher.
Advance Organiser	**Teacher Says:** Today you will learn to write a Show You Know sentence. You will learn to use vocabulary words in complicated sentences and express yourself in a clear, intelligent way. Show You Know sentences provide additional information about a word. They can also answer the questions who, when, where, why and how. Once you have learned to write more complex sentences, I will look for them during the writing you do in class.
I Do It: Teacher Models	**Teacher Does:** Display the transparency for the Show You Know organiser. Explain that the first task in writing a Show You Know sentence is to think about possible words and phrases that might go with the word. Questions can be helpful to get students started. Fill in the transparency while thinking aloud. **Teacher Says:** I will work with the word *bleak*. Even though there are many ways this word can be used, I will concentrate on only one way. What is the word? *Bleak.* Who or what is bleak? The sky. When might the sky be bleak? During a rainstorm. Where might I see a bleak sky? Outside my classroom window. How might the word occur? Suddenly. Why might the sky look bleak? A storm came through. I am going to use the phrases I've written on my organiser to compose my sentence. I won't use all of the words in the sentence, only the ones that relate to one another and make sense. You might need to write a sentence and then rearrange it a little to make it sound better. Here's my first try: *One spring day, a rainstorm suddenly began, and clouds rolled in, changing the blue sky to a bleak dark grey.* Or maybe this one would be better: *In the spring, the sky can quickly change from bright blue to a bleak and depressing grey.*
We Do It: Teacher and Students Work Together	**Teacher Says:** Let's work together to test the second sentence I wrote. Help me figure out if it answers the questions on the Show You Know organiser. *In the spring, the sky can quickly change from bright blue to a bleak and depressing grey.* Is the vocabulary word in the sentence? [Underline it.] Does the sentence answer these questions? Who or what? The sky. [Underline it.] When? In the spring. [Underline it.] How? Quickly. [Underline it.] Why? I can see that my sentence doesn't answer the why question. I need to add something to my sentence to tell why the sky quickly changed from bright blue to bleak grey. A storm. Here's my final sentence: *Before a springtime storm, the sky can quickly change from bright blue to a bleak and depressing grey.*

© 2009 Hawker Brownlow Education and Elaine McEwan-Adkins.

Figure 22.2: Show You Know form.

Show You Know

Directions: Write the vocabulary word. Answer the questions about the word. Write a sentence that uses the word in a meaningful way by including words and phrases from the answers to your questions.

Word _____

Who or what is (the word)?	
When might the word occur?	
Where might the word occur?	
How might the word occur?	
Why might the word occur?	
Show You Know sentence	

Source: McEwan & Bresnahan, 2008b. Used with permission.

Copyright © Hawker Brownlow Education. All rights reserved. Reprinted from *40 Reading Intervention Strategies for P-6 Students*, by Elaine K. McEwan-Adkins. Melbourne, Vic: Hawker Brownlow Education, www.hbe.com.au. Reproduction authorised only for use in the school site that has purchased the book.

INTERVENTION 23

Teaching Contextual Information About Words (Years 4–6)

> *If the goal [of vocabulary instruction] were to teach words in a way that would improve students' perfor-mance on multiple-choice vocabulary tests, the goal could be achieved through many simple and relatively undemanding methods. However, if the goal is to teach words in a way that will improve students' comprehension of text that contains these words, the methods become more labor- and time-intensive.*
>
> —Nagy (2005, p. 27)

This intervention ensures that students will process new words in a variety of ways to affix them into their long-term memories. A nine-square concept map includes visual imagery, use of a dictionary and original sentence writing. This strategy ensures that students are provided with the contextual information they need to improve comprehension and retention of important vocabulary. Before using this strategy, the Frayer Model (Intervention 21) and Show You Know (Intervention 22) strategies must be taught and practised.

Background Knowledge

As discussed in Intervention 19, students do not learn a word after hearing it and its definition just once. McKeown et al. (1985) suggest that it can take up to twelve encounters with a word for students to truly learn it. They also suggest that even as many as four "teaching encounters" with a word do not give learners enough knowledge to improve their reading comprehension in text containing that word; it may take as many as twelve experiences. Word and world knowledge are acquired incrementally (Nagy & Scott, 2000), hence the need to recursively teach words to help students make the connections. Students who have not had the benefit of high-quality early instruction or language-rich experiences in their homes will need to experience important words that will be appearing in their academic texts in multiple ways.

Sample Lesson for Teaching the Concept Map

Figure 23.1 is a sample lesson for teaching the nine-square concept map. Once students have mastered how to complete each of the nine squares over several days, the concept map can be completed in pairs or assigned individually for important words and terms. Figure 23.2 is a sample of the map for you to use with your students.

Figure 23.1: Sample lesson for teaching the concept map.

Lesson Objective	Students will learn how to construct a nine-square concept map for thoroughly analysing a vocabulary word in many different contexts.
Materials Needed for the Lesson	You'll need copies of figure 23.2 for students, and an overhead transparency for yourself.
Advance Organiser	**Teacher Says:** Today you will thoroughly learn one new vocabulary word by using antonyms, synonyms, a dictionary, prior knowledge and even your own drawings. Once you have mapped a word on a concept map, you will know it very, very well. I will look for correct usage in your everyday reading, writing and speaking. And when I use the word, I will expect you to understand what I am saying.
I Do It: Teacher Models	**Teacher Does:** Think aloud for students as he or she completes the concept map beginning at the top left box (dictionary definition) and moving left to right and top to bottom.
We Do It: Teacher and Students Work Together	**Teacher Does:** Provide students with a copy of the concept map (figure 23.2). Guide them to work with a new vocabulary word as you complete the top row of the concept map together.
You Do It: Students Work in Pairs or Individually	**Teacher Does:** Ask students to complete the middle and bottom rows of the concept map on their own as you monitor their progress and answer questions as needed.
Apply It: Students Complete Assignment Independently	**Teacher Does:** Repeat this activity at least once a week with a new word. At first you may need to model one or more maps for students. With enough guided practice, students should be able to complete the concept map on their own.

Source: McEwan & Bresnahan, 2008b.

Figure 23.2: Sample concept map.

Dictionary definition	Kid-friendly definition	Part of speech
Synonym	Write the word here.	Antonym
"Show You Know" sentence	When might you hear or use this word?	Illustration

Source: McEwan & Bresnahan, 2008b. Used with permission.

Copyright © Hawker Brownlow Education. All rights reserved. Reprinted from *40 Reading Intervention Strategies for P–6 Students*, by Elaine K. McEwan-Adkins. Melbourne, Vic: Hawker Brownlow Education, www.hbe.com.au. Reproduction authorised only for use in the school site that has purchased the book.

INTERVENTION 24

Facilitating Content Vocabulary Instruction (Years 4–6)

Vocabulary instruction is not just one of several important aspects of reading; it is a gift of words, a gift that one gives generously to others.

—Stahl (2005, p. 113)

This intervention combines the big ideas and essential vocabulary of a content unit with accessible text on students' independent reading levels to enable the mastery of content standards. It contains a five-day lesson plan for teaching content vocabulary, building reading fluency with that vocabulary in an original fluency-building passage, and providing consistent practice to master the reading, spelling and meaning of new content words each week.

Background Knowledge

All teachers know the importance of directly teaching new content vocabulary, but given the time constraints of teaching target objectives or content standards along with teaching all students to read, content-specific words are often overlooked.

Content-specific words from science, social studies and mathematics require multiple learning approaches (Pearson, Cervetti, Bravo, Hiebert, & Arya, 2005), including the following:

- Some type of hands-on-activity (conducting an experiment, seeing a video, looking at or drawing pictures, going through some motions or handling an artefact)
- A discussion about the word
- Multiple opportunities to read the word both in and out of context
- Opportunities to write the word

This "do it, talk it, read it and write it" approach to acquiring vocabulary results in meaningful learning that is more readily retrieved by students from their long-term memories.

Systematic vocabulary instruction has three characteristics: (1) it happens on a daily basis, (2) it provides routines for how words are understood and practised and (3) it gives students multiple opportunities to cognitively process new words. You might think you are systematically teaching vocabulary instruction if you hand out a list on Monday, assign definitions to be copied from the glossary to be handed in on Wednesday, and then give a test on Friday. However, even your best students are not likely to acquire critical academic vocabulary using this approach. Observations in twenty-three ethnically diverse classrooms found that only 6 per cent of class time was devoted to vocabulary instruction, and in the core academic subjects only 1.4 per cent of instructional time was used for building word knowledge (Scott, Jamieson-Noel, & Asselin, 2003). Bring words to life by directly teaching and talking about key academic terms and concepts.

Sample Weekly Lessons for Small-Group Intervention

Figure 24.1 is a five-day schedule for teaching academic content vocabulary. As you skim through the various activities shown in this schedule, you may get agenda anxiety. However, if you tighten up transitions, eliminate extraneous teacher talk and begin instruction promptly at the scheduled time (teach "bell to bell"), you will have all the time you need for vocabulary instruction. You *will,* however, be required to invest time outside of class preparing the materials and mastering the routines yourself. However, once students learn the routines, it shouldn't take more than ten or fifteen minutes each day—precisely the amount of time you reclaimed.

My content example uses mathematics, but the plan is generic and applicable to any content area and for any number of words. You can use the lesson with the whole class, or you can use some of the suggested activities with the whole class and have an interventionist or paraprofessional work with a small group on additional activities. Some of the activities refer to work with graphic organisers in Intervention 21.

Figure 24.1: Five-day lesson plan to teach content vocabulary.

Monday Day 1	Tuesday Day 2	Wednesday Day 3	Thursday Day 4	Friday Day 5
Whole Group Introduce the words you have chosen, using the poster you constructed. As needed, use the big word strategy shown in figure 10.1 to help students figure out how to pronounce multisyllabic words. Explain the words by giving student-friendly definitions and using the words in sentences that put the words in context. Use photos or illustrations to show meaning as appropriate. Display the poster in a prominent spot in your classroom so you can refer to it throughout the week, or post the words in appropriate categories on a word wall.	*Whole Group* Review the meanings of the words using figure 24.2. Introduce the fluency passage shown in figure 24.3. Read it chorally twice.	*Whole Group* Teach students the routine in figure 19.7 for reviewing the pronunciations and spellings of the words introduced on Monday. Everyone writes the words today. Use the routine in figure 24.3 for reviewing the meanings of the week's words.	*Whole Group* Use the routine in figure 19.8 to review the spelling, pronunciations and meanings of the words. Have students pair up and take turns reading the fluency passage aloud.	*Individual Students* Test out individual students on pronunciation, spelling and meaning of words to receive extra credit points.
Intervention Group Students make vocabulary cards for concept words by writing the vocabulary word on one side and the student-friendly definition on the back. The cards are hole-punched and placed on a ring.	*Intervention Group* Target students work in pairs to choose one word from the word list and complete a Show You Know organiser, shown in figure 22.2.	*Intervention Group* Practise reading the fluency passage three times (figure 24.3). Choose three words and draw an illustration of each word's meaning.	*Intervention Group* Practise reading the fluency passage (figure 24.3) two times. Help students develop an orthographic image of the word *mathematics* to ensure accurate spelling and reading using figure 12.1.	*Intervention Group* Practise the fluency passage sheet (figure 24.3) two times. Construct a semantic word map (figure 21.3) or a Frayer Model (figure 21.4) for one of the words.

© 2009 Hawker Brownlow Education and Elaine McEwan-Adkins.

Your first step is to select words that illustrate seven to ten critical concepts or big ideas in a chapter or unit. These are the words that your students will process in a variety of ways during the week. Students must see the words, say the words, read the words and spell the words (orally and in writing) many times to learn them. When students *orally* spell new words, it enhances their memory for pronunciations and meanings (Ehri & Rosenthal, 2007; Rosenthal & Ehri, 2008). Construct a simple poster on a piece of blank paper to anchor your practice activities during the week. The words chosen for the sample lesson are *mathematics, quantity, category, numeral* and *number*. Write the words in syllabicated form to help students pronounce them, and provide a sentence that shows the meaning of the word. Put up the poster and teach it on Monday. Once made, it can be used as long as you are using the textbook.

Figure 24.2 outlines a sample routine for reviewing and practising word meanings on Tuesday. The sample illustrates just three words. You will want to teach the meanings of all of your words on the first day. You may be tempted to stop and give impromptu lectures about something during the routine. Please don't! The purpose of a routine is to save time, cut out extraneous teacher talk or student interruptions and focus students' attention totally on the new words. Changing the wording or adding extraneous information to the definition defeats the purpose of practising the words in a routine. For more information about the importance of signals, see figure 1.4, which explains all of the presentation techniques used in this intervention. Signals save time and prevent students from calling out answers, thereby negating the power of a unison response to engage all students. If the content class (for example, maths) is scheduled to begin at 1:10, start this routine at that exact time every day. You can change the routine before you begin using it but not after you have taught it to students.

Figure 24.2: Sample routine for teaching and practising word meanings.

Teacher	Word 1 is *mathematics*. What word? [Give signal by dropping your hand, snapping your fingers or clapping your hands.]
Students	Mathematics.
Teacher	Mathematics is the study of numbers, shapes and quantities. What is the meaning of mathematics? [Give signal.]
Students	The study of numbers, shapes and quantities.
Teacher	Would we use mathematics in social studies? In science? Where at home would you use mathematics? [Teacher calls on individual students randomly to answer these questions.]
Teacher	Word 2 is *quantity*. What word? [Give signal.]
Students	Quantity.
Teacher	A quantity is an amount or number of something. What is the meaning of quantity? [Give signal.]
Students	An amount or number of something.
Teacher	If I bought one kilogram of potatoes at the store, would I have a large or small quantity of potatoes? What if I bought 5000 bricks to build an addition to my house? Would I have a large or small quantity of bricks? [Teacher calls on individual students randomly to answer these questions.]

Note: This sample routine shows only two of the words in the list. Follow this routine to teach all of the words, making up your own questions. If time permits, make up other questions so students can participate in miniconversations about new words.

Source: This routine was developed using research and information from Beck, McKeown, & Kucan, 2002; Bursuck & Damer, 2007; Carnine, Silbert, Kame'enui & Tarver, 2004.

A *fluency passage* gives students an opportunity to use the words in context as they orally read the passage several times during the week. Figure 24.3 contains an original sample fluency passage. You may find that writing your own fluency passages is too time-consuming or difficult, but this task can also be done by an interventionist or subject matter specialist. Another alternative is to locate books on a similar topic with a controlled vocabulary, such as *QuickReads* (Hiebert, 2003).

Figure 24.3: Sample fluency passage.

> Numbers are very important in everyday life. You have a phone number, a house or flat number, and maybe even a school ID number. Highways have numbers. Clothing is sized with numbers. The pages in books have numbers. Numbers are also important in the study of mathematics. In mathematics, a number stands for a quantity or an amount of something. A number answers the question, "How many?" If you have 2 apples, 5 oranges and 3 grapes, how many pieces of fruit do you have? The answer is 10, a number. When you write a number that you are thinking about on a piece of paper, it is then called a numeral. You are probably familiar with two kinds of numerals: Arabic numerals and Roman numerals. The numbers we use in everyday life and in mathematics class are called Arabic numerals. You will find Roman numerals on very old clocks, in very old books, and in the outlines you sometimes make in Enlgish class. Roman numerals look like capital letters, but they are actually a different set of symbols for numbers.

© 2009 Hawker Brownlow Education and Elaine McEwan-Adkins.

A note regarding figure 24.3: this fluency-building passage provides content and vocabulary knowledge at a more accessible reading level than the textbook. An alternative to writing your own passages is to find concept picture books that present the desired word and world knowledge at an easier reading level.

On Wednesday, use the routine found in Intervention 19 (figure 19.7) for practising the words' pronunciations and spellings. In addition, delve more deeply into the word meanings with questions and discussion that you have prepared ahead of time. Keep it short, and move through the routine quickly. Figure 19.8 shows a routine to take students deeper into the meanings and subtleties of the words. Apply the routine to your content words. Have some fun with the words on Wednesday and Thursday, but don't get carried away. Keep your eye on the clock. Do a few words on Wednesday, and save the rest for Thursday. No one knows your content better than you do. On Thursday, use the routine in figure 19.8 to practise spellings, pronunciations and meanings of the words and finish delving into word meanings more deeply, using statements and questions you have prepared in advance.

Note that a smaller intervention group does extra work with the words at another time during the day or the class period. They are also expected to make vocabulary cards, practise reading the fluency passage and complete graphic organisers.

Although the words you teach in content subjects have specialised meanings in the context of your classroom, alert your students to the fact that they may encounter these words in other contexts. Give students extra credit points for hearing, seeing or using new vocabulary in speaking or writing outside the classroom.

INTERVENTION 25

Playing the Word Power Game (Years 4–6)

> *Classrooms where students receive sound word in-struction are ones where lessons focus their attention on specific words and word-learning strategies, where opportunities to talk about words are many, and where occasions for applying what has been taught with engaging and content-rich texts and with motivating purposes occur with regularity and purpose.*
>
> —Kamil & Hiebert (2005, p. 10)

The Word Power game is an intervention strategy designed to develop word knowledge by creating an environment in which word learning is fun. Students choose the words from their own reading and experiences, thereby creating a more engaging list than the typical prepackaged list of words from a published book. The game has four distinct parts: (1) word nomination, (2) word selection, (3) word use and (4) word play. All parts work together to effectively build students' vocabularies. Introducing the game is best done at the beginning of a school year as part of teaching your classroom routine. Once students learn the various parts, you will be able to proceed through them effortlessly and incorporate them as a daily activity.

Background Knowledge

The gift of words that we give to students is a gift that keeps on giving. As a primary school educator, you are uniquely positioned to give the gift of words to your students on a daily basis. Word knowledge in its narrowest sense is simply knowing the meanings of lots of words. However, in a broader sense, word knowledge includes five specific kinds of linguistic information: (1) phonological awareness, (2) orthographic knowledge, (3) morphological awareness, (4) semantic knowledge and (5) mental orthographic images (Apel, 2007). Nagy and Scott (2000) call the information we store about specific words a *word schema,* and Crystal (2007) suggests that new word knowledge is not simply added to a list of words in long-term memory but rather is integrated with prior knowledge to create a more complex schema.

Rapp-Rudell and Shearer (2002) found that a vocabulary self-collection strategy similar to Increase Your Word Power was helpful to readers who were having difficulty comprehending text. Students who participated in the study generally chose more difficult words than the teacher would have selected for them and were excited about learning words and how the strategy helped them read better.

Sample Lesson for Playing the Word Power Game

Figure 25.1 is a sample lesson for teaching the Word Power game to your students. A suggested form for the Word Power poster described in the lesson is shown in figure 25.2, and the Word Power guidelines, also described in the sample lesson, are found in figure 25.3. Review the entire lesson before continuing to read.

Figure 25.1: Sample lesson for playing the Word Power game.

Lesson Objective	Students will increase their vocabularies by becoming more aware of words in their speaking, listening and reading.
Materials Needed for the Lesson	Prepare a large Word Power poster for the classroom using figure 25.2 as a model. Then prepare desk copies of the poster and guidelines (figure 25.3) for students. Mount an alphabetical class list on the wall next to the large Word Power poster. Procure a bucket and ask an artistic student to make a sign for the bucket.
Advance Organiser	**Teacher Says:** Today we are going to learn a game called Word Power that will increase your vocabulary. *Vocabulary* means the words you use and can understand when you read or when you hear someone use the words. It is called your lexicon, or the dictionary in your head. You must pay attention to interesting words. When you hear an interesting word, write it on a piece of scrap paper and put it into the Word Power bucket. Be sure to put your initials on the paper so we know it belongs to you. Each week I will pull one word out of the bucket and check to make sure it follows the guidelines. If the word follows the guidelines, I will write it on the Word Power poster. If your word is selected, I will give you a small reward. We will go over the guidelines in a minute. Later we will do a variety of activities with these words. We will play word games and keep track of how you individually use the words.
I Do It: Teacher Models	**Teacher Does:** Pass out copies of the Word Power guidelines (figure 25.3). **Teacher Says:** Any word you nominate must follow these guidelines, or it will be disqualified if I happen to draw the word out of the bucket. For example, I want to nominate the word *capricious*. I think my word meets the guidelines. I'm going to write it on a piece of paper, put my initials next to the word and put the paper in the Word Power bucket.
I Do It: Teacher Models	**Teacher Does:** Select the word you put into the bucket. Explain that if you were drawing out a word one of the students had put in the bucket, you would quickly decide whether that word met the guidelines because you are the judge of that. Go through each of the guidelines with *capricious* (or the word you selected from the bucket) to show students it follows the guidelines. Tell students that you will not reveal who put a word in the bucket until it has passed all of the guidelines and is deemed an impressive word. At that point, the nominating student will get a small reward. **Teacher Says:** Let's look up *capricious* in the dictionary. It means "changeable or unpredictable". What kinds of things would be changeable or unpredictable? Well, the weather in Hobart is certainly capricious. Last week the temperatures were in the 30s, and today it is raining. Hobart's weather is capricious. You can never tell what it is going to be. **Teacher Does:** Provide some nonexamples of the word, and ask students to think of their own. Providing negative examples is critical to clarifying the meaning of the word. For the word *capricious* you might say, "Here is something that is not capricious—the school bell. The bell rings at the same time every day. It is predictable." Name the part of speech for the word, and use it in an original sentence. Record the word on the class Word Power poster, and put your initials next to it to show that it is your word.

continued →

I Do It: Teacher Models	**Teacher Does:** Explain that to expand their vocabularies and make the word truly their own, students need to use the new word and be attentive to its use. Repeated exposure and practice will cement the word in their working vocabularies. Tell students that they can earn points for using the word in writing; seeing it written in material they read; hearing it used in conversation, on television or in another class; and using it themselves. Ask them to report word usage during a specified time of the day when you can meet with them individually. After reporting on the use of the word, have students write their initials on the class Word Power poster in the appropriate column. More than one set of initials can appear in each column. Distribute a copy of the Word Power guidelines. Explain each column using your example, capricious. **Teacher Says:** If you hear the word *capricious*, write your initials in the Heard It column next to the word. You must be able to describe the situation in which you heard the word. If you use the word *capricious* when talking to someone else, write your initials in the Said It box next to the word. If you claim to have said the word, you must be able to describe the situation in which you said it and to whom you were talking. If you read the word, you must show the text in which the word appeared before writing your initials in that column. Before writing your initials in the Wrote It column, you must produce a piece of writing in which you wrote the word. **Teacher Does:** Point out the class list that is displayed adjacent to the Word Power poster. Explain to students that each time they write their initials on the Word Power poster, they can put a tally mark next to their name on the class list. For individual accountability, have students keep track of their own use of the words by putting a tally mark in the appropriate column on their individual Word Power poster. When a student has marked three tally marks in each section, for a total of twelve marks, that word is closed out. Once an individual Word Power poster is filled, students can begin a new one with new words.
We Do It: Teacher and Students Work Together	**Teacher Does:** Ask the class to think about any words they have encountered recently that they think would be good ones for the whole class to learn. Take some nominations from the floor, and choose one word to go through the process together. Record the word on the poster and have the students record their word on their individual charts.
You Do It: Students Nominate Words on Their Own	**Teacher Does:** Invite each student to nominate one word per week. Draw a word from the bucket and add it to the poster if it qualifies. Have students add it to their poster and work toward marking twelve tally marks by hearing, saying, reading or writing the word. Gather students' individual Word Power posters and store them in a binder.

Source: McEwan & Bresnahan, 2008b.

Figure 25.2: Word Power poster form.

Word	Heard It	Said It	Read It	Wrote It
1.				
2.				

Source: McEwan & Bresnahan, 2008b.

Figure 25.3: Word Power guidelines.

Before you nominate a word:	1. Make sure that the word is a common noun, an adjective, a verb or an adverb (no proper nouns).
	2. Make sure that the word is general and not specific to one content subject.
	3. Make sure that the word is written legibly on a piece of scrap paper.
	4. Make sure that your initials are written next to the word.
After the teacher selects a word and writes it on the Word Power poster:	1. Write your initials next to the word to indicate that you have used it.
	2. Keep a personal record by adding a tally mark next to your name on the class list.
	3. Transfer the information to your personal Word Power poster. Write a tally mark on your personal poster to indicate that you have used the word. When a word has earned three tally marks in each section, for a total of twelve marks, that word is closed out. Once your poster is filled, you can get a new one.
How you can earn initials or tally marks:	1. If you hear a word, write your initials in the Heard It column next to the word. You must be able to describe the situation in which you heard the word.
	2. If you use the word in conversation with someone or in a class discussion or presentation, write your initials in the Said It column next to the word. You must be able to describe the situation in which you used (said) the word.
	3. If you read the word in a textbook, newspaper, magazine or a book you are reading, write your initials in the Read It column. You must be able to show the text in which the word appeared before writing your initials. A photocopy is acceptable if you read the word in text belonging to someone else.
	4. If you used the word in a piece of writing you did for this class or another teacher, write your initials in the Wrote It column. You must produce the piece of writing in which you wrote the word.

Source: McEwan & Bresnahan, 2008b.

Copyright © Hawker Brownlow Education. All rights reserved. Reprinted from *40 Reading Intervention Strategies for P–6 Students*, by Elaine K. McEwan-Adkins. Melbourne, Vic: Hawker Brownlow Education, www.hbe.com.au. Reproduction authorised only for use in the school site that has purchased the book.

The sample lesson in figure 25.1 led you and your class through the first three parts of the Word Power game: word nomination, word selection and word use. Once the game is underway and your large Word Power poster contains a dozen or more words, it's time for the fourth part: word play. As you use each of the following suggestions, be sure to keep students actively engaged in the process by either having them write individual responses on their dry-erase boards or cooperatively work with partners. You might wish to turn one of the activities into a game, awarding one point to the first pair who locates the word.

Have students spell the new word. If the word is an irregular word or contains an unusual spelling pattern, use the lessons in figure 9.1 to help students build an orthographic image of the new word. Ask students to find words in one or more of the following categories to review or to do a minilesson on some aspect of linguistic knowledge:

- Number of syllables (Example: Find a word with four syllables.)
- Types of syllables (Example: Find a word with an open syllable.)
- Word parts (Example: Find a word with a prefix that means "not".)

- Spelling conventions (Example: Find a word in which the *y* was changed to *i* before the suffix was added.)

Dig deeper into word meanings using the following prompts:

- Definition, synonym or antonym (Example: Find a word that is the opposite of *predictable*.)
- Analogies (Example: *Capricious* is to *predictable* as *hot* is to _____.)
- Words in context (Example: *I can never tell what my granddaughter will eat. One day she likes peas, and the next day she hates them. Her food tastes are* _____.)

Part 6

Interventions for Facilitating Comprehension

What the Research Says About Reading Comprehension

Comprehension is understanding what one reads. Adler and Van Doren (1972) refer to it as "reading with x-ray eyes". Extracting meaning from text involves enumerating the key facts, opinions or ideas in expository text or retelling a narrative. Students must extract meaning to answer questions or summarise. However, comprehension is also about constructing meaning, a process whereby the reader brings a unique set of experiences and knowledge to the text, and from reading and interacting with peers and teachers, develops new (to the reader) insights and ideas that help to affix the reading experience in long-term memory. The cognitive processes in which skilled readers engage are far more challenging to teach than discrete skills like word identification.

Our understanding of these cognitive processes comes from a fascinating qualitative study that asked expert readers to think aloud regarding what was happening in their minds while they were reading (Pressley & Afflerbach, 1995). The lengthy scripts recording the spoken thoughts (such as think-alouds) of skilled readers regarding their cognitive processing are called *verbal protocols*. These protocols were then categorised and analysed to answer specific questions, such as "What is the influence of prior knowledge on expert readers' strategies as they determine the main idea of a text?" (Afflerbach, 1990)

The protocols provide accurate "snapshots", and even "videos", of the ever-changing mental landscape that expert readers construct during reading. According to Pressley and Afflerbach (1995), reading is "constructively responsive—that is, good readers are always changing their processing in response to the text they are reading" (p. 2). Those who read this way are strategic readers. For students, whether struggling or gifted, to benefit from strategy instruction, teachers must daily and intentionally teach and model cognitive strategies.

Cognitive strategies are seen by some as mental tools, tricks or shortcuts to gaining meaning, understanding and knowledge. Duffy and Roehler (1987) call them "plans [that] readers use flexibly and adaptively depending on the situation" (p. 415). Cognitive strategies are also defined by Weinstein and Mayer (1986) as "behaviours and thoughts that a learner engages in during learning that are intended to influence the learner's encoding process" (p. 315). Such behaviours could include actions—note taking, constructing a graphic organiser, previewing the text, looking back to check on an answer, writing a summary, retelling a story—or thinking out loud and rehearsing the steps or the ideas that are unclear or need to be remembered. Thinking processes include activating prior knowledge, monitoring comprehension or inferring meaning.

Working with struggling readers requires that we also investigate the processes that are taking place in the minds of struggling readers. We must study their comprehension errors as closely as Pressley and Afflerbach studied the cognitive processes of skilled readers.

In another fascinating qualitative study of students who, despite their ability to read year-level text with some fluency, persisted in missing the point of what they were reading, Dewitz and Dewitz (2003) probed students' thinking to find out exactly where they had gone wrong. Students encountered the following difficulties:

- They failed to make causal inferences that required them to follow a chain of events throughout the narrative to identify a cause and effect.

- They failed to make causal inferences that required them to add some kind of background knowledge to what they read in the text.

- They made excessive elaborations with their own experiences, confusing them with what actually took place in the text.

- They had difficulties with relational (anaphoric) inferences, failing to determine how pronouns in the text matched up to actual people, thereby losing track of who did what and when in the story.

- They often had difficulties with comprehension at the sentence level because of the syntax (how the words and phrases are arranged in the sentence).

- Their lack of vocabulary knowledge kept them from fully understanding certain parts of the text, leading to confusion even in parts of the text that they could have understood.

Comprehension of text is undeniably our ultimate goal in reading instruction. If our efforts in word identification, vocabulary and fluency do not lead students to extracting and constructing meaning from text, we have laboured in vain. In spite of the vast body of cognitive research showing the power of teacher modelling accompanied by explicit and direct strategy instruction, Dewitz, Jones and Leahy (2007) concluded that while core programs do offer some guidelines for direct instruction, there is minimal guided practice for students and none of the explicit direct instruction that the cognitive research studies used to show the power of strategy instruction. Even if the basal contains scripted think-alouds, teachers often skip them, believing they are optional. The intervention strategies in this section use explicit, direct instruction to teach comprehension and include scripted think-alouds to use or adapt to the needs of your students.

Before you implement any of the comprehension intervention strategies in part 6, "Interventions for Facilitating Comprehension", make sure that you have data from a reliable and valid assessment instrument to inform your decision. Such data can help you in targetting specific students as well as in making needed adjustments to the sample lessons that are provided. As you implement, informally assess the individual students in your group on specific skills as part of every lesson to adjust instruction for the next day. Also, give the regular curriculum-based progress-monitoring tests to collect more definitive data. If needed, be open to scheduling more time or decreasing the size of an intervention group.

INTERVENTION 26

Scaffolding Year-Level Reading Texts for Struggling Students (Years 3–6)

> *Lack of exposure to year-level concepts, vocabulary, and syntax may prevent children from acquiring information that contributes to their development of language, comprehension, and writing.*
>
> —McCormack, Paratore, & Dahlene
> (2004, p. 119)

This intervention is designed for students who have been heavily supported throughout the primary years but whose year-level attainment remains tenuous. It provides the scaffolding they need to continue to access year-level text in homogeneous "pull-aside" groups at the same difficulty and pace as their on-year-level peers.

Background Knowledge

This intervention was developed by a reading specialist and her colleagues in a primary school to meet the needs of year three students who, although strongly supported in the primary years, were reported to be struggling in year three reading.

There are conflicting schools of thought regarding how best to differentiate instruction for struggling students. Juel (1988, 1990) found that children do best when they are taught with materials at their instructional level and when the teacher differentiates instruction by changing the reading materials used. However, one consequence of doing so is that these students will experience even further handicaps in the form of knowledge deficits (Fielding & Roller, 1992).

In this intervention, the reading specialist, special education teachers and classroom teachers designed what they called a pull-aside intervention. In this intervention, students left the regular classroom for reading instruction but continued to read the same story at the same pace as the students in the regular classroom. They constructed their intervention as an action research project around the following question (McCormack et al., 2004):

> When children enter third-grade reading substantially below grade level, what are the effects of grouping children homogeneously for part of their literacy instruction and providing instruction using year-level text in combination with explicit, systematic, and intensive instruction in both word and comprehension strategies? (p. 120)

The authors found that although teachers were expected to differentiate instruction for students who were struggling, they seldom did it with the intensity or the kinds of decoding and comprehension instruction that were required. Below-year-level students often spent long periods of time simply listening or watching and not nearly enough time engaged in real reading.

This intervention was designed around the evidence from research in several key areas of reading instruction:

- Explicit, systematic and intensive instruction in word-identification strategies (Adams, 1990, 1998; Ehri, 1997; Torgesen et al., 1997)

- Preteaching of vocabulary (Beck & McKeown, 1991)

- Discussion of background knowledge (Pearson & Fielding, 1991)

- Repeated readings (Dowhower, 1987; Rasinski, 1990; Samuels, 1979)

- Explicit instruction in reading comprehension strategies (Pearson & Fielding, 1991)

Daily Schedule for Pull-Aside Homogeneous Reading Groups

This is the sequence of events that took place daily in the pull-aside reading group taught by the reading specialist:

- Before reading, students reviewed and practised retelling what they had read the previous day. All of the children in the group struggled with being able to retell stories from the beginning of the school year.

- The students were introduced to new vocabulary needed for comprehending the day's selection.

- Irregular words were introduced and practised. (See Intervention 9 for a research-based approach to teaching irregular words.)

- Decodable words were introduced, and word-study strategies and activities were used. (See Intervention 10 for descriptions of two big word strategies.)

- The reading specialist read the text aloud while students followed along in their own copies of the book. As she read, the reading specialist used frequent think-alouds to model various comprehension strategies. (Many of the upcoming comprehension interventions have sample teacher think-alouds.)

- After the read-aloud, the students shared their reactions to the story, returned to and discussed their predictions, and attempted to answer any questions they had posed before reading.

- At this point, the students read the selection with a peer, using a variety of oral reading strategies, including echo reading, choral reading, Reader's Theatre and buddy reading.

- After peer reading, students reread a small portion of the story to the reading specialist, either individually or in pairs.

This intervention offers far more opportunities for struggling students to do real reading with an emphasis on oral reading and fluency building in year-level text than would have been possible in the heterogeneous large-group instruction. McCormack and colleagues (2004), the researchers who developed this intervention, concluded that "the fact that children achieved high levels of performance on text that was judged 'too difficult' for them reminded us that reading difficulty does not reside in the text alone, but that text difficulty interacts with the linguistic characteristics of the text and the actions of the teacher" (p. 130). Especially noteworthy from this study were the achievement results of special education students who were included in this scaffolded group.

INTERVENTION 27

Teaching the Seven Cognitive Strategies of Highly Effective Readers (Years 3–6)

> *Good strategy use is complex and thus calls for prolonged and detailed instruction.*
>
> —Pressley, Goodchild, Fleet, Zajchowski & Evans (1989, p. 301)

This intervention is a comprehensive one that will take months, if not years, to adequately teach. Its complexity, however, should not deter you from beginning immediately. Teaching and facilitating the use of cognitive strategies is very different from teaching the discrete skills of phonemic decoding and blending. There is a beginning and an end to teaching discrete reading skills. However, teaching cognitive strategies is an ongoing process that is situational—that is, dependent on the characteristics of the text.

Background Knowledge

Cognitive strategies are the mental processes that skilled readers use to extract and construct meaning from text and to create knowledge structures in long-term memory. When these strategies are directly taught to and modelled for struggling readers, their comprehension and retention improve.

Struggling students often mistakenly believe they are reading when they are actually engaged in what researchers call "mindless reading" (Schooler et al., 2004), zoning out while staring at the printed page. The opposite of mindless reading is the processing of text by highly effective readers using cognitive strategies. Figure 27.1 defines the seven cognitive strategies of highly effective readers.

Figure 27.1: Seven cognitive strategies of highly effective readers.

Strategy	Definition
Activating	"Priming the cognitive pump" in order to recall relevant prior knowledge and experiences from long-term memory so as to extract and construct meaning from text
Inferring	Bringing together what is spoken (written) in the text, what is unspoken (unwritten) in the text, and what is already known by the reader from relevant prior experiences and learning in order to extract and construct meaning from the text
Monitoring-Clarifying	Thinking about how and what one is reading both during and after the act of reading for purposes of determining if one is comprehending the text combined with the ability to clarify and fix up any mix-ups if necessary

continued →

Strategy	Definition
Questioning	Engaging in learning dialogues with text (authors), peers and teachers through self-questioning, question generating and question answering
Searching–Selecting	Searching a variety of sources in order to select appropriate information to answer questions, define words and terms, clarify misunderstandings, solve problems or gather information
Summarising	Restating the meaning of text in one's own words—different words from those used in the original text
Visualising–Organising	Constructing a mental image or graphic organiser for the purpose of extracting and constructing meaning from text

Source: Adapted from McEwan, 2004.

According to the research, the most effective way to teach the seven strategies is directly and explicitly using the following steps:

- **Define and explain the cognitive strategy.** To do this, you must settle on a definition that makes sense to you, uses the vocabulary and processes set forth in your relevant standards, and can be explicitly modelled for students.

- **Explain the purpose that the cognitive strategy serves for students during their own reading of text.** Sell your students on the usefulness of cognitive strategies in their reading.

- **Describe the critical attributes of the cognitive strategy, and provide concrete examples and nonexamples of the strategy.** If the strategy is activating prior knowledge, model for students how to activate relevant prior knowledge that relates to the text and helps them to make solid inferences. Conversely, model for them how activating knowledge that is not connected in any way to the text can confuse them, causing them to totally miss the meaning of what they are reading.

- **Model the strategy by thinking aloud.** This is an essential aspect of comprehension instruction. It is a metacognitive activity in which you reflect on your behaviours, thoughts and attitudes regarding what you are reading and then describe your behaviours and attitudes and speak your thoughts aloud for students.

- Finally, **guide your students in the beginning steps of using the strategy using easy-to-read text.** This process takes weeks, not days. For struggling readers, focus on one strategy at a time.

You will note that some of the cognitive strategies receive more attention than others in the upcoming interventions. As I work with teachers and principals, they routinely tell me that the most difficult strategy to teach is inference, particularly with struggling readers. I therefore chose to pay more attention to inference in this book. Two strategies receive no further mention: activating prior knowledge and searching-selecting. Most teachers spend more time on activating prior knowledge than on any of the other six strategies. Although searching-selecting is important when skimming text or the Internet and looking for information, summarising, questioning and inferring are more important for the struggling student in overall reading comprehension.

INTERVENTION 28

Teaching Students About Inferences (Years 3–6)

A fully explicit text would not only be very long and boring, but it would destroy the reader's pleasure in imposing meaning on the text—making it their own.

—Oakhill, Cain, & Yuill (1998, p. 347)

This intervention approaches the topic of teaching inference from the students' point of view. It begins with leading students to consider the inferences they make on a daily basis and then transitions them to making inferences based on four different kinds of evidence: (1) the printed word in the text, (2) what the author means but doesn't actually state in the text, (3) what the reader knows from real-life personal experiences and (4) what the reader has learned both from reading texts and academic experiences. While all students can benefit from this intervention, the most needy students are those who have chronic comprehension difficulties despite being able to read the text with a fair degree of fluency. These students can fool you with their fluctuating comprehension scores, but they do not have a solid understanding of what it means to comprehend text and frequently mix in their own stories in an effort to cover up their lack of understanding.

Background Knowledge

Teaching students how to make inferences begins with explicitly and directly teaching what an inference is. To do that, you need to settle on a student-friendly definition of *inference*, one that you and your students can understand and talk about regularly. If your definition is too complicated, students won't get it. However, if it's missing critical attributes of the term, your students won't get it either. The *New Oxford American Dictionary* defines an *inference* as "a conclusion reached on the basis of evidence and reasoning". The terms *evidence* and *reasoning* suggest a process of deduction much like a detective would use in building a case to take into the courtroom. Detectives don't need to know everything about how and why a crime was committed, but they cannot build solid cases out of thin air. One can make an inference based on some assumptions, but eventually there must be some evidence for making those assumptions. Princeton University's WordNet 3.0 defines an *inference* as "the reasoning involved in drawing a conclusion or making a logical judgment on the basis of circumstantial evidence and prior conclusions rather than on the basis of direct observation based on evidence". This definition clearly spells out that an inference is a cognitive process (thinking, reasoning, deducing, judging, figuring out) that uses circumstantial evidence and prior knowledge rather than direct observation. When making an inference while reading, the student uses circumstantial evidence and prior knowledge rather than any direct statements the author has made.

When you directly teach students how to make inferences, be as explicit and direct as possible. Cut out all extraneous teacher talk, and strive for complete clarity. If you prefer the idea that an inference is a puzzle that one must assemble without having all of the pieces and then decide what is pictured with chunks of the puzzle missing, your definition could be "My thinking about what the puzzle will look like if I could find the missing pieces is . . ." The student statement would be "I think the picture looks like this . . ."

You can use artefacts to gain students' attention, such as a Sherlock Holmes hat, puzzle pieces or a special "inferential calculator" that adds up information from four different sources rather than numbers. Choose an approach that will motivate your students, and stick with it.

Here is another way to approach the teaching of inference. Hansen (1981) suggests a weaving metaphor to explain inference to students. After the teacher helps students activate their prior knowledge related to a specific text, students write down what they know about the subject on long strips of grey paper (for grey matter in their brains) to symbolise their known experiences and background knowledge. Next, the students preview the text and write on brightly coloured strips of paper what the text or story might say. Finally, they weave the grey strips of background knowledge and the coloured strips of their predictions about the text to symbolise the process of making inferences.

Weaving is a lovely metaphor, but it could leave students with the mistaken impression that formulating an inference is a creative art activity rather than a serious problem-solving exercise that demands cognitive processing. When confronted with inferential questions (in class discussions, informal silent reading assessments or standardised tests), the default strategy for many struggling readers is *imagining* rather than inferring. Dewitz and Dewitz (2003) speculate, "It may be a coping strategy, or it may be learned, as teachers have overstressed what students know without directing them back to the text to justify their understandings and their interpretations" (p. 428). As you teach students what an inference is, continue to focus their attention on the evidence in the text.

Sample Lesson for Teaching Inference

Figure 28.1 is a sample lesson for teaching students the definition of an inference. You are not teaching them *how* to make inferences yet. Before they can do that, they have to know what an inference actually is. At the end of the lesson, you will think aloud about making inferences as you read the sample text in figure 28.2. Figure 28.3 is an organiser with question prompts for helping students figure out what the evidence means.

Figure 28.1: Sample lesson for teaching inference.

Lesson Objective	Students will be able to define an inference and give examples of inferences they have made in their everyday lives.
Materials Needed for the Lesson	You'll need the text from which to model inferring. This sample lesson uses text from *Call of the Wild* (London, 1903). You have the option of choosing your own text.

continued →

Teaching Students About Inferences

Advance Organiser	**Teacher Says:** Today we're going to learn about one of the seven strategies that very good readers use whenever they read. The strategy is called *inferring*. Say that with me. *Inferring*. When readers infer, we say they have made an inference. Now making inferences may sound very complicated, but you make inferences every day. Let me give you an example. Suppose you get up in the morning and you come out to the kitchen and your mother gives you that "look". [Illustrate the upset, angry look for students.] She doesn't say good morning. She is totally quiet. What do you think is happening here? [Students offer answers: She is mad at me. She just figured out that I didn't finish my homework. She discovered the mess I made in the refrigerator and didn't clean up.] Congratulations. You have just made an inference. Did your mother say she was angry? Did she explain what was going on? No. You had to figure it out on your own based on what you already know. We're going to learn more about what an inference is and how you make inferences when you are reading.
Define and Explain an Inference	**Teacher Says:** I'm going to give you the definition of an inference, and we will use that definition whenever we're talking about inferences either in our daily experiences or in our reading. An inference is a decision you make about what the evidence means. What is an inference? [Students respond chorally: An inference is a decision you make about what the evidence means.] The decision could be your decision or my decision or your partner's decision or a decision you and your partner made together. But an inference is always a decision that somebody makes about what the evidence means. If you're ever in doubt about what an inference is, look at the definition on the bulletin board. What is an inference? **Students Say:** An inference is a decision you make about what the evidence means. **Teacher Says:** First, let's make sure we know what a decision is: it's something that you decide. You could decide to have vanilla ice-cream for a snack or potato chips or an apple. You get to decide. You are in charge of making the choice. It's your decision. So what's an inference? **Students Say:** An inference is a decision you make about what the evidence means. **Teacher Says:** Second, let's make sure we know what evidence is. If you watch those crime shows on TV, you already know what evidence is. Evidence is the proof or the facts. Evidence on a TV show could be fingerprints or eyewitness reports. That's factual evidence. You can see it and hear it. But there's also another kind of evidence: circumstantial evidence. What's an inference? **Students Say:** An inference is a decision you make about what the evidence means. **Teacher Says:** So we can have factual evidence. But detectives can also have circumstantial evidence. Circumstantial evidence is "evidence based on inference". Ah, there's our word. What is an inference? **Students Say:** An inference is a decision you make about what the evidence means. **Teacher Says:** Right. But it's evidence based on an inference. Remember your experience with your mother. Your evidence was circumstantial. You made an inference about why your mother didn't speak to you and looked so angry. But you didn't really have any factual evidence. You made your decision based on circumstantial evidence. When you make a decision based on circumstantial evidence, you have to use all of your brainpower to reason out an inference. It's more difficult to do when you are reading than when you are doing it in your own life. But once you understand the process, you'll be able to make inferences more quickly when you're reading. **Teacher Says:** Before we move on, tell me once again what an inference is. **Students Say:** An inference is a decision you make about what the evidence means.
Explain the Purpose That Inferences Serve	**Teacher Says:** Making inferences is one of the most important things readers do. If you can infer, you can comprehend. If you can infer, you can answer questions about what is happening in the story. If you can infer, you can tell me what the main idea is or who the main character is. Knowing how to infer is very important.

continued →

Describe Critical Attributes of a Good Inference	**Teacher Says:** Tell me once again what an inference is. **Students Say:** An inference is a decision you make about what the evidence means. **Teacher Says:** In order to make a good inference you first have to have evidence. A good inference doesn't just rely on one source of evidence. A good inference is based on adding up evidence from several different places and seeing if all of the evidence makes sense together. A good inference requires thinking and reasoning.
Provide Concrete Examples and Nonexamples of Inferences	**Teacher Says:** Let's look at some examples of good inferences and inferences that can cause what I call "comprehension confusion". Bad inferences are made when you make a decision about the evidence before you have all of the evidence. A good inference uses the text that the author has written. If you're trying to make a decision about what the evidence means, first rely on the factual evidence in the text. Suppose you read the first sentence in a book: "Buck did not read the newspapers, or he would have known that trouble was brewing." As you read this first part of the sentence about Buck not reading the newspapers, you might decide right away that Buck is a person who doesn't read the newspapers. That's not a good inference because by the time you get to the end of the sentence, you'll find out that the text identifies Buck as a dog and states that all the dogs who live along the western coast are going to have trouble. A good inference also considers what the author means but doesn't come right out and say—evidence that isn't right there in the text but can be figured out if you read carefully. The author doesn't come right out and say what kind of trouble Buck and other dogs would be having, but let me read a bit further for you. **Teacher Does:** Continue reading from p. 1 from "Call of the Wild" (London, 1903). **Teacher Says:** There were several phrases in what I read that provide clues—"men had found a yellow metal", "men wanted dogs with strong muscles and furry coats"—that give us clues about what is going to happen to Buck. What is the author telling us about Buck and his future? Right, he is going to be kidnapped. The author didn't come right out and say Buck was going to be kidnapped. That would have taken all of the suspense and excitement out of the story. So that was a good inference because it looked for what the author meant but didn't come right out and tell us. A good inference uses the reader's personal experiences, if they are related to the story. You have to be very careful when you start thinking about your own experiences. They have to be connected to the story in some way or you could confuse your story with the author's story, which doesn't make for a good inference. For example, suppose someone who was reading this story had a dog named Buck, and he decided to relate what happened to his dog and how it got run over by a car. He decided that because the dog in the story is named Buck and his dog was named Buck, that the dog in the story is going to get run over by a car. That is an example of a very bad inference. The reader's experiences with his own dog don't tell us anything that will help us figure out the story we are reading. A good inference uses information the reader has read in other books or learned in school that is related to the story. Suppose that the reader had learned the meaning of the word *tidewater* in social studies class, and the minute he read the expression "tidewater dog", he knew that the dog must live in an area near an ocean, along the seacoast. That information will help the reader make good inferences about what might happen in the story. A good inference adds up all of the important and connected evidence and then makes a decision based on what the evidence means. I've put a chart up on the wall that shows the four kinds of evidence that you need to add up to make a good inference. You can look at it when you need to remind yourself.
I Do It: Teacher Models the Strategy	**Teacher Says:** I am going to model for you how I make inferences while I'm reading by thinking aloud. **Teacher Does:** Use the think-aloud shown in figure 28.2.

© 2009 Hawker Brownlow Education and Elaine McEwan-Adkins.

Figure 28.2: Think-aloud for making inferences.

Read-Aloud Text

Grahame, K. (1908). *The Wind in the Willows:* The Mole had been working very hard all the morning, spring-cleaning his little home. First with brooms, then with dusters; then on ladders and steps and chairs, with a brush and a pail of whitewash; till he had dust in his throat and eyes, and splashes of whitewash all over his black fur, and an aching back and weary arms. Spring was moving in the air above and in the earth below and around him, penetrating even his dark and lowly little house with its spirit of divine discontent and longing. It was small wonder, then, that he suddenly flung down his brush on the floor, said "Bother!'" and "O blow!" and also "Hang spring-cleaning!" and bolted out of the house without even waiting to put on his coat. Something up above was calling him imperiously, and he made for the steep little tunnel which answered in his case to the gravelled carriage-drive owned by animals whose residences are nearer to the sun and air.

Teacher Think-Aloud: The first thing that is puzzling is that the Mole says "something" not "someone". So he can't be referring to a person (or to one of his animal friends). What could be calling him? The evidence tells me that this is not a literal statement. He is not saying I hear a voice calling to me. He is saying, I have a strong feeling inside of me that is telling me to get out of this dark hole I live in and go up into the sunshine. I can relate to that. There are times in my life when I just get a strong feeling like that.

The second puzzling thing is when the Mole says "up above". I don't think that he is talking about the ceiling of his hole in the ground, which would be dirt. I don't think he's talking about the sky either, because he can't see the sky from his hole in the ground. I think he's talking about the wide world above ground level, the part of the earth where humans live. There is his world under the ground where he and lots of other animals live and then there's the world above the ground.

Finally, there is that word *imperiously*. The text says that the "something up above was calling him imperiously". I am going to check my dictionary for the meaning of *imperious*. I think that word means that this was not a feeling that the Mole could ignore. It was more like an order from a higher authority, like a general or a king or queen. Sure enough, when I look up *imperious* in the dictionary, one of the meanings is "commanding", and the other meaning is "authoritative". So the Mole gets a very strong feeling that is telling him to crawl out of his hole.

The second half of the last sentence says, "He made for the steep little tunnel which answered in his case to the gravelled carriage-drive owned by animals whose residences are nearer to the sun and air." I have to closely examine the text and read that sentence again. I have to figure out what the word *which* refers to in the phrase "which answered in his case". If I go back to immediately before "which", I find the words *steep little tunnel*. That tells me I can substitute the words *steep little tunnel* for the word *which* to help me make sense of this sentence.

So if I substitute *steep little tunnel*, here's what it would say: "the steep little tunnel answered in his case to the gravelled carriage-drive". This is very confusing. I know the meaning of the word *answered*, but it doesn't seem to fit in this context. The tunnel can't be answering a question for the carriage-drive. I wonder if there's another word that makes more sense to me, but actually means the same thing the author is trying to say. I know when I'm reading books that were written a long time ago, the language can be used in very different ways and I have to do some clever inferring to get the true meaning. It seems to me that the author is comparing the Mole's steep tunnel to a gravelled carriage-drive, but I'm not sure what's alike about a Mole's tunnel and a gravel driveway. I'm going to keep reading in that sentence where it says that the carriage drive is owned by animals whose residences are nearer to the sun and air. What kind of animals could he be talking about? Well if I picture a gravel driveway it probably leads up to somebody's house. Could those be the animals that the Mole is talking about? Are humans animals? Well, I have heard an expression somewhere, maybe I read it, "the human animal" so that seems to make sense. So the Mole is saying that his tunnel down to his little "home" is just like the driveway would be to a house. It's how you get to the house if you want to go inside.

© 2009 Hawker Brownlow Education and Elaine McEwan-Adkins.

Figure 28.3: Four sources of evidence on which to base an inference.

What does the author directly state in the text?		
What does the author mean, but doesn't actually state in the text?		
What do you know from your real-life experiences that could help you make a decision about the evidence?		
What have you learned from classes in school and reading books that might help you make a decision about what the evidence means?		

© 2009 Hawker Brownlow Education and Elaine McEwan-Adkins.

Copyright © Hawker Brownlow Education. All rights reserved. Reprinted from *40 Reading Intervention Strategies for P–6 Students*, by Elaine K. McEwan-Adkins. Melbourne, Vic: Hawker Brownlow Education, www.hbe.com.au. Reproduction authorised only for use in the school site that has purchased the book.

INTERVENTION 29

Teaching Pronouns to Improve Inferential Comprehension (Years 2–6)

> *[An inference is] information that is activated during reading yet not explicitly stated in the text.*
>
> —van den Broek (1994, p. 556)

This intervention teaches students how pronouns in the English language stand for other words and models how to identify the referents of pronouns in text for the purpose of comprehension. Struggling readers of all types have difficulties making connections between English pronouns and their referents. English language learners as well as students at risk and those with reading disabilities, whose opportunities for the natural acquisition of English are often limited, are candidates for the direct instruction of anaphoric relationships.

Background Knowledge

Anaphora are words or phrases in a text that stand for other words, and *anaphoric relationships* are how these words relate to their referents in the text. Literature would be very boring if every time the author wanted to refer to Grandma in his story, he could use only the word *Grandma*. Instead, the author can use pronouns like *she, her* and *hers*. If Grandma is speaking, the author can use *I, my* and *mine*. Or the author can draw upon an almost unlimited supply of phrases that can also stand for Grandma in the text: an elderly lady, my father's mother, a geriatric genius, a senior citizen or a role model. When asked to select a main idea or write a short sentence about what the story is mainly about, students may not recognise that Grandma is the star of the show unless they understand the role of anaphoric relationships. Although this intervention will be limited to pronouns, once you have used it, you will want to give your struggling readers advance warning of how synonymous and descriptive words and phrases also function as anaphora in the stories they read. In other words, cue readers to synonyms and adjectival clauses that stand for people, animals and things in the text.

Few (if any) reading programs teach anaphora as part of their curriculum. I am only aware of *Reading Success* (Dixon et al., 2002). Popular core programs assume that average students, for whom their lessons are designed, will pick up anaphoric relationships gradually as they read widely in well-written and authentic narrative and expository texts. The most important reason to explicitly teach anaphora is the role they play in helping readers to determine the main idea in text.

Sample Lesson for Teaching Pronouns

Figure 29.1 displays the pronouns that stand for other words. In advance of teaching the lesson, prepare a similar chart as a poster to place on a classroom bulletin board.

Figure 29.1: Pronouns: words that stand for other words.

Personal Pronouns That Stand for People or Talking Animals	Pronouns That Stand for Females	Pronouns That Stand for Males
	I, we, me, us, she, her, they, them	I, we, me, us, he, him, they, them
Reflexive Personal Pronouns That Stand for People or Talking Animals	myself, herself, yourself, ourselves, themselves	myself, himself, yourself, ourselves, themselves
Possessive Personal Pronouns That Stand for Ownership by People or Talking Animals	my, mine, hers, your, yours, our, their	my, mine, his, your, yours, our, their
Pronouns That Stand for Things, Actions or Ideas	Pronouns That Stand for Things, Actions or Ideas (Neutral)	
	it, they, them	
Reflexive Pronouns That Stand for Things, Actions or Ideas	itself, themselves	
Possessive Pronouns That Stand for Ownership by Things, Actions or Ideas	its, their	

Source: Al-Jarf, 2001; Baumann, 1986.

Figure 29.2 is a sample lesson for teaching students in years 2–6 how pronouns stand for other words in a story. The text example is an easy picture book (*The Little Red Hen*). Once you understand the lesson objective, you can choose other text samples that may be more relevant for your students.

Figure 29.2: Sample lesson for teaching the function of pronouns.

Lesson Objective	Students will know (1) what pronouns are (words that stand for other words in a story), (2) which words are pronouns and (3) how to find the words that pronouns stand for in a story.
Review Prior Learning	**Teacher Says:** We've been talking about and making inferences in our reading a lot lately. Remind me again: what is an inference? A decision you make about the evidence. We talked about adding up evidence from four places: (1) what is written in the text, (2) what the author means but doesn't come right out and say, (3) what you know from your personal experience that is connected to what you're reading and (4) what you have learned in school or read in a book that is connected to what you're reading.
Advance Organiser	**Teacher Says:** Today we're going to learn about a category of words that stand for other words in stories. These words are called *pronouns*. The reason authors use words like pronouns to stand for other words is to make what they are writing more interesting.

continued →

Teaching Pronouns to Improve Inferential Comprehension

Explain the Purpose That Pronouns Play	**Teacher Says:** Let me read something aloud to you two different ways and see if you can figure out the difference between these two paragraphs. "Mrs Bannister was easy to spot. Mrs Bannister was a good 30 cm taller than any of the other adults on the playground and was wearing a huge sunhat. Springy grey curls stuck out around the edges of the hat, and Mrs Bannister was wearing gym shoes. Mrs Bannister had a whistle, a pair of glasses and one of those mechanical pencils all hanging around Mrs Bannister's neck. Mrs Bannister wasn't going to waste any time looking for what Mrs Bannister needed." Now listen to the second version: "Mrs Bannister was easy to spot. She was a good 30 cm taller than any of the other adults on the playground and was wearing a huge sunhat. Springy grey curls stuck out around the edges of the hat, and she was wearing gym shoes. She had a whistle, a pair of glasses and one of those mechanical pencils all hanging around her neck. She wasn't going to waste any time looking for what she needed." What was the difference between the two paragraphs? Yes. That first version was pretty boring when I kept saying Mrs Bannister's name over and over again. What words did I use in the second version to stand for Mrs Bannister? Right. The words *she* and *her* on our chart are called personal pronouns, and they stand for people and talking animals in stories. It's important to pay attention to them because they will help you understand what you are reading and often can help you find the main idea of a story.
Model Figuring Out Which Words the Pronouns Represent	**Teacher Says:** Remember that the pronouns on our chart stand for people and talking animals in stories. I am going to read aloud one of my favourite folktales. It features three talking animals: a little red hen, a rooster and a cat. This story contains many of the pronouns shown in the chart I've put up. "One day the little red hen found a grain of wheat lying on the ground. 'Look what I have found,' she said to the rooster and the cat." I see two words that stand for the little red hen. *I* and *she*. I'm going to underline them on my copy of the story on the overhead. The pronoun *she* is used because a hen is a female chicken. The next sentence says, "I will plant it in the soil. Who will help me?" There are two words in this sentence that also stand for the red hen. *I* and *me*. I am going to underline those two words also. Now, there is another pronoun in that sentence, *it*. I need to figure out what *it* stands for in this sentence. What is the little red hen going to plant in the soil? I have to go backward in the story until I find the words *a grain of wheat*. The pronoun *it* stands for the grain of wheat. I'm going to substitute the words *a grain of wheat* for *it* and see if that makes sense. "I will plant the grain of wheat in the soil." Yes, that makes sense. Follow along with me as I read: "'Not I,' said the rooster." There is another pronoun in this sentence, *I*. This word stands for the rooster. He is a talking animal. I used the word *he* because the rooster is a male chicken. I'm going to underline the *I*. *I* is a pronoun that stands for the rooster in this sentence. The rooster is a talking animal, and we treat animals just like people in imaginary stories. Follow along as I read the next sentence: "'Not I,' said the cat." I can tell that *I* stands for the cat, so I'm going to underline the word *I*. The next sentence says, "'Then I will do it myself,' said the little red hen." I see two words that stand for the little red hen: *I* and *myself*. I underline them. I also see another pronoun that is on our chart: *it*. It doesn't stand for people or talking animals. *It* stands for a thing or an action. I will need to look back in the story to find a thing or an action that the word *it* stands for. I can see I have two choices. *It* could stand for the grain of wheat. But we already found another sentence where *it* stood for the grain of wheat. But the sentence says that the little red hen is going to "do it". That means that *it* stands for an action of some kind. The cat and the rooster will be able to watch the little red hen doing it.

continued →

© 2009 Hawker Brownlow Education • SOT4749

Model Figuring Out Which Words the Pronouns Represent (continued)	When I move my finger back up the page from where she said, "I will do it," to the last sentence where the little red hen was talking, it says, *"Who will plant it in the soil?"* I think that's what she is going to do by herself: plant the seed in the soil. Notice that the *it* in the sentence "who will plant it in the soil" stands for the seed. *It* is a very handy word, but sometimes it is a very confusing word.

© 2009 Hawker Brownlow Education and Elaine McEwan-Adkins.

Picture books are a good way to model cognitive strategies for upper-yewrs students. They often contain challenging themes and new words, but students are familiar with the plot lines and can concentrate on how the strategy works.

There are dozens of versions of *The Little Red Hen*. See if you can find one so each student can have an individual copy of the story to read several times for independent practice. Any version you choose will contain a variety of personal, possessive and reflexive pronouns that stand for the hen and her friends.

Figure 29.3 is a sample lesson that provides additional practice in the identification of pronouns in an upper-year story. The text and answer key are found in figures 29.4 and 29.5. Figure 29.6 is a blank thinksheet on which students can write their descriptions of each of the characters. Figure 29.7 is a suggested list of answers that students might provide. However, creative students may come up with others that are appropriate to the text.

Figure 29.3: Sample lesson for practicing pronouns.

Lesson Objective	Students will use what they know about how pronouns stand for other words in a story to make inferences about two characters in a story.
Materials Needed for the Lesson	Prepare and give copies to students of page 1 of the novel they will be reading together (figure 29.4). Prepare an enlarged overhead version (sample is illustrative of text that could be used and contains the answer key). Choose easy-to-read text containing many examples similar to the sample.
Advance Organiser	**Teacher Says:** Today we're going to be detectives and figure out what the author of our story means but doesn't come right out and say. So put on your detective hats, and away we go.
Review	**Teacher Does:** Review the pronoun chart (see figure 29.1) you have posted on your wall.
I Do It: Teacher Models Coding Pronouns	**Teacher Says:** I have put the first page of a story up on the overhead, and you have a copy to help you keep track of what I'm doing. This text is the first page of a novel we are going to read together. The first page is a big mystery. There are no names. Just lots and lots of pronouns—words that stand for other words in the story. On this page, the pronouns stand for two characters. My assignment as I read this page is to figure out who these characters are and learn something about them as individuals. What kind of people are they? Are they adults, small children, teenagers? As you listen to me think aloud, I want you to be thinking about these characters.
We Do It: Teacher and Students Work Together	**Teacher Does:** Pass out figure 29.5 to the class. Explain that you will work with them to get this exercise started and then will expect them to work in partners to finish it today and tomorrow.
You Do It: Students Work in Pairs	**Teacher Does:** After modelling what students are expected to do three or four times, ask them to team up with their assigned partners to find one thing they know about Character 1 and one thing they know about Character 2. Check for understanding by asking various students to give their examples. If students understand, let them proceed to work in partners. If not, go back to the We Do It part of the lesson and continue to scaffold students' practice.

© 2009 Hawker Brownlow Education and Elaine McEwan-Adkins.

In the sample lesson, there are two characters speaking to each other in the first page of an easy reading novel for upper-years students found in figure 29.4. Begin by coding the first pronoun (I) with 1 and the second pronoun (me) with 2. Pronouns and other words that stand for the main character, Joshua McIntire, are coded 1. Pronouns and other words that stand for Wendell (who becomes Josh's best friend later in the five-book series) are coded 2. You would not share this information with students ahead of time.

Figure 29.4: Text for pronoun practice lesson (McEwan, 1991, p. 1).

> "Hey, you wanna go to the library with me?"
>
> The voice came from the other side of the fence, but I couldn't see its owner through the overgrown shrubbery.
>
> "It's me! Over here. Do you wanna go to the library with me or not?"
>
> Who goes to the library in the summertime? Ugh! That's almost as bad as taking a shower every day.
>
> I only take showers when my mother nags at me—and even then I sometimes just run water over my hair so it looks like I've showered.
>
> "I can't!" I called back. "I have to help my mum unpack."
>
> "Well, maybe you can make it tomorrow. See you later." The voice and its owner vanished.
>
> What kind of weirdo was my next-door neighbour? Not only did this oddball go to the library in the summertime, he went two days in a row. We were definitely not living on the same planet.

© 2009 Hawker Brownlow Education and Elaine McEwan-Adkins.

Copyright © Hawker Brownlow Education. All rights reserved. Reprinted from *40 Reading Intervention Strategies for P-6 Students*, by Elaine K. McEwan-Adkins. Melbourne, Vic: Hawker Brownlow Education, www.hbe.com.au. Reproduction authorised only for use in the school site that has purchased the book.

Figure 29.5: Answer key for pronoun practice lesson (McEwan, 1991, p. 1).

> "Hey, you (1) wanna go to the library with me (2)?"
>
> The voice (2) came from the other side of the fence, but I (1) couldn't see its owner (2) through the overgrown shrubbery.
>
> "It's me! (2) Over here. Do you wanna go to the library with me (2) or not?"
>
> Who (2) goes to the library in the summertime? Ugh! That's almost as bad as taking a shower every day.
>
> I (1) only take showers when my (1) mother nags at me (1)—and even then I (1) sometimes just run water over my (1) hair so it looks like I've (1) showered.
>
> "I (1) can't!" I (1) called back. "I (1) have to help my (1) mum unpack."
>
> "Well, maybe you (1) can make it tomorrow. See you (1) later." The voice (2) and its owner (2) vanished.
>
> What kind of weirdo (2) was my (1) next-door neighbour (2)? Not only did this oddball (2) go to the library in the summertime, he (2) went two days in a row. We (1 and 2) were definitely not living on the same planet.

© 2009 Hawker Brownlow Education and Elaine McEwan-Adkins.

Copyright © Hawker Brownlow Education. All rights reserved. Reprinted from *40 Reading Intervention Strategies for P-6 Students*, by Elaine K. McEwan-Adkins. Melbourne, Vic: Hawker Brownlow Education, www.hbe.com.au. Reproduction authorised only for use in the school site that has purchased the book.

Figure 29.6: Student thinksheet.

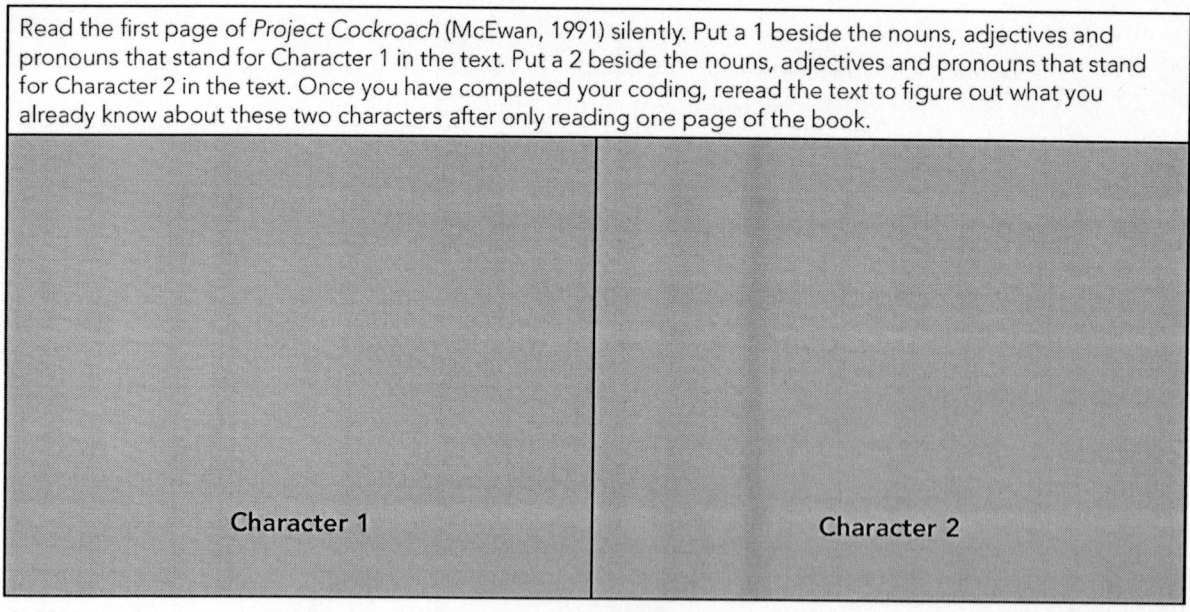

Read the first page of *Project Cockroach* (McEwan, 1991) silently. Put a 1 beside the nouns, adjectives and pronouns that stand for Character 1 in the text. Put a 2 beside the nouns, adjectives and pronouns that stand for Character 2 in the text. Once you have completed your coding, reread the text to figure out what you already know about these two characters after only reading one page of the book.

Character 1	Character 2

© 2009 Hawker Brownlow Education and Elaine McEwan-Adkins.

Copyright © Hawker Brownlow Education. All rights reserved. Reprinted from *40 Reading Intervention Strategies for P-6 Students*, by Elaine K. McEwan-Adkins. Melbourne, Vic: Hawker Brownlow Education, www.hbe.com.au. Reproduction authorised only for use in the school site that has purchased the book.

Figure 29.7: Answer key for student thinksheet.

Character 1	Character 2
could be boy or girl	is a boy
doesn't like to read	goes to the library in the summertime
doesn't like to take showers	is friendly
is helpful to his or her mother	lives next door to "I" whoever "I" is
doesn't seem that eager to make friends	feelings weren't hurt when "I" said he or she couldn't go to the library
is very judgmental about his or her neighbour	
just moved in	must love to read

© 2009 Hawker Brownlow Education and Elaine McEwan-Adkins.

Copyright © Hawker Brownlow Education. All rights reserved. Reprinted from *40 Reading Intervention Strategies for P-6 Students*, by Elaine K. McEwan-Adkins. Melbourne, Vic: Hawker Brownlow Education, www.hbe.com.au. Reproduction authorised only for use in the school site that has purchased the book.

INTERVENTION 30

Thinking Aloud to Teach Inference (Years 3–6)

> *We do not teach our children wisely and well if certain keystone stances are not topmost in our minds and hearts. Modelling is one of those keystone precepts. The only thing worse than faulty modelling is a teacher who does not credit the power of modelling.*
>
> —Pickard (2005, p. 35)

By listening to their teachers make inferences from texts during daily think-alouds, students will learn about the multiple ways to make inferences during their own reading. This intervention shows how to think aloud about inferential thinking from a variety of classroom texts, read-alouds and supplementary materials. It is based on the cognitive apprenticeship model in which students are the apprentices and teachers are the cognitive masters (Collins, Brown, & Holum, 1991; Collins, Brown, & Newman, 1990). Teaching students how to infer is a long-term, several-step endeavour, of which this intervention is only a part. If you have not already discovered the other interventions designed to help you teach your students how to infer, look at Interventions 28 and 29.

Background Knowledge

To model cognitive strategy usage for students, teachers must think aloud, or as Pressley, El-Dinary, and Brown (1992, p.112) described it, "[show] students exactly how a good reader would apply [a particular] strategy". If you have never engaged in thinking aloud for students, your initial attempts may feel awkward and artificial, but with practice, you can readily become a strategic teacher who routinely thinks aloud (Davey, 1983). Thinking aloud requires three simultaneous acts: (1) comprehending the text, (2) figuring out what you had to do to construct meaning since the cognitive processing happens in split seconds and (3) articulating for students what was going on in your mind. Herber and Nelson call it the "artificial representation[s] of a real experience; a contrived series of activities which, when taken together, approximate the experience of the process that ultimately is to be applied independently" (quoted in Herber & Herber, 1993, p. 140).

Thinking Aloud for Students

Although we saw in Interventions 28 and 29 that inference can be directly taught, your students can only understand it completely if you model it for them—not just once or twice, but every day for just a few minutes. Thinking aloud (modelling) is one of the most challenging teaching moves to implement, but it is also one of the most powerful for struggling students. I recommend writing scripts the first few times you think aloud, something similar to the one following. The biggest pitfall during the initial stages of thinking aloud is slipping out of the metacognitive mode and sliding into the "teaching trap". Be careful not to let these *nonexamples* of thinking aloud creep into your think-alouds:

- Explaining what the text means
- Giving a short synopsis of the text
- Teaching what a concept or idea in the text means
- Giving the impression that students should be getting the same meaning from the text as you are
- Lecturing to students about the importance of cognitive strategy usage (save that for another time)
- Giving the impression that you never have any comprehension problems when you read

Figure 30.1 is a sample teacher think-aloud for the opening paragraphs of *The Adventures of Tom Sawyer* by Mark Twain. Showing students how the teacher makes inferences while reading is the objective of the think-aloud.

Figure 30.1: Teacher think-aloud for *The Adventures of Tom Sawyer*.

The Adventures of Tom Sawyer Mark Twain (1876)	Teacher Think-Aloud
"TOM!" No answer. "Tom!" No answer. "What's gone with that boy, I wonder? You. TOM!" No answer.	The first thing I am wondering about is who does the pronoun *I* refer to? I don't know yet, but whoever it is, this person is quite upset. I can tell from the capital letters and exclamation points that are used as punctuation. I do wonder where Tom is. It's a little early to start making an inference about where he might be, since I have no evidence from the text to give me any clues.
The old lady pulled her spectacles down and looked over them about the room; then she put them up and looked out under them. She seldom or never looked through them for so small a thing as a boy; they were her state pair, the pride of her heart, and were built for "style", not service—she could have seen through a pair of stove lids just as well.	I now know who *I* refers to—an old lady. I don't know whether she's an aunt, a grandmother or a babysitter. The story hasn't told me that, but it does give me a clue by describing her spectacles in great detail. I know *spectacles* is another word for *eyeglasses*. There are several words and phrases in this section that I need to figure out if I'm going to make sense of this story. Sometimes when I don't have an exact meaning, I think about some words I could use in place of the hard words (they are the ones I have underlined) that would give me an idea of what the author is saying here. Here's what I think Mark Twain, the author, means. When he says they were her "state pair", I think he means that the spectacles were her good glasses that she only wore for "show". "They were built for style" probably means "they weren't that useful". I had to ask somebody what stove lids were, somebody who grew up in a house where the cast-iron stove had lids to cover the burners when the cooking was done so the heat didn't escape and kids didn't burn their hands. The stove lids were solid. Mark Twain is writing that the old lady's spectacles were about as useful for seeing through as the solid stove lids.

continued →

The Adventures of Tom Sawyer Mark Twain (1876)	Teacher Think-Aloud
She looked perplexed for a moment, and then said, not fiercely, but still loud enough for the furniture to hear: "Well, I say, if I get hold of you I'll—"	The author, Mark Twain, has quite a sense of humour, and you can hear it coming out when he says the old lady talked loud enough for the furniture to hear. I know he's making a little joke there. I know when I read I have to pay attention to pronouns so I can keep track of the characters and what's happening in the story. When the old lady says, "if I get hold of you", the "you" is Tom.
She did not finish, for by this time she was bending down and punching under the bed with the broom, and so she needed breath to punctuate the punches with. She resurrected nothing but the cat. "I never did see the beat of that boy!"	I can figure out that the old lady is getting pretty upset at not being able to find Tom. And she has used another one of those old-fashioned expressions: "I never did see the beat of that boy." I think that she means: "I haven't seen or heard Tom around anywhere." That makes sense in this context.
She went to the open door and stood in it and looked out among the tomato vines and "jimson" weeds that constituted the garden. No Tom. So she lifted up her voice at an angle calculated for distance, and shouted: "Y-o-u-u, Tom." There was a slight noise behind her and she turned just in time to seize a small boy by the slack of his roundabout and arrest his flight.	I can infer that it's summertime because there are tomato vines growing in the backyard. The old lady said something that I can't take literally. It must be figurative language: "she lifted up her voice at an angle calculated for distance". Now I know that the author doesn't literally mean she lifted up her voice. When I visualise what she might be doing, I can see her raising her head to shout. That's what Twain must mean. I've got to be a detective once again and solve the mystery of what Mark Twain means by "seize a small boy by the slack of his roundabout and arrest his flight". I'm visualising what this would look like. Tom is running behind the old lady, and she turns around just in time to grab him. But she misses his body and just grabs hold of his trousers and is holding him off the ground like he's flying. That's what "arresting his flight" means. She has stopped him from going any further. Wow, reading Mark Twain is slow going with all of these old-fashioned expressions and unusual words!

© 2009 Hawker Brownlow Education and Elaine McEwan-Adkins.

Thinking Aloud With Students to Solve Their Comprehension Difficulties

In addition to simply thinking aloud from the text you are reading aloud every day, you can also think aloud with students in a supportive way through text they are finding difficult. Figure 30.2 describes the difficulty that one struggling reader has in reasoning his way through the first page of the novel *Hatchet* (Paulsen, 1987). Gary Paulsen is a popular writer among upper- and middle-years students, but struggling students cannot immediately appreciate his popularity when they pick up one of his books for the first time. In fact, many struggling readers left on their own will never be able to solve the mystery of *who or what was driven* that is posed by Paulsen on the first page of *Hatchet*.

Figure 30.2: Making inferences from *Hatchet*.

Source of Information	What It Means to the Reader
The Printed Word	The actual text on page 1 of the novel *Hatchet* (Paulsen, 1987) provides the following information about the main character, Brian: Brian is thirteen; he is taking a trip in a small aeroplane; there is a pilot named Jim or Jake who is about forty years old; Brian and the pilot are flying over an endless green northern wilderness. Even struggling readers with some preteaching of vocabulary would be able to figure this much out.
	However, struggling readers will likely become completely confused when they read the last sentence on the first page where it says, "In fact, since Brian had come to the small airport in Hampton, New York, to meet the plane—driven by his mother—the pilot had spoken only five words to him" (p. 1). This brief flashback suddenly plucks Brian from being a passenger in the plane and takes him back to his arrival at the airport.
	For a struggling reader trying to visualise the sequence of the story, flashbacks are extraordinarily confusing. To further confuse struggling readers, they encounter the underlined words in the flashback. The struggling reader suddenly has to make a mental shift from flying with Brian and the pilot to being at the airport meeting a plane driven by his mother. None of this makes any sense at all, and struggling readers tackling this text on their own will surely close the book in frustration.
What the Author Means but Doesn't State	What the author means but doesn't actually say in so many words is that Brian's mother drove him to the airport in the family automobile so he could board a small plane to go somewhere by himself. While he was flying in the plane, he reconstructed his departure in his mind. All of this the reader must infer from four words (the participial phrase, "driven by his mother"), which should have been placed as close as possible to the word it is modifying (Brian). The author has made it exceptionally difficult for struggling readers. As the text stands, the only hope for struggling readers is to hear a teacher think aloud about how he or she made sense of it.
What the Reader Knows From Personal Experience	The reader has no personal experiences to bring to this text. He has never seen an endless green northern wilderness, flown in any plane, much less a small one. He doesn't know what a Cessna 406 bush plane looks like, and he cannot envision what the scene looks like at all. He does not know the demographics or the geography of Hampton, New York, details that add another layer of meaning to the text.
What the Reader Has Learned in School	The reader has learned little in school to prepare him for understanding this text. The concepts of north and south have not yet been mastered. Much of the vocabulary in the text is unfamiliar, and he has received no instruction about "flashbacks" or participial phrases.

© 2009 Hawker Brownlow Education and Elaine McEwan-Adkins.

First, take some time to read the information in the previous figure, and then we'll walk through how the reader and his teacher used thinking aloud to solve the mystery.

Stefan has no difficulty decoding text, and if you hear him read aloud from *Hatchet*, he would seem to be an excellent reader. The only clue to his lack of comprehension might be his lack of prosody. He loves the exercise of bringing his own knowledge and experiences to bear on the text to such an extent that his elaborations and experiences take over the story. Stefan can pick out important details if they are clearly stated by the author. However, the syntax of the last sentence on the first page totally confused him. Paulsen writes, "In fact, since Brian had come to the small airport in Hampton, New York, to meet the plane—driven by his mother—the pilot had spoken only five words to him." Stefan got completely confused by Brian's flashback and the awkward placement of the phrase "driven by his mother", and he threw down his book in frustration. Now it's up to the teacher to talk Stefan through his misunderstanding and put him back on track. Stefan is positive that the author has said Brian's mother is driving the aeroplane.

The teacher says, "Let's stop and think about the idea of exactly who was driving the aeroplane. Who does the text actually say was 'driving the aeroplane'?"

Stefan is forced back to the text to confirm that knowledge. He finds the information and answers, "The pilot."

The teacher then pushes him a bit further by asking, "Does a pilot actually drive an aeroplane? What does a pilot do with an aeroplane?"

Stefan looks a bit embarrassed as he answers, "No, the pilot flies an aeroplane."

The teacher now addresses the matter of that awkward clause "driven by his mother". "What do you think Brian's mother might be driving?" she asks the student.

"A car, a ute, or a four-wheel-drive," Stefan replies.

"Excellent!" says the teacher. "So put what you know together with what the text says to figure out what is going on. You know that his mother is not driving the plane. To 'solve this case', you have to figure out what the phrase 'driven by his mother' means. You have to find who or what this phrase refers to."

Stefan answers, "It refers to a car or ute."

The teacher persists in holding Stefan accountable for what is actually stated in the text. Until he becomes a more careful reader, he will be unable to make accurate inferences. "Stefan, look at that text again. Is there a car or ute mentioned anywhere?"

Stefan admits, "No."

"So if this phrase is not telling us what was driven by his mother, it must be telling us who was driven by his mother. Who does *his* refer back to? Go back to the text and find the answer to that question."

Stefan once again pores over the words on the page. Finally, he gets an "aha!" "Brian," he says with a smile. "Why didn't you tell me that in the first place?"

The teacher smiles sweetly and says, "Then I'd be doing all the work. In my class, the students do the work of comprehending. And believe me, I share your frustration! Comprehension is hard work. But you did it. And the next time you find a phrase like this, you'll pay more attention to those pesky pronouns like 'his'."

Stefan needs a small scaffolded silent reading group in which students read small sections of the text and then stop to think aloud with each other and the teacher about what they have read and what inferences they can make.

INTERVENTION 31

Facilitating Cooperative Comprehension (Years 3–6)

We should not only use the brains we have, but all that we can borrow.

—Wilson

This intervention teaches students a routine in which partners work to-gether to comprehend text they have heard read aloud, read in cooperative pairs, or read independently orally or silently. This intervention can be used to scaffold the reading of narrative or expository texts and helps students increase their listening comprehension and their note-taking abilities. Once taught, this routine can be used once or twice a week as a way to both strengthen and assess students' listening and reading comprehension.

Background Knowledge

All students can benefit from working cooperatively with partners to cognitively process important vocabulary and content knowledge. However, the cooperative learning model is a particularly powerful one for scaffolding struggling readers in your classroom (Kagan, 1997; Slavin, 1990, 1996). Cooperative learning differs from group work in two important ways: (1) individual and group accountability are built into every activity so all group members are required to participate and produce, and (2) group members are taught and then expected to fulfil certain roles during the cooperative process.

Sample Lesson for Teaching Cooperative Comprehension

If students arrive in your classroom without cooperative skills, consider using a simple activity like scripted cooperation in dyads (Dansereau, 1988). This activity involves teaching only two roles to your students: *recaller* and *listener*. Figure 31.1 is a sample lesson for teaching students how to use the cooperative comprehension routine. Figure 31.2 is a blank cooperative comprehension form on which students can take notes and answer questions. The text that the lesson refers to is in figure 31.3.

Figure 31.1: Sample cooperative comprehension lesson.

Lesson Objective	Students will learn the cooperative comprehension routine and use it to read, understand and summarise what they have read.
Advance Organiser	**Teacher Says:** Today we're going to learn a process called *cooperative comprehension*. In this process, two students work together to help each other read, understand and remember. This process uses a script, kind of like a play. The script will help you remember exactly which part you are playing and what steps you need to follow. While we learn the process, we're going to use part of a story that we have already read. That way you will already know what the story is about and you can concentrate on figuring out what you are supposed to do.
Explain the Purpose of Cooperative Comprehension	**Teacher Says:** The reason we are learning this process is so that you can work in pairs reading and comprehending stories. Two heads are better than one. Together you will come up with better answers than either one of you alone can.
Define the Two Roles in the Process	**Teacher Says:** There are two roles: a recaller and a listener. They both take notes while the story is being read aloud or later while each one is reading the story silently. When the story has been read, the recaller has to tell some details from the story without looking at his or her notes. The listener uses his or her notes to add any details that the recaller forgot or to correct any errors that the recaller might have made. Then together you talk about what you think is the best answer for the question.
We Do It: Model the Process With a Student	**Teacher Says:** I'm going to model this process with a volunteer. I'm going to read the story aloud, and I'm going to play the part of the recaller. So, if you volunteer, you will be the listener. You will take notes while I'm reading the story. Then I'll recall some of the things I remember from reading the story. I won't get to take notes, but since I'm reading, I think I'll be OK. Then, the listener—whoever volunteers—will look at the notes he or she took and tell me if I left anything out. Then we'll talk with each other to figure out what the answer to the question is. I'm going to read aloud a couple of pages in *Murphy's Mansion* that we read yesterday. Who would like to be my volunteer? **Carmen Does:** Raise her hand and the teacher gives her a copy of the cooperative comprehension form found in figure 31.2. **Teacher Says:** Carmen, the question you and I have to answer after we finish reading, taking notes, and talking about what we read is this, "What is Joshua's goal in this part of the story?" [The text for the lesson can be found in figure 31.3.] **Teacher Says:** Class, even though you're not modelling this with me, you can pretend you are and jot down some notes to help you remember what I read aloud. If we leave anything out, you can remind us. [The teacher reads the story while Carmen listens and takes notes. After reading the story, the teacher—who is the recaller—lists several details from the story, leaving out one or two important details that she should have included.] [Carmen is the listener and gets to use her notes to remind the teacher of what she might have forgotten. The teacher asks the class if they have any additional ideas and two people add more details. Then Carmen and the teacher talk about what they think Josh's goal is. The teacher tells Carmen what a goal is and asks Carmen if she has any ideas. Carmen thinks his goal might have something to do with the mysterious house, but she isn't sure. The teacher wonders if anyone else in the class might have an idea about what Josh's goal is. George is sure that Josh's goal is to find out who lives in the house. So, if he and Carmen had been teammates, they would have come up with the right answer.]

continued →

We Do It: Two Students Model the Process With Teacher Support	**Teacher Says:** Now I'd like to have two students model the process together. I'll read the story again, but this time the question will be different. The question is, "What are the advantages and disadvantages of being a postman?" [Two other students volunteer, and the teacher rereads the same section of text. Familiarity with the text builds confidence and helps students become comfortable with note taking and talking about their notes. Once students learn the process, using it with unfamiliar text will seem much easier to them. Charlie and Sam volunteer this time and repeat the process. They both do an excellent job of taking notes. Sam is the recaller and takes good notes, especially about the postman and what he does. Charlie is the listener and adds some good inferential information about people getting statements from their bank and credit card companies in the mail. The two of them talk about their answer, and with Charlie's good inference, they answer the question correctly.]
You Do It: Have All Students Pair Up and Work Supervised	**Teacher Says:** Class, now it's your turn to try out cooperative comprehension. This time, I want each pair to take turns reading sentences in the story excerpt. You should sail through the reading since we've been through it several times. I've passed out the forms [figure 31.2]. The person whose first name comes first in the alphabet will be the recaller. The other person will be the listener. Next time we'll trade. You'll be working with the same partner for about two weeks and then we'll switch partners. The question for our first read-through is this, "Does Josh accomplish his goal? How does he accomplish it?"

© 2009 Hawker Brownlow Education and Elaine McEwan-Adkins.

Figure 31.2: Cooperative comprehension form.

QUESTION: _____

Pair: Write your name and the name of your partner in the box. Decide who will be the listener and who will be the recaller.

Read: Write the title of the text in the box. Read the text as directed by the teacher, stopping to take brief notes two or three times.

Write: Write notes in the box to help you remember the important details that you heard or read.

Recall: The recaller summarises what was read from memory without looking at his or her notes. The listener uses his or her notes to provide feedback on errors or material omitted by the recaller.

Answer the Question: After you have shared your information, reread the question and decide on an answer. You must agree on the answer you both write down on your sheets. Your answer must be in a complete sentence.

© 2009 Hawker Brownlow Education and Elaine McEwan-Adkins.

Copyright © Hawker Brownlow Education. All rights reserved. Reprinted from *40 Reading Intervention Strategies for P-6 Students*, by Elaine K. McEwan-Adkins. Melbourne, Vic: Hawker Brownlow Education, www.hbe.com.au. Reproduction authorised only for use in the school site that has purchased the book.

Figure 31.3: Text for cooperative comprehension lesson (McEwan, 1994).

> I leaned over to pick up my bike, and a flutter of movement at that upper-storey window caught my eye. I gave a cry of surprise. The windows were covered with grime, but I could see a shadowy outline of someone standing there. I gave a half wave of my hand, but the person dropped the curtain and vanished.
>
> I was curious. Maybe I could pretend to be selling magazines and ring the doorbell. But what if the door opened and the mysterious figure grabbed me and pulled me inside? I shivered, picked up my bike and headed for town.
>
> Back in familiar territory again, I waved to the postperson. (I have to call him that, even though he's a man, because my friend Tracy at school insists on it.)
>
> "Hi, Joshua," he called. "Sorry I didn't deliver any important mail to your house today."
>
> Last year I'd written to the governor, and everybody in town seemed to know about it.
>
> "Hey!" I called to him. "Wait up." I pushed my disabled bike as fast as I could down the path.
>
> "That tyre looks as flat as a pancake!" He laughed uproariously at his humour. It was a good thing he was delivering mail for a living and not telling jokes.
>
> "Do you know who lives in that big house on James Court?" I asked. "The one with the jungle in the front yard?"
>
> The postperson pushed back his safari hat and wiped his brow with a grimy red bandanna.
>
> "Shore do," he said. "I been deliverin' mail on this route in Grandville for twenty-five years." He turned and started to push his cart on down the sidewalk.
>
> "Wait a minute," I said. "Who?"
>
> "Who what?" he asked.
>
> I was beginning to feel as though I were talking to a five-year old.
>
> "Who lives in the house?" I asked.
>
> "Aw, shucks, Joshua," he replied. "I can't tell you that."
>
> "Why not?"
>
> "Confidentiality," he said softly.
>
> "What's that?"
>
> He lowered his voice still further. "Can't talk about people on my route."
>
> "I don't get it."
>
> "Well, how would you like it if I blabbed all the secrets I know about you to the neighbourhood?"
>
> "Whaddya mean?" I asked.
>
> "Well," he drawled, "We mail carriers know an awful lot about the people we deliver mail to. We know where your relatives live, how often they write, if you haven't paid your bills, and where you keep your money. It's all stored up here." He tapped the hard surface of his safari hat.
>
> I wondered if he remembered that I'd only gotten three letters from my dad in the whole year we'd lived in Grandville.

continued →

"And that's where it's going to stay," he affirmed, smacking his hat once more for emphasis. "You'll have to find out who lives at 816 James Court from somebody else."

"What if I asked you a question, and you could blink once if the answer's yes and twice if it's no?" I suggested. "You wouldn't have to say a word."

"I wasn't born yesterday, Joshua," he said. "My lips are sealed."

© 2009 Hawker Brownlow Education and Elaine McEwan-Adkins.

Copyright © Hawker Brownlow Education. All rights reserved. Reprinted from *40 Reading Intervention Strategies for P-6 Students*, by Elaine K. McEwan-Adkins. Melbourne, Vic: Hawker Brownlow Education, www.hbe.com.au. Reproduction authorised only for use in the school site that has purchased the book.

INTERVENTION 32

Mastering the Five Cs of Summarising (Years 4–6)

> *Summarising, the ability to recursively work on information to render it as succinctly as possible, requires judgment and effort, knowledge, and strategies.*
>
> —Brown & Day (1983, p.1)

Of the seven cognitive strategies, summarising is one of the most challenging to teach and learn. This intervention is a five-step process for writing a summary of an article or story. Once the process has been introduced, modelled and practised together over several weeks, students will have internalised a set of prompts to use when they are expected to write a summary of something they have heard or read.

Background Knowledge

Restating the meaning of what one reads in one's own words—different words from those used in the original text—is a challenging assignment for all readers and writers. Readers of all ages and ability levels regularly resist investing the time and cognitive effort that is essential, no matter how smart we are, to struggle with extracting and constructing meaning from text. The University of Washington Psychology Writing Centre (2003) gives this advice to its students regarding the summarising of text:

> If you can't put the information into your own words, you aren't ready to write about it [or talk about it]. To learn how to paraphrase what you want to write, try to explain it to someone else without referring to your source. (p. 2)

Summarising has its roots in a time-honoured tradition of reading comprehension instruction: finding the main idea. In days gone by, main-idea instruction consisted of little more than reading short selections and circling the best title for the selection. That was then, but this is now. Today's high-stakes assessments demand that students know how to summarise as appropriate to their year levels. Prep and year one students are expected to retell (or act out the order of) important events in stories, whereas year two and three students are expected to produce summaries of text selections. In the upper years, year four and fives are expected to determine the main idea and how it is supported with details, and year four to eights are expected to paraphrase and summarise text to recall, inform or organise ideas.

© 2009 Hawker Brownlow Education • SOT4749

Sample Lesson for Teacher-Directed Small-Group Intervention

Figure 32.1 is a sample lesson for teaching the five Cs of summarising. Figure 32.2 shows examples of well-written summaries. Figure 32.3 is a chart showing the five Cs of summarising that can be reproduced for students to keep in their folders or converted to a poster for your bulletin board. Figure 32.4 is a graphic organiser summarising the teacher's life as described in the sample lesson. Figure 32.5 is a graphic organiser summarising the life of one student as described in the lesson. Figure 32.6 is a sample graphic organiser to use or adapt with your students.

Figure 32.1: Sample lesson for teaching the five Cs of summarising.

Lesson Objective	Students will be able to write a one- to three-sentence summary in their own words of a story, book or article they have read or of a video or movie they have seen.
Advance Organiser	**Teacher Says:** Class, during the next few weeks, I am going to teach you how to summarise. I promise you that if you are here every day and turn on your cognitive processing units (CPUs), you will be able to summarise just about anything when we finish—a basketball game, your summer holiday, or most importantly for this class, anything that you read. A summary is one or two sentences (or sometimes a very short paragraph) that tell the main idea of a story, book, chapter, video, movie or article. Summarising is restating the meaning of something you have read or heard or watched in your own words—different words from those used in the story or article that you read. If you look around, you'll find summaries everywhere.
Define and Explain the Summarising Strategy	**Teacher Says:** Most students (and adults) have problems with summarising because no one has ever shown them how to do it. Summarising is the ability to read, or hear or experience something "long" or "big" or "complicated" and then reduce it to one or two sentences. A summary is short, to the point, contains the "big idea" of the story, doesn't include trivial and unimportant details, collapses lists of information into one word or phrase and is not a "retelling" of a story or text.
Explain the Importance of Summarising	**Teacher Says:** Knowing how to summarise will help you pick out the most important parts of what you are reading, hearing, seeing or experiencing and write about them. Summarising is one of the most useful strategies you will ever learn. If you can write (or orally give) a summary, you'll be able to take notes in your own words from a book or encyclopedia for a research report. You can tell a friend about a book you read or a movie you watched and actually have more to say than, "It was really awesome." You'll be able to write a short answer on a test and know that you have included the most important ideas. If you look around, you'll find summaries everywhere. There are even summaries of people's lives written after they die: obituaries.
Describe the Critical Attributes of a Summary	**Teacher Says:** Let's review: a good summary is short and contains the most important idea. A good summary is not long and does not contain unimportant information or details.
Provide Concrete Examples of Summaries	**Teacher Says:** I've put three examples of summaries up on the overhead [figure 32.2]. [If you have some excellent examples of student summaries from prior years, use them. Student nonexamples are also very helpful for students to see.]
Explain the Five Cs	**Teacher Says:** We're going to use what I call the five Cs of summarising to help us write our summary. They are steps that we will follow whenever we want to write a summary of a story or an article. I've put up a poster containing the five Cs, and we'll leave it up all during the year to remind us of the steps [figure 32.3].
The First C: Comprehend	**Teacher Says:** The first C stands for *comprehend*. Before we can write a summary we have to know what an article or story or a person's life is mainly about. We spent several weeks learning about the main idea of very short stories and articles. The five Cs will help us summarise a book for a book report or summarise longer articles.

continued →

Mastering the Five Cs of Summarising

The Second C: Chunk	**Teacher Says:** The second C stands for *chunk*. When you are asked to summarise a story or article that is very long, it helps to divide it into smaller chunks, just like you would cut up a big piece of cheese into smaller chunks if you wanted just a little bit at a time.
The Third C: Compact	**Teacher Says:** The third C stands for *compact*. When we were talking about main idea, we learned that the details aren't the main idea. When we're writing a summary, we try to get rid of the unimportant information or details by deleting them or by collapsing a long list of details into one word rather than trying to put the whole list in our summary.
The Fourth C: Conceptualise	**Teacher Says:** The fourth C stands for *conceptualise*. That means to think of one word (a concept) that stands for each chunk of the story.
The Fifth C: Connect	**Teacher Says:** The fifth C is *connect*. Suppose I have three chunks of my story or article and I've thought of really good keywords for each chunk. Now I need to write a sentence or two that connects my keywords.
Model Writing a Summary Using the Five Cs	**Teacher Says:** I am going to model writing a summary for you. You'll be surprised when you hear what I'm going to summarise—my life. Now I've lived for quite a while and done quite a few things so my life is a pretty big subject to summarise. But it will be easy if I use the five Cs. Remind me what the five Cs are once again. **Students Say:** Comprehend, chunk, compact, conceptualise and connect. **Teacher Says:** We're going to be working with these five Cs almost every week during the school year and by the end of the year, you are going to be champion summarisers. When you're summarising a movie, you have to watch the movie carefully and understand (comprehend) what's going on. The same thing is true for something you read. Well, I do understand my life. After all, I have lived it. So the first step, comprehend, is taken care of. Now the second step, chunk, could be challenging. I have to decide how to divide my life into some categories or chunks so I can be organised about writing my summary. I can't write everything if I only get three sentences. There are several possibilities for chunking my life. I could divide it up into states where I have lived. That would be three chunks. I could chunk my life into roles I've played in my life. I've been a daughter, a sister, a wife and a mother. That would be four chunks. Or, I could chunk my life into kinds of books I've written. I've written books for parents, books for kids and books for educators. Since I still haven't hit on an idea I want to use, I had better fill in the thought balloons attached to the comprehension boxes to help me comprehend. **Teacher Does:** Fill in the thought balloons in the first step: Comprehend as shown in figure 32.4. [AUTHOR'S NOTE TO TEACHER: I have modelled this summary of my life for you, so you can model writing a summary of your life for your students.] **Teacher Says:** What I've just decided to do is chunk my life into three time periods: childhood, adulthood and retirement. I'm going to compact what happened in those three periods of my life to one thing: how I felt about the weather. **Teacher Says:** Now that I have three ideas or concepts about those three time periods in my life, I'm ready to write some sentences that connect all of those thoughts. [Teacher writes the sentence in the rectangular box at the bottom of the figure. When modelling the writing of a summary, carefully think about what you will write and experiment with various sentence constructions. Save one or two of your draft sentences to show students how you kept rewriting until you wrote a sentence you liked.] [AUTHOR'S NOTE TO TEACHER: You can keep going with this lesson at this point, or end it with a summary statement and begin the next day with the student work.]

continued →

© 2009 Hawker Brownlow Education • SOT4749

Work With a Student to Write a Summary	**Teacher Says:** Who knows what a "ghost writer" is? **Jamie Says:** It's somebody who writes ghost stories. **Teacher Says:** That's a very creative answer. But it's not the one I was hoping for. A ghost writer is someone who helps someone else with her writing. When famous people write books, many of them don't actually write their own books. They hire a ghost writer to do it for them. The famous person just talks, and the ghost writer takes notes and then goes home and writes the book. I am looking for a famous student in this class who would like to hire me as her ghost writer. Together we will write about that student's life. She will get to put her name on the paper, and since I'm the ghost writer I won't get any credit. But this is my way of showing you how you can write about your life. Who is willing to be famous today? **John Says:** I am. **Teacher Says:** Have you been thinking about your life? Look at the boxes across the top of the graphic organiser. They say: activate prior knowledge, make connections to experiences, clarify confusion, make emotional connections. Here's a question for you, John. Tell me about an experience in your life that was really exciting or sad, or made you feel proud. **John Says:** Well, when I was eight, I broke my arm when I fell off my bicycle and had to go to the hospital in an ambulance. That was exciting and scary at the same time. **Teacher Says:** Good, I'm going to write that down in the Activate Prior Knowledge box. Have you had any other experiences that were exciting? **John Says:** Well, my soccer team won the league championship last year. That was even better than my broken arm. **Teacher Says:** How did you feel when you won the championship? **John Says:** I felt proud of my team, but I also felt a little sad because I didn't score a goal. **Teacher Says:** I'm going to write that in the thought balloon under Make Emotional Connections. So far you've told me about two experiences you had where you had mixed emotions. You were both excited and scared when you rode in an ambulance. And you were proud and a little sad when your team won the championship. Can you think of any other experiences you have had in your life where you felt two ways at the same time? **John Says:** Yes. My mum just had a baby. I was really happy about having somebody else in my family since I was the only child. But I was a little disappointed that we got a girl instead of the boy I wanted. **Teacher Says:** We have some confusion here to clarify. I am wondering how you can feel two emotions at the same time. I'm going to write that in the thought balloon attached to the Clarify Confusion box. John, how do you like being a famous person? **John Says:** I like it just fine. Do you think the TV will want to interview me? **Teacher Says:** You never know. When the story of your life is published, you may be on the 6:00 news. But first we have to get this written. It seems to me that while we were talking, we just sort of automatically compacted your life. We didn't pay any attention to any other experiences you had when you didn't experience two emotions at the same time. So, let's write these three experiences in the numbered boxes. We will have a box left over, but that's OK. You don't have to have four chunks.

continued →

Work With a Student to Write a Summary *(continued)*	So, in the first box, I'm going to write *ambulance ride*. In the second box, I'm going to write *soccer championship,* and in the third box, I'm going to write *new baby*. Now we have to conceptualise the ideas from these three events in our famous person's life. It seems that the thing all of these experiences have in common is that you felt two emotions at the same time. That's called having mixed emotions. So, I will have to write something about mixed emotions. In the first box, I will write *feeling excited and scared at the same time*. In the second box, I will write *feeling proud and sad*. In the third box, I will write *happy and disappointed*. I'm getting a thought here about what I'm going to write for John's summary. Now as I write, remember I'm the ghost writer, so I have to pretend I'm John when I write. I am a person who seems to experience a lot of mixed emotions in my life. When my arm was broken, I felt excited about the ambulance ride. When my team won the championship, I felt sad because I didn't score a goal. And when my sister was born, I was disappointed because she wasn't a boy. I am a very complicated person. [See figure 32.5 for a graphic organiser of John's life.] **Teacher Says:** Tomorrow I'm going to choose another famous person. If you have time to think about your life, jot down some ideas on your blank organiser. When I ask for a volunteer tomorrow, it will help you to get chosen if you've done some thinking ahead of time. Let's all give John a silent cheer for being such a good sport. Tell me, John, how did you feel about this experience? Do you have mixed emotions? **John Says:** I feel a little embarrassed, and I also am feeling happy.

© *2009 Hawker Brownlow Education and Elaine McEwan-Adkins.*

Figure 32.2: Sample summaries.

Type	Summary	Length
My Brilliant Career	Sybylla is a young woman who lives in the outback. Sybylla's poor family sends her to her rich grandmother's house. Instead of becoming a rich housewife as expected of her, Sybylla chooses a 'brilliant' career over love and getting married, getting a book published in 1901. (Gillian Armstrong, *My Brilliant Career*, 1979)	100 minutes
	In this persuasive and gently humorous novel, the discovery of a newborn baby girl left in a cardboard box creates opportunities for redemption and renewal for the handyman who finds her and for the dowager on whose estate she was abandoned (*Blessings* by Anna Quindlen, New York Times Notable Books 2002).	250 pages
John Button	John Button, federal Minister for Trade for ten years under the Hawke and Keating governments, Member of Parliament for two decades and Senator for Victoria, died today of pancreatic cancer. Mr Button, who was born in Ballarat, Victoria, was 74.	74 years

© 2009 Hawker Brownlow Education and Elaine McEwan-Adkins.

Figure 32.3: The five Cs of summarising.

Comprehend		Read and understand the text.
Chunk		Divide the text into parts.
Compact		Make each chunk smaller.
Conceptualise		Think of a keyword for each chunk.
Connect		Combine the keywords into a summary sentence.

© 2009 Hawker Brownlow Education and Elaine McEwan-Adkins.

Copyright © Hawker Brownlow Education. All rights reserved. Reprinted from *40 Reading Intervention Strategies for P-6 Students*, by Elaine K. McEwan-Adkins. Melbourne, Vic: Hawker Brownlow Education, www.hbe.com.au. Reproduction authorised only for use in the school site that has purchased the book.

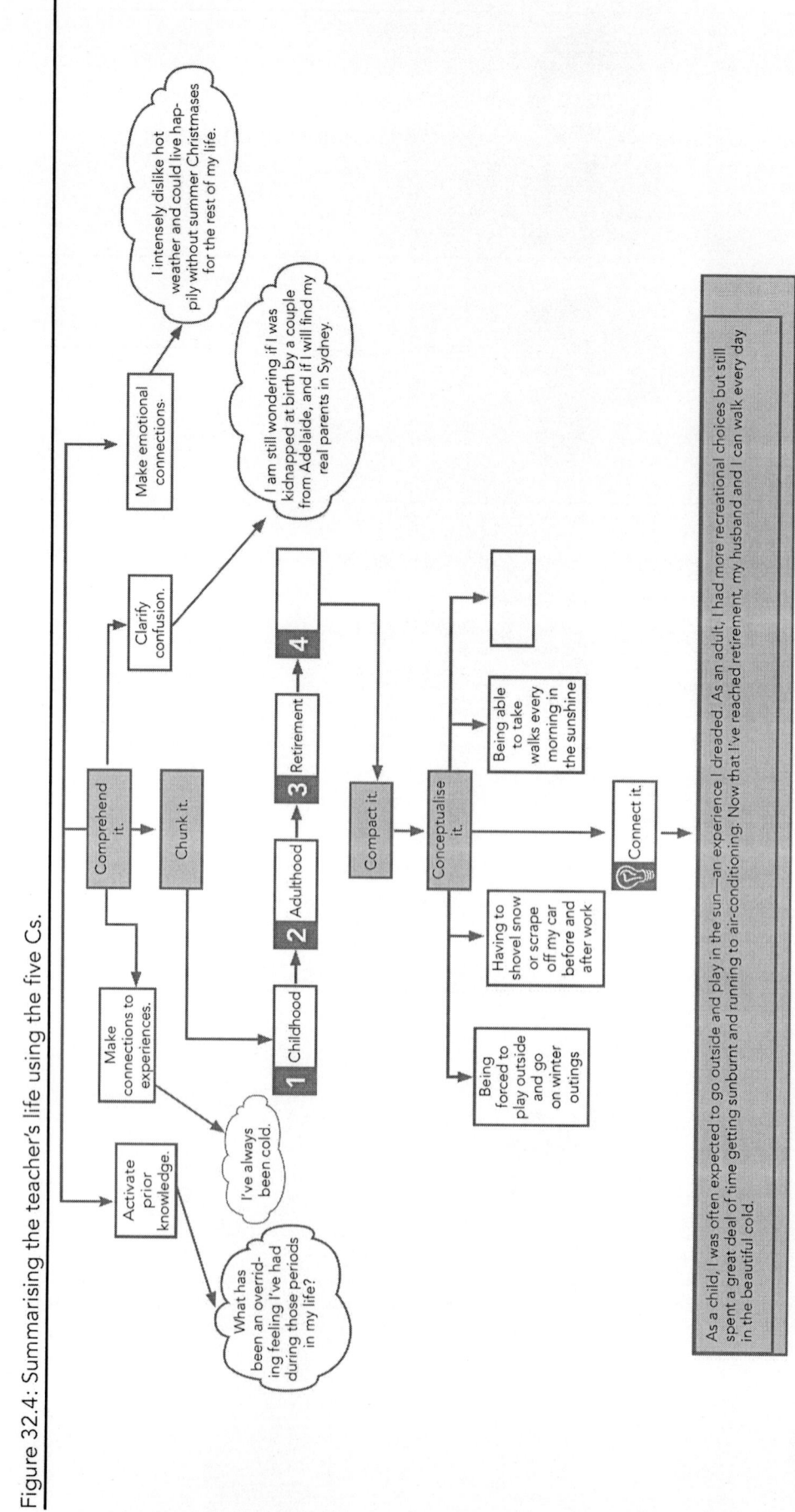

Figure 32.4: Summarising the teacher's life using the five Cs.

```
Activate prior knowledge. → What has been an overriding feeling I've had during those periods in my life?
Activate prior knowledge → I've always been cold.

Make connections to experiences. → I've always been cold.

Comprehend it. → Make emotional connections. → I intensely dislike hot weather and could live happily without summer Christmases for the rest of my life.

Comprehend it. → Clarify confusion. → I am still wondering if I was kidnapped at birth by a couple from Adelaide, and if I will find my real parents in Sydney.

Chunk it: 1 Childhood → 2 Adulthood → 3 Retirement → 4

Compact it

Conceptualise it →
  • Being forced to play outside and go on winter outings
  • Having to shovel snow or scrape off my car before and after work
  • Being able to take walks every morning in the sunshine

Connect it. →
As a child, I was often expected to go outside and play in the sun—an experience I dreaded. As an adult, I had more recreational choices but still spent a great deal of time getting sunburnt and running to air-conditioning. Now that I've reached retirement, my husband and I can walk every day in the beautiful cold.
```

© 2009 Hawker Brownlow Education and Elaine McEwan-Adkins.

Mastering the Five Cs of Summarising

Figure 32.5: Summarising John's life using the five Cs.

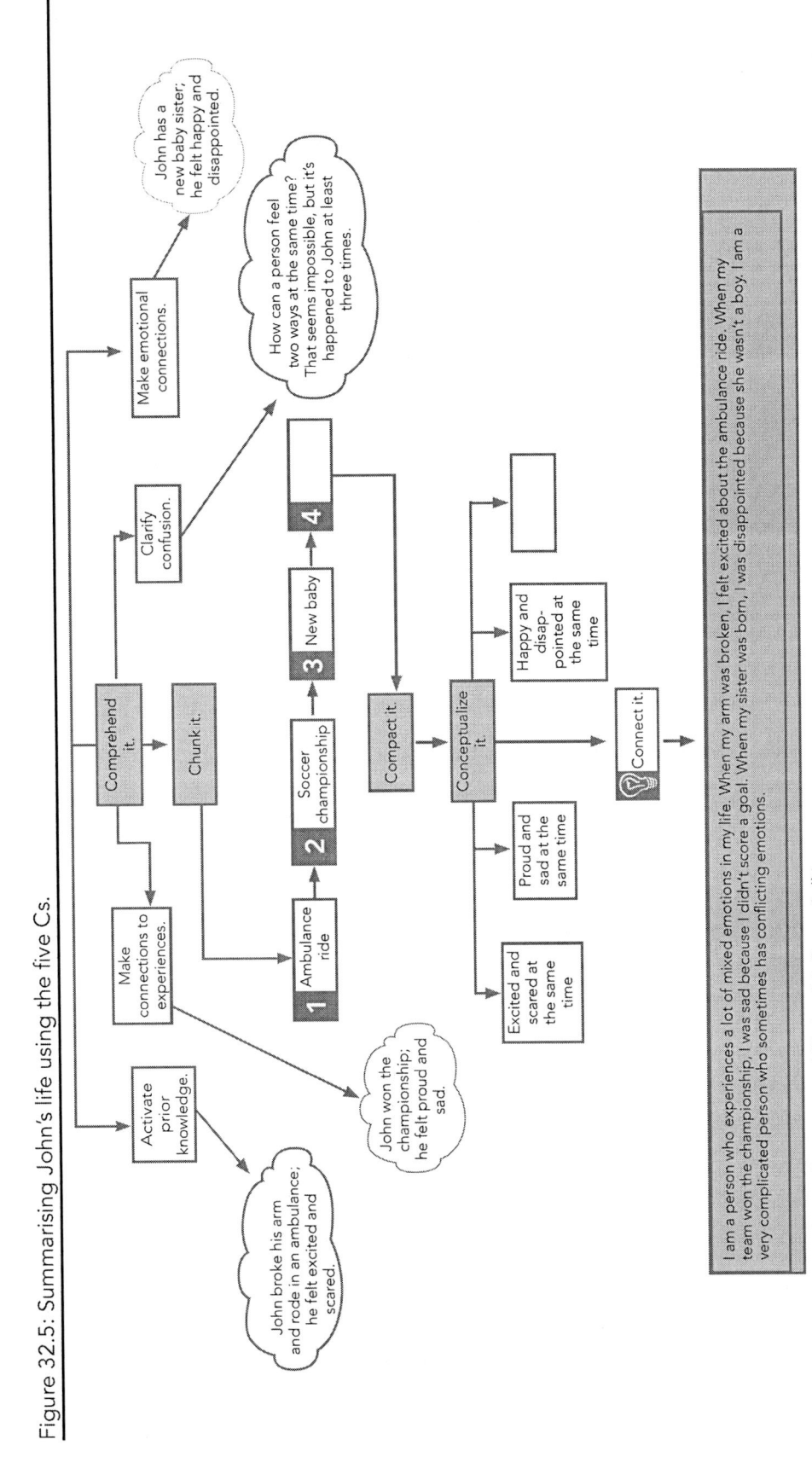

John has a new baby sister; he felt happy and disappointed.

How can a person feel two ways at the same time? That seems impossible, but it's happened to John at least three times.

Comprehend it.
Make emotional connections.
Clarify confusion.
Chunk it.

| 1 Ambulance ride | 2 Soccer championship | 3 New baby | 4 |

Compact it.

Conceptualize it.
- Excited and scared at the same time
- Proud and sad at the same time
- Happy and disappointed at the same time

Connect it.

Make connections to experiences.
Activate prior knowledge.

John broke his arm and rode in an ambulance; he felt excited and scared.

John won the championship; he felt proud and sad.

I am a person who experiences a lot of mixed emotions in my life. When my arm was broken, I felt excited about the ambulance ride. When my team won the championship, I was sad because I didn't score a goal. When my sister was born, I was disappointed because she wasn't a boy. I am a very complicated person who sometimes has conflicting emotions.

© 2009 *Hawker Brownlow Education and Elaine McEwan-Adkins.*

© 2009 Hawker Brownlow Education • SOT4749

40 Reading Intervention Strategies for P–6 Students

Figure 32.6: Graphic organiser for the five Cs.

Comprehend

Activating: make connections between background knowledge and experience to what you are reading in the text.
Visualising: make mental images of important scenes and characters (fiction), events (history) or processes (science).
Monitoring-clarifying: ask questions about what you don't understand. Clarify your confusion.
Questioning and inferring: determine the underlying meaning of what the author is saying.
Organising: figure out how best to chunk (divide up) the text.

Compact

Delete what is trivial and redundant from a piece of text, thereby reducing the number of words.

Chunk

Divide up and organise a large piece of text into smaller, more manageable sections to make it easier to understand and remember.

Conceptualise

Think of a keyword (concept or idea) that describes or sums up each chunk.

Connect

Connect the keywords (adding other words as needed) to create a summary sentence.

© 2009 Hawker Brownlow Education and Elaine McEwan-Adkins.

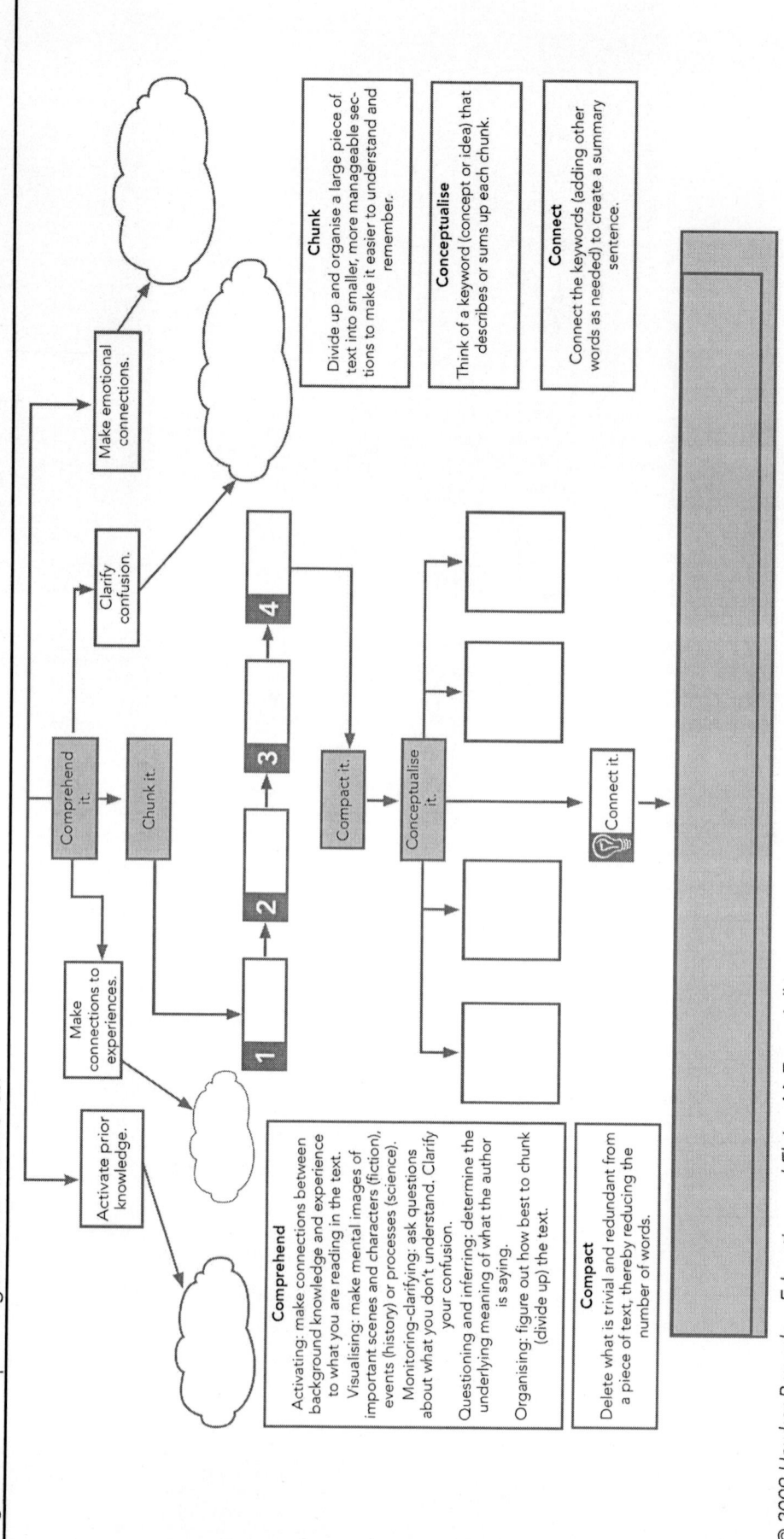

Copyright © Hawker Brownlow Education. All rights reserved. Reprinted from *40 Reading Intervention Strategies for P–6 Students*, by Elaine K. McEwan-Adkins. Melbourne, Vic: Hawker Brownlow Education, www.hbe.com.au. Reproduction authorised only for use in the school site that has purchased the book.

© 2009 Hawker Brownlow Education • SOT4749

INTERVENTION 33

Using Graphic Organisers to Summarise Stories (Years P–2)

> *Any sort of systematic attention to clues that reveal how authors attempt to relate ideas to one another or any sort of systematic attempt to impose structure upon a text, especially in some sort of visual representation of the relationships among key ideas, facilitates comprehension as well as both short-term and long-term memory for the text.*
>
> —Pearson & Fielding (1991, p. 832)

In this intervention, students will acquire two graphic organisers to scaffold their ability to organise a story's events, sequence and elements so they can retell or summarise the story in a brief sentence. The organisers are intended to be used regularly to help students extract and construct meaning from classroom read-alouds, core program selections or independent reading.

Background Knowledge

The visualising-organising cognitive strategy is one way to reduce the cognitive overload that beginning readers often experience as they juggle their emerging reading skills while extracting and constructing meaning from text. Visualising-organising gets my vote for the most misused, underappreciated and untapped treasure among the seven strategies of highly effective readers. Make no mistake, there are dozens of stunning graphic organisers and hundreds of beautiful illustrations and photos in every published basal reading series and content-area textbook on the market. Pretty pictures and glitzy organisers do not necessarily contribute to students' understanding and retention of text. Visual images and organisers are of little value to students unless they have personally unleashed their own cognitive powers on visualising and organising the text. It is only when students develop their own personal concept maps that the structure of a discipline or the complexity of an idea or proposition sticks with them. In fact, one of the biggest pluses of graphic organisers is the way they can reduce cognitive overload by keeping concepts more visible.

A graphic organiser or graphic representation is a "visual illustration of a verbal statement" (Jones, Pierce, & Hunter, p. 20) and involves the following tasks or abilities:

- To read text

- To determine which type of graphic organiser would best be suited for constructing a personal schema in order to better understand and remember large bodies of information

- To choose the frames or labels for the parts of the organiser

- To construct the organiser by drawing it either manually or using a software program designed for that purpose

Comprehension Strategy Cards

Comprehension strategy cards provide an interactive way for students to monitor their own reading when they read independently. Cut out, laminate and hole-punch several sets of cards and place them on a ring. Figure 33.1 shows a sample of a card, and the following are some other possible prompts to put on individual cards:

- What was the setting?
- What were you visualising?
- What was the story about?
- Did the pictures tell you more about the story?
- What did the story remind you of?
- How did the story make you feel? Why?
- Do you have any questions?

The laminated cards can be used as an activity in a year one or two centre where students read a short book and then work with a partner to take turns answering the questions on the cards.

Who were the characters?

Figure 33.1: Sample comprehension strategy card.

Source: McEwan, Judware, Carino & Darling, 2008.

Story Elements Graphic Organiser

Keep an ongoing story elements graphic organiser on a wall in your classroom to keep track of the various stories you read aloud. Emphasise the meaning of every read-aloud story as you review the story elements. As students gain skill at identifying story elements and have heard and seen you model both oral and written summaries of a story, gradually release the responsibility for orally summarising stories to partners or individual students (Pearson & Gallagher, 1983). The next step is for students to write their summaries. When students are regularly expected to gain meaning and remember the elements of a story, the process will become routine for them. Figure 33.2 contains a sample story elements graphic organiser summarising two classic fairytales and a familiar song. Familiar nursery rhymes and songs provide excellent texts for introducing and practising the story elements graphic organiser.

Figure 33.2: Sample story elements graphic organiser.

Characters	Setting	Problem	Solution
pigs/wolf	straw/stick house	house blown down	brick house
girl/wolf	woods	hungry wolf	hunter
spider	waterspout	washed out	sun came out

Source: McEwan, Judware, et al., 2008.

INTERVENTION 34

Teaching Students How to Monitor Their Silent Reading Comprehension (Years 4–6)

> *Monitoring one's reading comprehension and fixing up the mix-ups that inevitably occur is a habit—much like putting dirty dishes in the dishwasher or brushing your teeth. If you can't be bothered, there will be a price to pay.*
>
> —McEwan (2004, p. 96)

This intervention has two parts: (1) it teaches students a variety of ways to keep track of comprehension and (2) provides several strategies for "fixing the mix-ups" that struggling readers have on a daily basis. It also provides a scaffolded silent-reading opportunity in which to practise the monitoring strategy.

Background Knowledge

Struggling readers are often like lost motorists who refuse to admit they are lost and ask for directions. In fact, most struggling readers use comprehension confusion as an excuse to stop reading: *The book was boring. I didn't get it. It was a dumb book.* There is no guarantee that this intervention will increase the likelihood of your struggling reader actually reading an entire book, but you cannot let that keep you from intervening immediately. Nagging struggling readers doesn't work. Making them sit with a book for thirty minutes in a classroom where everyone else is reading hard books and they are reading easy books doesn't work. Making them sit with a book for thirty minutes when they have chosen a hard book doesn't work, either. They need total privacy in which to read and talk about their mix-ups with a trusted teacher. They desperately do not want to be perceived as incapable. Bravado keeps them from facing the unpleasant reality of their inability to comprehend what they read.

Sample Lesson for Teaching Monitoring

This intervention depends on chemistry and solid reading instruction. Bond with your struggling readers so they will trust you with their insecurities about reading. Begin small with this intervention. Identify up to five of your most reluctant readers, and then remove your "teacher" hat and put on your "psychologist/salesperson" hat. Find a way to meet with this small group when nobody else is around, possibly after school or during the lunch hour. Ask the reading specialist or interventionist to do some informal testing to determine where these students have gaps in their reading knowledge to give you a sense of each student's independent reading level. Find a way to "sell" easy reading to these students while simultaneously giving them the skills they need to become better readers. They are caught in a vicious cycle.

Enlist the help of the school librarian or media specialist in finding materials for these students to read. This is a big challenge, since there is no single way to match up the reading level of the student with the reading level of the text. Scholastic assigns a Lexile value to all of the books they sell. When students take the Scholastic Reading Inventory, their reading level is reported in a Lexile value. Visit www.mylexile.com.au for more information. Accelerated Reader has its own way of measuring the difficulty of books: students earn points when they read the book and answer a certain number of questions correctly. That works for many students, but it probably won't work for your reluctant readers. These students will immediately figure out that no matter how many of the "easy" books they read, they will never gather enough points to win the contest or purchase the item they want from the school shop, etc. That is where your selling skills come in. You need to convince these students that reading books that are easy to read will gradually give them the skills to read more challenging books. Beginning skiers can't ski the highest slopes, and struggling readers can't read *War and Peace*. Engage the media specialist in some sleight of hand to develop an alternative point system for struggling readers. You have to constantly give them *reasons* to read. Most struggling readers are not fond of fiction because they have to work too hard to figure out what's going on. For some students, understanding fiction requires too much background knowledge. Use nonfiction to entice those struggling readers to do more "real" reading.

Someone—the teacher, a highly motivating and energetic aide or a media specialist—must meet with these students daily. Each student will bring to the group the book he or she is silently reading. Bring a book of your own to read. Make it an easy book so your students can see that adults choose easy books, too. For the first five minutes of the thirty-minute period, talk about any mix-ups the students have fixed on their own. For every one they can describe, they get ten points. Then ask if anyone has a current mix-up that is keeping them from going on with their reading. Ask the student to articulate what the problem seems to be. Any students who are willing and able to describe their comprehension mix-up also get ten points. The first student to get fifty points is awarded a token he or she can use to buy things in the school store (or something similar that works with your school's behaviour or reading incentive plan).

Struggling readers must battle a two-headed monster: the inability to monitor their comprehension and not knowing how to fix their mix-ups, even when they acknowledge that they are confused. To scaffold struggling readers through comprehension mix-ups, pick and choose from the following menu of suggestions, combining them as necessary, or use another approach that has worked with students in the past. Although we know a great deal about what skilled readers do, you must still do your own action research to determine what your unskilled readers typically do and then endeavour to get them back on the road to reading.

Figure 34.1 shows the first approach: a sample lesson for teaching students how to use sticky flags to mark their mix-ups as they read.

Another way to scaffold silent reading for comprehension is to teach students six signals that indicate a need for comprehension repair (Tovani, 2000):

1. The inner voice inside the reader's head stops its conversation with the text, and the reader only hears his voice pronouncing the words.

2. The camera inside the reader's head shuts off, and the reader can no longer visualise what is happening as she reads.

3. The reader's mind begins to wander, and he catches himself thinking about something far removed from the text.

4. The reader cannot remember or retell what she has read.

5. The reader is not getting his clarifying questions answered.

6. Characters are reappearing in the text, and the reader doesn't recall who they are.

Figure 34.2 is an abbreviated sample lesson for teaching these signals to your students. The "signals" function as prompts for struggling readers to help them internalise and routinise comprehension monitoring.

Figure 34.1: Sample lesson for teaching students how to monitor their comprehension.

Lesson Objective	Students will learn how to keep track of their comprehension using sticky flags.
Advance Organiser	**Teacher Says:** I want to teach you a way to keep track of your comprehension while you are reading that I regularly use: sticky flags. **Teacher Does:** Show students a sample of a package of sticky flags that you have purchased at an office supply shop. Tell them that you will be giving each of them a package to use when the lesson is over. **Teacher Says:** I keep the sticky flags in my purse or right on my desktop so when I am reading and I come to something that confuses me, I put one on that page. I'm going to show you how the process works and how it helps my reading comprehension.
I Do It: Teacher Models Using Flags With Text	**Teacher Does:** Put text on the overhead that contains some moderately challenging vocabulary and offers opportunities for teacher modelling of comprehension breakdowns. **Teacher Says:** When I am reading, it is very easy for me to get confused, especially if I am not focused or paying close attention. I know that happens to you, too. Using the sticky flags helps me to keep focused because I am doing something with my hands. It's much easier than taking notes, but it serves the same purpose. It makes me stop and think about my confusion. It forces me to fix up my mix-ups. **Teacher Says:** Look up at the screen. I read this book, *Rebecca of Sunnybrook Farm* [Wiggins, 1903], when I was a child, but I don't remember the story at all. On page 1, as you can see up on the screen, the text mentions "one passenger in the stagecoach—a small dark-haired person in a glossy buff calico dress." I don't know who this person is, so I'm going to put a sticky flag on that page to remind me that I need to keep track of this description in my mind. The text mentioned the stagecoach driver's name, Mr Cobb, but not the name of his passenger. This person may be important to the story. As I turn the page and keep reading, I hope to find some more information about this person. But suddenly, the story shifts backward in time. These flashbacks are confusing. Now the story seems to be about a woman who was at the stagecoach stop earlier in the day. Then I begin to understand: the woman is the mother of a child. The child is the passenger on the stagecoach. But the author did a very clever job of making me wonder. In fact, I was so sure that the passenger was a woman that I turned back the page and reread the beginning of the story again. Then I peeled off my sticky flag and put it on my desk for the next comprehension problem I encounter. Often you will put down a sticky flag because you were confused about something and find that your problem has been solved or your question answered further on in your reading. The physical act of putting the sticky flag right where the comprehension breakdown occurred will remind you to keep looking for the answer as you read. If you get to the end of a section or chapter and still haven't found the answer, it's time to get help from your teacher, a friend or the Internet. **Teacher Does:** Continue modelling in the text you have chosen. Then select text that students will be reading and work together with them.

© 2009 Hawker Brownlow Education and Elaine McEwan-Adkins.

Figure 34.2: Sample lesson for teaching brain signals.

Lesson Objective	Students will understand the six brain signals as described in this lesson and be able to think aloud about using these signals for monitoring comprehension.
Advance Organiser	**Teacher Says:** Do you ever get signals in your brain? I'm not talking about signals you can actually hear, but a thought will come to you about something important. Today I'm going to tell you about six different brain signals that I get while I'm reading, and then we're going to choose one of them to help us monitor our reading comprehension today. **Teacher Does:** Introduce the six signals described in the text.
Explain to Students How the Brain Signals Work	**Teacher Says:** Now, I want to make sure you understand that I am not hearing actual voices, but often I visualise exactly what I am reading about to help myself understand and remember what I read. These signals are very quiet, and it is very easy to ignore them and keep on reading. But if I ignore them, I will become totally confused. Does anybody else have that same experience of getting lost when they are reading? Tell me what it feels like to you. [Hopefully, if the group is small and you have been very transparent about your own comprehension breakdowns, your students will share their experiences with you.]
I Do It: Teacher Models the Brain Signals for Students	**Teacher Does:** Select text that you are reading and model for students what happens when your eyes glaze over and your mind starts wandering. Let them know that when that happens you know you need to stop reading and do something. When any of the brain signals kick in, students need concrete examples of what to do. That is when you can introduce the clarifying checklist (figure 34.3).

Source: Brain Signals adapted from Tovani, 2000.

If you are tempted to give your struggling students a handout with these six signals and announce that whenever these things happen, they need to refocus their attention, don't do it! Struggling readers won't know what you are talking about. They hear no inner voices. They see no cameras or video recorders. Start from scratch, and think aloud for students about one signal at a time. Explain very clearly what your inner voice is saying to you at various times. Tell them precisely where you zoned out and started thinking about what you were going to have for lunch. Then, as you work with them in scaffolded, silent reading groups, stop the reading every five minutes to talk about what their inner voices were saying when you called time. After spending a week or two with the "inner voice" prompt, try the "camera" prompt. These will be new insights for your students and perhaps even for you as a reader.

Figure 34.3 is a clarifying checklist that lists specific strategies for fixing mix-ups. Again, teaching each of the items on the list as a separate lesson is the most effective way to convince students of their worth. Post the clarifying checklist on a bulletin board that you and your students can refer to on a regular basis. Prior to beginning a reading assignment, review the prompts with students and remind them to use them to fix comprehension breakdown during reading.

Figure 34.3: Clarifying tools.

Is there something specific you don't understand: a word, phrase, concept or idea?	1. Ask someone: an adult, an expert, a classmate, the author or your teacher. 2. Look it up: in the dictionary, an encyclopedia, the index, the glossary or on the Internet. 3. Make an inference based on your background knowledge: "This must be what the author means. I'm going to keep reading and see if I'm right." 4. Make an inference about the word's meaning based on the context or the word's structure.
Is the text poorly written, disorganised or very long?	1. Chunk it physically: divide the text into smaller sections, and work on one section at a time. 2. Chunk it conceptually: divide the text into big ideas or concepts that fit with the subject or the subject matter that you're reading. 3. Draw a picture, diagram or graphic organiser.
Are you confused about the meaning of the text?	1. Connect what you have read to your own experience: "This reminds me of the time that . . ." 2. Read the back cover copy, the blurb on the inside front jacket, the preface, a chapter summary, the introduction or a review of the book on Amazon.com for more clues. 3. Read the text again or even two or three more times if necessary. 4. Stop and think aloud to yourself about what you have read. 5. Talk to someone: think aloud to a friend, family member or classmate. 6. Ignore temporarily the part you don't understand and keep reading.

Source: Adapted from McEwan, 2007. Used with permission.

Copyright © Hawker Brownlow Education. All rights reserved. Reprinted from *40 Reading Intervention Strategies for P-6 Students*, by Elaine K. McEwan-Adkins. Melbourne, Vic: Hawker Brownlow Education, www.hbe.com.au. Reproduction authorised only for use in the school site that has purchased the book.

INTERVENTION 35

Coding Text to Improve Comprehension (Years 4–6)

[The student's] most common response was to insert or invent knowledge that was not in the passage. If he could not recall explicit information or if he could not generate an inference, he constructed his own plausible answer of excessive elaboration from his prior knowledge and experiences. At times he seemed to invent the knowledge.

—Dewitz & Dewitz (2003, p. 323)

This intervention teaches students an alternative framework for marking text in addition to the following one that is more commonly taught: text-to-self, text-to-text and text-to-world. This intervention seeks to refocus the students away from their personal generations and elaborations of personal experience that are often confused with the meaning of the text and help them focus on specific parts of the text that may be interfering with their ability to make inferences based on the evidence sources in the text:

- Coding pronouns and their referents (P)
- Coding for connections to the main idea (M)
- Coding single sentences where the meaning is not clear (S)
- Coding for unknown vocabulary (W)

Background Knowledge

Keene and Zimmermann (1997) suggest that students comprehend more readily when they make three kinds of connections as they read: text-to-self (the reader's personal experiences); text-to-text (other things the reader has read); and text-to-world (background knowledge the reader has acquired from school and other educational experiences). Harvey and Goudvis (2000) suggest teaching students to place sticky notes on the text to indicate where they have made the specific connections suggested by Keene and Zimmermann. They do caution that when students lack background knowledge to make appropriate and meaningful connections, teachers need to teach vocabulary and background knowledge in advance of reading. Regrettably, some struggling readers only focus on information from their own experiences and background knowledge that is unrelated to the text, totally missing the point of what they are reading. This intervention focuses on multiple text features that often interfere with students' comprehension, particularly making inferences, pronouns and their referents, the main idea, and complex sentences and vocabulary (Dewitz & Dewitz, 2003).

Sample Lesson for Teaching Text Coding

Figure 35.1 is a sample lesson for teaching students how to code text as they read. Figure 35.2 is a poster showing the four codes, figure 35.3 is a text sample and figure 35.4 is the coded text.

Figure 35.1: Sample lesson for teaching students how to code text.

Lesson Objective	Students will learn a method for helping them monitor their comprehension by coding the text in four ways: P (a pronoun that needs an antecedent), M (information to help me figure out the main idea), S (a sentence that I don't understand) and W (a word I don't know).
Materials Needed for the Lesson	Students will need photocopies of text to mark or sticky notes on which they can write their codes. They will also need copies of figure 35.2.
Advance Organiser	**Teacher Says:** Today you are going to learn about a way to code text. [If you have taught students to code text using Harvey and Goudvis (2000), explain how this is different.] This method will help you focus on what you are reading and help you to monitor your comprehension. If you do not stop to ask questions when you are confused, you will get frustrated and then give up. Even when you have become skilled at marking the text and making good decisions about the evidence, you will still want to take notes to help you remember what you read. When I read things that are hard to understand at first, I still code the text as I am reading. I promise you that this method will help you understand what you are reading.
Review	**Teacher Says:** Let's take a minute and review what an inference is. Tell me. Together. **Students Say:** An inference is a decision you make about what the evidence means. **Teacher Says:** Right. When you are reading, you must think like a detective who is trying to solve a mystery. The mystery you are solving is this: what is this story about? When I finish reading the story, will I be able to tell about it in just a few words or choose a main idea for it? Unless you are a good detective, you may get confused by what you are reading and will get frustrated. Good detectives do get frustrated once in a while, but they persevere, keep trying to figure it out, and are able to make good decisions about the evidence. Coding the text will help you figure out the places you need to make inferences as you are reading.
Define and Explain the Four Ways to Code the Text	**Teacher Says:** There are four codes that you will mark in your text. Detectives often take notes in little notebooks to help them remember important information, and sometimes they use a code so no one will be able to read their notes. We will use four different letters for our codes: *P*, *M*, *S* and *W*. Let me tell you what these mean. *P* stands for pronouns. We have been working with the pronouns we find in the text that stand for other words [Intervention 29]. We learned that it's very important to figure out who or what the pronouns stand for. So anytime we come to one of those words—pronouns in our chart—we will put a *P*. The second letter, *M*, stands for the main idea, what the story is about. When you come to a person or an idea that you think might have something to do with the main idea, you will write *M*. The third letter, *S*, stands for sentences that you don't understand. As we read together in our group, I don't want you to skip any sentences that you don't understand. I want you to write the letter *S*. We'll think aloud about what the sentence means. The fourth letter is *W*, and that stands for words you can't figure out. If you don't know the meanings of important words, you can't make good decisions about the evidence. So, once again, we're going to figure those words out together.
I Do It: Teacher Models Use of Four Codes During Reading	**Teacher Does:** Place the text shown in figure 35.2 on the overhead. Model coding the text for students as shown in figure 35.3, (text from *Murphy's Mansion*), thinking aloud about the reasons for coding.

continued →

Coding Text to Improve Comprehension

We Do It: Teacher and Students Work Together to Practise Coding Text	**AUTHOR'S NOTE TO TEACHER:** The facilitation of guided practice can take place immediately, or can be held over for the following day (depending on group progress and time available). More modelling may be needed before moving on. **Teacher Says:** Today we're going to read the next few pages of our story, and while you read, we're going to practise coding the text. I'll be working with you to help you. [Display chart with the codes written on it.] We're going to do assisted reading today. That means I'll read a section of the story aloud, and then you'll read those same sentences silently. While you are reading silently, I want you to think about the four codes and really focus on what you are reading to see if there are places in the text where it would help you to place one of those codes. You might not need to write all of them, but I want you to write down at least one code. These codes will remind you that you need to make inferences—to pay attention to the evidence—in those places to comprehend. **Teacher Does:** Read aloud the text on page 8 of the book. Students then read page 8 silently. Students then read silently to the first break. **Teacher Says:** Turn to your partner and share what codes you marked for that section of text. [Students talk to partners.] **Teacher Says:** Marissa, tell me where your partner wrote a code. **Marissa Says:** Patrick wrote a *W* on the word *mangy*. **Teacher Says:** You knew how to pronounce the word because you heard me read it aloud. But even after you heard the word, you didn't know its meaning. So, class, we need to make an inference, use the context here, to figure out the meaning of this word. We know some details about this dog from what the author has written. The dog barked at Josh. The dog was drinking water from a dirty bucket. The dog is tied to the porch railing. Does this sound like a well-loved dog that has had a bath and gotten his hair clipped at a grooming salon? No. So what kind of evidence do we have here that we can put together to decide what the meaning of *mangy* is? Patrick, what do you think? **Patrick Says:** The dog might be kind of ugly and dirty and nobody cares about him. **Teacher Says:** Good detecting, Patrick. Carmen, tell me where your partner wrote a code. **Carmen Says:** Tim wrote an *S* on the sentence that says "The school looked like it felt . . . lonely." **Teacher Says:** There's something about that sentence that is confusing, and we need to read it once or twice more to see if we can figure out what it means. Look backward in the sentence, and find the first thing or place that *it* could stand for. *It* stands for the school. How could a school be lonely? Give me some details that might describe a lonely school. **Students Say:** It is summer, and there are no students there. No one has played on the playground, so the weeds have taken over. **Teacher Says:** Tim, are you getting this picture in your mind of how a school feels in the summertime? Now a school doesn't have feelings like a person, but we can put all the evidence together and figure out the meaning the author is trying to convey. Let's do one more, and then we'll move on. Who has a code they are willing to share with us? [Sam volunteers.] Sam, thanks for volunteering. What code did you put down? **Sam Says:** I put an *S* on the sentence "He'd given me a great idea." I don't know how a dog can give a person an idea.

continued →

© 2009 Hawker Brownlow Education • SOT4749

We Do It: Teacher and Students Work Together to Practise Coding Text *(continued)*	**Teacher Says:** Did anyone else mark this sentence? If not, then you must all have ideas about what the meaning is here. Let's have some volunteers. Good, John, we haven't heard from you today. Have you been hiding over there? **John Says:** The author doesn't mean that the dog talked to Josh and gave him the idea. The author means that while he was looking at the dog drinking, he felt thirsty, and that made him think of going to the ice-cream shop. **Teacher Says:** Very good decision making, John.
You Do It: Students Practise Independently	**Teacher Says:** We're going to read silently now for ten minutes. This is not a race. I don't care how far you get. Our goal is to be good detectives and find evidence in the text so we can understand what's going on. Please code the text as you read. Don't forget that rereading something you don't understand can often help you to understand it. After our ten minutes of silent reading, we'll talk about what evidence you found on your own.

Source: Codes adapted from Dewitz & Dewitz, 2003.

Figure 35.2: Four ways to code text.

Codes
P (Who does this pronoun refer to?)
M (This information will help me figure out the main idea of this story or article. I know a few things about the main character and the setting but nothing about the problem yet.)
S (What does this sentence mean?)
W (What does this word mean?)

© 2009 Hawker Brownlow Education and Elaine McEwan-Adkins.

Figure 35.3: Sample text from *Murphy's Mansion*.

Adapted Text from *Murphy's Mansion* (McEwan, 1994, pp. 1–2)
I rode my bike aimlessly around the neighbourhood. Mum wouldn't be home from work for another couple of hours. My next door neighbour and best friend, Will, was away at camp. Even my grown-up friend Sonny didn't need me. His leather shop had been closed for most of the summer so he could tour with his band, the Messengers. Sonny was the drummer.
The humid, hazy summer afternoon seemed endless. Perspiration trickled down my forehead, and I swatted the flies away as I rode.
I could clean my room, I thought. Mum had been bugging me since school was out to do that.
"You did a great job on toxic waste in Grandville," she had reminded me. "Now how about some action on that pile of rubbish in your bedroom?"
I crossed that idea off my list. Too much work.
I thought of riding over to the library to see if they had any new books. I'd been reading a lot this summer. The best book so far was *Dear Mr Henshaw* (Cleary, 1994). It was about a kid whose parents were divorced, just like mine.

© 2009 Hawker Brownlow Education and Elaine McEwan-Adkins.

Copyright © Hawker Brownlow Education. All rights reserved. Reprinted from *40 Reading Intervention Strategies for P–6 Students*, by Elaine K. McEwan-Adkins. Melbourne, Vic: Hawker Brownlow Education, www.hbe.com.au. Reproduction authorised only for use in the school site that has purchased the book.

Figure 35.4: Coding text from *Murphy's Mansion*.

Adapted Text from *Murphy's Mansion* (McEwan, 1994, pp. 1–2)
I (P) rode my bike aimlessly (W) around the neighbourhood. Mum wouldn't be home from work for another couple of hours. My next door neighbour and best friend, Will, was away at camp. Even my grown-up friend Sonny didn't need me. His leather shop had been closed for most of the summer so he could tour with his band, the Messengers. Sonny was the drummer.
The humid, hazy summer afternoon seemed endless. Perspiration trickled down my forehead, and I swatted the flies away as I rode.
I could clean my room, I thought. Mum had been bugging me since school was out to do that.
"You did a great job on toxic waste in Grandville (S)," she had reminded me. "Now how about some action on that pile of rubbish in your bedroom?"
I crossed that idea off my list. Too much work.
I thought of riding over to the library to see if they had any new books. I'd been reading a lot this summer. The best book so far was *Dear Mr Henshaw* (Cleary, 1994). It was about a kid whose parents were divorced, just like mine (M).

© 2009 Hawker Brownlow Education and Elaine McEwan-Adkins.

INTERVENTION 36

Asking and Answering Questions (Years 3–6)

> *Asking one's own questions is a form of making predictions and is essential to comprehension—it forces one to construct meaning rather than passively accept the text as it is encountered.*
>
> —Cecil (1995, p. 3)

This intervention teaches students how to ask and answer four different types of questions:

1. Factual questions, the answers to which can be found directly in the text

2. Factual questions, the answers to which can be found in multiple places in the text

3. Inferential questions, the answers to which can be found by combining what the text says with one's own background knowledge and experience

4. Inferential questions, the answers to which can be generated by connecting one's relevant personal experiences and knowledge to the text

This intervention is an adaptation of Raphael (1984) and Raphael and Wonnacott (1985).

Background Knowledge

Questioning is as common in schools as homework and tests, and often it is just as ineffective in promoting meaningful learning. That's because the wrong individuals are asking the questions: the teachers. Students are supposed to come up with correct answers as evidence of their comprehension, but more often than not, teachers end up answering their own questions. Beck, McKeown, Hamilton and Kucan (1997) suggest that the typical initiate-respond-evaluate questioning model (Dillon, 1988; Mehan, 1979) leaves much to be desired when it comes to uncovering students' comprehension breakdowns. Further, hearing classmates give *correct* answers to questions usually does nothing for the student who may have no clue as to why the answer *is* correct. Just and Carpenter (1987) believe that generation and answering of higher-level questions by students "encourage[s] deeper processing and more thorough organisation" (p. 422).

Questioning, whether in the asking or answering mode, is a powerful strategy for processing text, but students need explicit instruction regarding all types of questions combined with daily opportunities for hearing teachers think aloud about how they self-question, generate questions and find answers to the questions others ask. The cognitive benefits of teaching a variety of questioning approaches to students include improved memory for text, the ability to answer questions with more accuracy, and the ability to more easily find answers to questions, as well as to discriminate among types of questions and how to access the answers to them (Trabasso & Bouchard, 2002).

The questions that students ask after they have read a story or an article can be placed in the four categories discussed earlier. All students need is explicit instruction about the *critical attributes* of these types of questions, prompts to help them generate their own questions and ample teacher modelling to show them how it's done. If your students never ask you or one another any questions, they are missing out on an entire dimension of learning: getting answers to questions about what they read.

Sample Lesson for Teaching Questioning

Figure 36.1 is a sample lesson for teaching students about the four types of questions. Figure 36.2 is part of the teacher's think-aloud for modelling this intervention. Figure 36.3 is a blank question-answer quadrant form. Figure 36.4 provides some question prompts in each of the four quadrants to help students generate their questions.

Figure 36.1: Sample lesson for teaching students to question.

Lesson Objective	Students will be able to explain the four types of questions, where answers can be found for these questions, and write one of each kind of question based on a story or article they have read.
Materials Needed for the Lesson	You'll need a copy of figure 36.3 for each student, and an overhead of figure 36.3 for the teacher.
Advance Organiser	**Teacher Says:** Today we're going to learn about another one of the strategies that very good readers use whenever they read. The strategy is called questioning. Now, I know that all of you have been asking questions since you could talk. Why? What? When? Who? Where? You no doubt drove your family a little crazy because you never stopped asking questions. Well, that's not quite true. When you got to school, you stopped asking questions, and some of you stopped answering them, too. Sometimes when teachers ask questions, the same people put up their hands every time. We will have none of that in this group. Everyone is going to ask and answer questions every day.
Explain the Purpose That Questioning Serves	**Teacher Says:** Questioning is a very important strategy when you are reading. You might think that the teacher asks the questions and the kids are supposed to answer. But that's not true. Very good readers ask questions continually as they read. When you are asking questions, your comprehension improves. Once you ask a question, then you want to keep on reading to see if the story or article gives you the answer.
Define and Explain the Four Types of Questions	**Teacher Says:** When you read, there are four kinds of questions and answers. That's easy to remember. I've put a chart up on the overhead, and I'll be giving you a copy of this later. There are four quadrants, sections on this chart, to help you keep track of the questions you need to ask or answer. Look at the chart.
Quadrant 1	**Teacher Says:** The top left-hand quadrant has a picture of a book with an arrow pointing to the page. This quadrant is where we will write questions that have answers right in the book, called "In the Book" questions. You can point to the sentence that answers the question. They are the easiest kind of questions for teachers to ask students and for students to answer. Here's a quick example. In the story we're reading right now, what is the name of the town where Josh lives? If you don't remember, you can turn right to page 1 and point to it.

continued

Asking and Answering Questions

Quadrant 2	**Teacher Says:** The second type of question in the top right-hand quadrant is a little harder than the In the Book question, but it's easier than those inferential questions we've been working on. In this quadrant, the answer to the question that is asked is in the book, but it's not just in one place in the book. You have to find details in different places and then summarise them to give the answer. For example, in the Josh story we're reading right now, if I asked you what kind of a person Josh was, you would have to skim over several pages and write down several details and then think about how you could summarise them to tell me what Josh is mainly like as a person. I think we could say that he is always asking questions, so I could pick a word that summarises that. I would say he is inquisitive or that he would make a great detective.
Quadrant 3	**Teacher Says:** The third type of question is one that you know very well. We have been working on making inferences for two months, and now you know what an inference is as well as you know your own name. What is an inference? Together. **Students Say:** An inference is a decision you make about what the evidence means. **Teacher Says:** Thank you. To make an inference, you have to put four sources of evidence together. You are nodding your heads because you know the four kinds of evidence. The questions in this quadrant are inferential questions. Now if you know how to answer inferential questions, and you do, you also know how to ask them.
Quadrant 4	**Teacher Says:** The fourth quadrant has a picture of a brain. That's your brain. The questions in this quadrant are questions that can only be answered in your brain. Let me explain. The question has to relate to the story, but the answer would have to do with your personal experiences that relate to what happens in the story. For example, have you ever felt the way Josh did about doing homework? To answer that question, you need to connect your own personal experiences and feelings with the text. Remember what you connect from your brain has to be relevant (that means it has to make sense) to the text. You can't ask a question like, "Do you play in a band?" That question is completely unconnected to anything in the story.
Teacher Models Questioning	**Teacher Says:** There are four quadrants, four kinds of questions and four different kinds of answers. I'm going to model asking those four different kinds of questions. We'll use some text from the story we're reading about Josh. [The teacher develops questions from an excerpt of a story she has been reading aloud to the class as shown in figure 36.2.]
Facilitate Guided Practice	The students and teacher develop some In the Book questions together.
Independent Practice	The teacher assigns a short segment of the text to be read with partners. If the text is at students' independent reading level, the partners can take turns reading it aloud sentence by sentence. If the text is difficult, read the excerpt aloud before asking students to make up questions.

Source: Question Quadrant adapted from Raphael, 1984.

Figure 36.2: Questions generated by the teacher and students during the lesson.

Why does Tracy insist that Joshua call the postman a "postperson"? (Brain and Book) What idea did Joshua have for finding out who lived in the house? (Book)	I leaned over to pick up my bike, and a flutter of movement at that upper-storey window caught my eye. I gave a cry of surprise. The windows were covered with grime, but I could see a shadowy outline of someone standing there. I gave a half wave of my hand, but the person dropped the curtain and vanished. I was curious. Maybe I could pretend to be selling magazines and ring the doorbell. But what if the door opened and the mysterious figure grabbed me and pulled me inside? I shivered, picked up my bike and headed for town. Back in familiar territory again, I waved to the postperson. (I have to call him that, even though he's a man, because my friend Tracy at school insists on it.)
Why was it a good thing the postman wasn't trying to make a living telling jokes? (Brain and Book)	"Hi, Joshua," he called. "Sorry I didn't deliver any important mail to your house today." Last year I'd written to the governor, and everybody in town seemed to know about it. "Hey!" I called to him. "Wait up." I pushed my disabled bike as fast as I could down the path. "That tyre looks as flat as a pancake!" He laughed uproariously at his humour. It was a good thing he was delivering mail for a living and not telling jokes. "Do you know who lives in that big house on James Court?" I asked. "The one with the jungle in the front yard?"
Why was the postman wearing a safari hat? (Brain and Book) Why did Josh feel like he was talking to a five-year-old? (Brain and Book)	The postperson pushed back his safari hat and wiped his brow with a grimy red bandanna. "Shore do," he said. "I been deliverin' mail on this route in Grandville for twenty-five years." He turned and started to push his cart on down the sidewalk. "Wait a minute," I said. "Who?" "Who what?" he asked. I was beginning to feel as though I were talking to a five-year-old. "Who lives in the house?" I asked. "Aw, shucks, Joshua," he replied. "I can't tell you that." "Why not?" "Confidentiality," he said softly. "What's that?" He lowered his voice still further. "Can't talk about people on my route."
How would a postman know where somebody kept their money? (Brain and Book) Do you have any character traits in common with Josh? (Brain) What did the postperson mean when he said he wasn't born yesterday? (Brain and Book) Write two details that describe a postperson's job. (Book—more than one place)	"I don't get it." "Well, how would you like it if I blabbed all the secrets I know about you to the neighbourhood?" "Whaddya mean?" I asked. "Well," he drawled. "We mail carriers know an awful lot about the people we deliver mail to. We know where your relatives live, how often they write, if you haven't paid your bills, and where you keep your money. It's all stored up here." He tapped the hard surface of his safari hat. I wondered if he remembered that I'd only gotten three letters from my dad in the whole year we'd lived in Grandville. "And that's where it's going to stay," he affirmed, smacking his hat once more for emphasis. "You'll have to find out who lives at 816 James Court from somebody else." "What if I asked you a question, and you could blink once if the answer's yes and twice if it's no?" I suggested. "You wouldn't have to say a word." "I wasn't born yesterday, Joshua," he said. "My lips are sealed."

Note: This text was previously used in Intervention 31. Using familiar text to teach a new strategy lessens the cognitive overload for struggling readers.

© 2009 Hawker Brownlow Education and Elaine McEwan-Adkins.

Asking and Answering Questions 207

Figure 36.3: Blank question-answer quadrant.

In the 📖	In the 📖
In Your 🧠 and in the 📖	In Your 🧠

Source: Adapted from Raphael, 1984.

Copyright © Hawker Brownlow Education. All rights reserved. Reprinted from *40 Reading Intervention Strategies for P-6 Students*, by Elaine K. McEwan-Adkins. Melbourne, Vic: Hawker Brownlow Education, www.hbe.com.au. Reproduction authorised only for use in the school site that has purchased the book.

© 2009 Hawker Brownlow Education • SOT4749

Figure 36.4: Question-answer quadrant with sample question prompts.

In the 📖

1. Who is the main character?
2. Where does the story take place?
3. When does the story take place?
4. What happened first in the story?
5. How did the main character respond to the problem he encountered?
6. Point out an example in the story of _____.
7. Who was it that _____?

In the 📖

1. What are the different kinds of _____ described in this story?
2. What are the important _____ of _____?
3. What are some characteristics or qualities of _____?
4. Tell us about the beginning, middle and end of the story in sequence.

In Your 🧠 and in the 📖

1. What caused _____ to happen?
2. What do you think will be the outcome or the result of _____?
3. If _____ does _____, what will happen?
4. How are _____ and _____ alike?
5. Compare _____ and _____ with regard to _____.
6. Why did _____ act that way?

In Your 🧠

1. What happened in this story that is similar to something from your own life?
2. How did you feel when you read about the main character's experience?
3. Would you have made the same choice that the main character did? Why or why not?
4. What did you learn from this story that might change the way you act in certain situations?

Source: Adapted from Raphael, 1984. Question prompts have been added by the author.

© 2009 Hawker Brownlow Education • SOT4749

INTERVENTION 37

Previewing Text to Improve Comprehension (Years 3–6)

> *Teachers must weigh the benefits gained by students with their use versus the amount of time and energy they expend in their creation. However, research on text previews seems to show that the effort is well worth it. Students report that previews help them to understand the text selection better.*
>
> —Tierney & Readence (2000, p. 341)

This intervention (Graves, Cooke, & LaBerge, 1983) can be used with short stories, novels and chapters from content text. Text previews are an excellent way to scaffold the comprehension of struggling upper-year readers, particularly ESL students. The teacher provides background and vocabulary knowledge, helps students make connections between their lives and the text, and directly states and explains the theme of a story or novel or the important ideas and concepts of a science or social studies unit. The original research for the text preview intervention took place in middle school classrooms, but the learning theory behind it—reducing the cognitive load so students can pay attention to the story and construct meaning for themselves—works equally well in years 4–6.

Background Knowledge

In an earlier related intervention on teaching inference, we explored the difficulties that struggling readers have with understanding short novels (for example, *Hatchet*) that have unusual text structures or that require background knowledge that struggling students are unlikely to have. Typically, in the getting-ready-to-read segment of a lesson, the teacher spends time finding out what students already know and helping to connect that information to the upcoming assignment. Teachers are often reluctant to fully explain the story's characters, problems and resolutions before students have an opportunity to read the story. Struggling students report, however, that their reading experiences are less stressful and more enjoyable when they have an extensive preview of the text (Graves, Penn, & Cooke, 1985; Graves et al., 1983). An ideal use of the text preview would be to provide it as a small-group intervention during another class period or time of the day prior to the introduction of the story or novel in class. Struggling students would have had time to hear the text preview and take the book home and look through it. Preparing text previews is time-consuming but well worth the payoff in increased student motivation to actually grapple with more challenging text.

Sample Lesson for Using Text Previews

The following steps are recommended for preparing a text preview:

1. Read the text at least once, and preferably twice, to become thoroughly familiar with it so you can help students move from their real world to the world of the characters and setting in the story.

2. Next, write a short summary of the story to include a brief description of the characters, setting, point of view and plot of the story up to the climax.

3. Finally, determine what students should be looking for as they read: how the author keeps the story suspenseful, how the character changes as the story develops and how the theme or big idea is developed. Alert students to any difficulties they might encounter along the way.

You may want to enlist the help of your school media specialist/librarian to provide novel text previews. Sending a small group of struggling readers to the library for a text preview will be a change from heading off to the special education or remedial reading room for extra help.

Figure 37.1 is a text preview for *Hatchet* (Paulsen, 1987) using the steps recommended by Graves et al. (1985).

Figure 37.1: Sample text preview for *Hatchet*.

Preview Steps	Text Preview Script
Introduce the novel.	**Teacher Says:** We are always glued to our TVs when an exciting story of rescue occurs. A walker gets lost in the bush, and a group of searchers find her. Have you ever wondered what it would be like to be a survivor—someone who experienced a serious emergency and lived to tell about it?
Read the interest-building section of the preview to the students.	**Teacher Says:** In the story you are about to read, entitled *Hatchet*, the main character is a thirteen-year-old boy. He is a bit older than you are, but not by much. When the story opens, he is the passenger on a small plane flying over the wilderness in Canada. The view from his window consists of solid evergreen trees. Brian is supposed to be flying to meet his dad. However, the pilot suffers a fatal heart attack and slumps dead in his seat, while Brian goes down with the very small plane. As you read the story, you will have a chance to find out what it's like to be a survivor, without having to actually experience it firsthand. You will have what's called a vicarious experience. Brian is going to survive using a very special tool that his mother gave to him as a gift.
Give students a few minutes to discuss prior knowledge.	**Teacher Says:** Can you think of a time when you had to take charge and do something that even some adults would find difficult to do? Think for a few seconds, and then turn to your partner and share what happened. [Students quickly share with their partners.] **Teacher Says:** Did anyone's partner share something really exciting? Tell us what your partner said.
Read the remainder of the text preview.	**Teacher Says:** As you read the story about Brian's exciting adventures, the main plot of the story, you will also find what is called a *subplot*. As you might guess, the subplot isn't as important. In fact, sometimes you might wish that Brian would stop going back in his mind to think about the subplot. It has to do with his parents' divorce and what he calls the "secret". You might guess the secret right away if you have had an experience like it in your family. But I'm going to tell you the secret ahead of time, so you won't be worrying about what it is. Brian saw his mother kissing someone else (not his father), and he thinks that is the reason they are getting a divorce. We all have sad things like that in our families, but that subplot isn't the important thing about this story. The important thing is how Brian grows up and learns how to solve problems and think for himself in a very hostile and unfriendly environment. As you read, you will be able to see Brian gradually change from a timid and even frightened person into someone who has met the challenge of surviving on his own without anything but a few clothes and the hatchet his mother gave to him just before he got on the plane. Pay attention to the part that the hatchet plays in helping Brian survive.

© 2009 Hawker Brownlow Education and Elaine McEwan-Adkins.

Part 7

Interventions for Teaching Students to Read a Lot

What the Research Says About Reading a Lot

Do students become skilled readers because they read a lot, or do they read a lot because they are skilled readers? Actually, the answer is yes to both questions. Students who begin year two with strong reading skills read increasingly more books, which results in fluency and increased vocabulary. The combination of fluent reading and knowing the meaning of lots of words leads to increased reading comprehension. When students understand what they are reading, reading is a more rewarding experience. This sense of enjoyment and fulfilment quite naturally leads to a desire to read more. As students' reading volume increases, their skills become stronger. And so it goes. The good readers soar to the top of the charts. Of course, most of the reading that proficient readers do, except for some oral reading in school at certain stages, is silent.

In contrast, students who begin year two with weak reading skills have fewer opportunities to read accessible text and generally spend much less time reading in school than their "reading rich" counterparts (Allington, 1984; Cunningham & Stanovich, 1998; Nagy & Anderson, 1984). Their phonemic decoding skills are often laboured, and they have far fewer sight words available in their long-term memories for instant retrieval. Therefore, their fluency is marginal, and they know the meanings of fewer words. This sad state of affairs leads to diminished comprehension. For struggling readers, reading is a frustrating and unrewarding experience to be avoided at all costs. They have almost no motivation to read, so they read less and less. The poor readers are left at the end of the school year with seemingly fewer reading skills than they had at the beginning, and the gap between them and their reading-rich peers grows even wider.

To break this depressing cycle for struggling readers, something must happen to turn them on to reading. Sometimes a teacher can help students break through some instructional barrier and begin to experience success. Sometimes the librarian provides the "just right" book that makes interesting reading accessible for the first time. Sometimes it's a strong interest in a topic that students want to learn about. But above all, there must be success. Success in any field of endeavour, whether basketball, ballet or reading, engenders more success. Struggling readers of any age need high-success reading experiences to keep them practising until they get better. How long does anyone fail before giving up? Variables like a strong interest in a subject, an opportunity to have a choice about what to read, or a growing sense of self-efficacy engendered by effective instruction are essential components for engaging upper-year struggling readers. The interventions for reading a lot combine a strong dose of preventive interventions and a great deal of explicit instruction to give students the skills they need to become voluminous and voracious readers.

Before you implement any of the three intervention strategies in part 7, "Interventions for Teaching Students to Read a Lot", make sure that you have data from a reliable and valid assessment instrument to inform your decision. Such data can help you in targetting specific students as well as in making needed adjustments to the sample lessons that are provided. As you implement, informally assess the individual students in your group on specific skills as part of every lesson to adjust instruction for the next day. Also, give the regular curriculum-based progress-monitoring tests to collect more definitive data. If needed, be open to scheduling more time or decreasing the size of an intervention group.

INTERVENTION 38

Teaching Reading a Lot (Years P–2)

> *Reading a lot is characterized by the mindful and engaged reading of a large volume of text both in and out of school, at increasing levels of difficulty, with personalized accountability.*
>
> —McEwan (2009)

This intervention is designed to encourage students in years P–2 to read a lot every day, beginning on the first day of school. In the beginning, reading a lot will take the form of teachers, aides, older students, peers, parents and other caregivers reading aloud to students in a systematic way. As students acquire beginning reading skills, they will begin to independently read aloud from simple decodable books to their parents. Some children never outgrow their desire for a read-aloud bedtime story. Others can't wait to read on their own. Eventually these students will begin to engage in the kind of reading a lot described in the epigraph.

Background Knowledge

Few schools seem to teach all of their students to read a lot. Often, teachers focus so much on teaching their students to read and achieving the various benchmarks that are indicators of future reading achievement that they forget that teaching students to read a lot every day is essential for academic success. Think of this intervention as preventive in nature. Students who get in the reading habit early are less likely to fall through the cracks later.

Sample Plan for Whole-Class (or Whole-School) Intervention

Teaching students to read a lot begins in the first year of school. Begin teaching students to read a lot on the first day of their schooling. I developed a methodology to do that as a media specialist in two different schools and took it with me when I became a principal. When I first suggested it, I got raised eyebrows from both the teacher and media specialist. They believed that a once-a-week visit to the library was sufficient, but I convinced them that to teach students to read a lot, you had to get them in the habit of reading daily.

Here's how the system works. On the first day of school, every prep student goes to the library for the first time. There they are assisted in checking out a picture book. There are plenty of volunteers to help them select their books and sign their names on the checkout cards. When they get back to the classroom, they put their books into their backpacks. Their parents are notified at the parent orientation about the books that would be coming home, and they are given instructions on how to read the book aloud to their child just before bedtime. As soon as the book is read, it goes right back into the backpack and is brought to school the next day.

The teacher carefully teaches students the routine for returning their books to school, getting a star on the chart for the story they "read" before bedtime, "writing" their name on the easel using a scribble or symbol that is meaningful to them, and then going to the library to return their book and check out a new one at the appointed time. Of course, there are always a few glitches, like the child who returns his book with the alarming news that nobody read a story to him. The teacher does some checking to find out if the parent understood the directions and to encourage the parent to read to the child—all the while empathising with how frantic and busy life can be and emphasising how reading is just as important as brushing your teeth before bedtime. (I always said it is easier to fill cavities than it is to teach children to read.)

The teacher (hopefully someone who is fluent in the parent's language) can also suggest these other options:

- Read to the child in the parent's native language.

- Use a tape player so the child can be in charge of the read-aloud process if the library has no picture books in the parent's language.

- If there are older English-speaking children in the home, have one of them read to the child.

- If the child attends an after-school program, ask the supervisor to read to the child; other children can also benefit from the reading.

Many students love having the flexibility to hear their story read aloud multiple times while they follow along in the book, especially if their parents are not reading to them. Once the program has been introduced, it takes one or two weeks to get all of the glitches out of it. However, most children are telling the teacher and other adults about their stories, getting their stars on a simple chart and checking out another book. This program is powerful because it builds a reading-before-bedtime habit that you will reinforce for the rest of the child's primary school career. You are also "training" the parents to read every evening. When they don't, their children will remind them over and over. Figure 38.1 contains a checklist for setting up your reading a lot program.

Figure 38.1: Checklist for setting up a program for reading a lot.

✔	Steps
	1. Meet with your year-level colleagues to explain what you would like to do. Ideally, the entire year level will participate. Choose one or two individuals to present your plan to your administrator.
	2. Meet with your administrator to explain your idea. You'll need your administrator's help, and hopefully he or she will attend the meeting with the librarian to convey his or her support for the project. The librarian will have many questions and concerns. Often these questions and concerns focus not on students and reading but on logistics, work and time. The presence of your administrator is required to articulate the basic principle: nothing should stand in the way of bringing students and books together. Once you have secured the support of colleagues, administrator and librarian, the most difficult aspects of implementing this intervention are behind you.

continued →

✔	Steps
	3. Schedule a parent meeting to explain the program. Be ready to give the rationale for the program. The more reading students do both in and out of school, the greater the likelihood that they will become skilled readers. Explain that every student needs a backpack that will go back and forth between home and school every day. Inform parents that if anyone needs help with procuring a backpack, you have some extras that you would be willing to share (if that is the case). If needed, make sure to have translators present to explain the program to parents. Take parents on a tour of the library, and show them where the picture books are shelved. Read aloud a sample story to demonstrate how they should read to their children. Empathise with how tired and busy they are, but remind them that this is one of the most important things they can do for their children in terms of future academic success. If you have the sense that some parents would be more comfortable with a tape player and book bag, offer to provide them from the start.
	4. Purchase charts and stars at the teachers' store. Print all of the students' names on your chart.
	5. Make sure the librarian has plenty of parent volunteers available to help on the first day of checkout.
	6. Explain the routine to students: Check out a book. Put it in your book bag immediately. Take it home. Take your book out of the book bag and show it to your mother, father, babysitter or older sibling, and tell them this is your read-aloud and that they have to read it aloud to you before bedtime. Explain that parents are busy people and often need to be reminded to read stories. However, if no one reads the story aloud to them, they will not get a star the next day, and they won't be able to check out a new book.
	7. Schedule the first checkout day with the librarian. Send no more than five students from one class at a time.
	8. On the second day, ask students about their read-aloud experience the night before. Who read a story to them? What was the story about? Did anybody have a problem getting their story read? If there are students who did not return a book, find out why and give them another chance the next day. If a student admits that he brought his book back even though no one read it to him, remind him that he won't get a star unless the book has been read aloud. If in doubt, ask the student what the story was about.
	9. Make telephone calls to any parents who are having difficulty with the routine. Find out if they would rather have a book bag and tape player so the student can take responsibility for his or her own reading. Check in with the librarian to give appreciation and affirmation for a job well done.

© 2009 Hawker Brownlow Education and Elaine McEwan-Adkins.

Copyright © Hawker Brownlow Education. All rights reserved. Reprinted from *40 Reading Intervention Strategies for P–6 Students*, by Elaine K. McEwan-Adkins. Melbourne, Vic: Hawker Brownlow Education, www.hbe.com.au. Reproduction authorised only for use in the school site that has purchased the book.

INTERVENTION 39

Facilitating REAL Reading in the Classroom (Years 1–3)

> *Children can learn a great deal about the language and content of texts through listening to experienced readers read texts aloud, but unless children's eyes are making contact with print and translating that print into language, they can't be described as reading.*
>
> —Hiebert (2008, p. 1)

Although implementing this intervention in your classroom will build fluency in your targetted students, it is not a fluency-building program per se. There are no marked passages, charts or forms. This intervention is designed to ensure that all students are reading on their independent reading level for at least seventy-five minutes every day: forty-five minutes of REAL reading (reading accessible text with a high degree of success—95 per cent) at school and thirty minutes at home.

Background Knowledge

REAL (Reading Everyday At Level) reading takes place when students identify words independently, either analytically (through phonemic decoding, analogy or context) or increasingly as they gain fluency, through the rapid identification of words stored in their mental dictionaries as sight words. Although the following literacy activities are beneficial for building word and world knowledge in the earliest literacy experiences, they do *not* qualify as REAL reading because they do not provide reading practice that builds fluency:

- Rereading and memorising predictable big books
- Listening to read-alouds
- Writing predictable books as a class, based on predictable books that have been read aloud
- Looking at pictures in books
- Drawing pictures about stories that have been read aloud to them
- Dramatising books
- Sharing student-authored books
- Writing stories with the teacher

Unfortunately, these activities, along with art projects that have students constructing nested Russian dolls after reading a story set in Russia or making a torn paper collage in the style of a popular illustrator, are all too common in basal programs.

To become fluent readers, students must read independently. They must *personally* process the text, decoding unfamiliar words enough times through repeated oral readings to store the mental orthographic images in their long-term memories as sight words. Each student will move through the stages from slowly sounding out words aloud to sounding them out subvocally to saying them fast to fluent silent reading on a slightly different timetable. Unfortunately, far too many students will never achieve fluency because they have limited opportunities to engage in REAL reading.

For many students, the "scaffolded" or "guided reading" that takes place during the reading block is not REAL reading because the text is too difficult for them to read independently. Even after a week of fluency-oriented reading instruction and vocabulary lessons, the story remains incomprehensible without help. Guided reading groups can help students build vocabulary and background knowledge, but without seventy-five minutes of independent reading every day, the chances are slim for any kind of meaningful progress.

A group of researchers wanted to increase the time that students spent reading accessible texts, but first they had to determine how much students were actually reading (Brenner, Tompkins, Hiebert, Riley, & Miles, 2007). They used a methodology that had been used previously to determine if students were reading: they intently watched the eyes of six students in each classroom to calculate the amount of time each student spent looking at the page, observing each child for thirty seconds every three minutes (Adler & Fisher, 2001). They then computed the amount of time that this selected sample of year three students (both boys and girls at three different achievement levels) in sixty-five schools spent actually reading during the reading block. Using the data from their sample, they extrapolated the findings to a whole class. During the reading blocks, which ranged from 90 to 120 minutes in the various schools, the actual time spent reading averaged between 18 and 19 minutes—just 17.5 per cent of the average time allocated for the reading block. The most distressing finding was that no reading took place at all for one-quarter of the recorded observation period.

Having determined a baseline amount of reading, the team then set out to increase the amount of reading time in classrooms in these schools. They provided professional development for literacy coaches in the form of seven modules focused on varying topics related to how to increase the amount of time students read: partner reading, repeated reading, reading with a purpose, and the difference between reading-rich and reading-poor activities. Literacy coaches in turn presented the modules to their faculty members. During a follow-up assessment of the amount of time students were reading, the actual time spent reading went from 18 minutes to 29 minutes. Eleven minutes per day times about 176 days of the year adds up to a lot more reading practice for students who need it most!

As part of their research, the team also carefully examined the various core reading programs being used to determine how well they supported reading time for students. They discovered that the programs suggested many more reading-poor activities (what I call "unreal reading") and that the teachers' manuals devoted little space to time spent reading. Following is the outline of an intervention to ensure that your students at risk do more real reading.

The lesson plan for your intervention students will be individualised. Con-structing a plan that builds in seventy-five minutes of real reading each day will take some clever scheduling. However, to build fluency, this intervention is essential. REAL reading can come in various forms:

1. Repeated oral reading

2. Guided or coached reading with a paraprofessional or teacher, in which stories at the student's instructional level are read together, with the student assuming a large share of the reading responsibility

3. Reading in the regular reading group

4. A period of shared reading with a reading buddy from another classroom two or three times per week

5. Choral reading with two students in the intervention group reading together

6. A period in the library reading along with a tape at the student's instructional level (supervised by a volunteer in the library)

7. Reading aloud with a small group during the lunch hour (supervised by anyone who is available)

As you can see, this individualised plan is complicated and will require the cooperation of many individuals. It will, however, be worth every minute of every individual's time. I suggest nominating a reading aide who has a passion for both students and books to help gather the books that will be used and to keep the schedule running smoothly.

It's a good idea to begin this intervention with only two students at risk who are somewhat reluctant readers. Experiment with different formats to see what works best in your setting. Many schools have book rooms where hundreds of books from previous programs or even current programs are gathering dust. Get these books out and into the hands of teachers and students at risk. For this intervention, you'll need decodable books, books with controlled vocabulary (for example, *QuickReads*), and books that are short, interesting and *new*. Once you have students reading for forty-five minutes per day, begin to work on the at-home reading program as described in Intervention 38.

INTERVENTION 40

Teaching Reading a Lot (Years 4–6)

Pervasive reading in every subject, in every physical space, reading just about anything, just about all the time—is the key to reading success.

—Peter Temes (personal correspondence, 2001)

This intervention combines scaffolded instruction in book selection as well as weekly monitoring of students reading by themselves and with their teacher. The intervention builds fluency, personal reading habits and vocabulary. Teaching students to read a lot may seem like something teachers shouldn't have to do. However, as Meichenbaum and Biemiller observe, "High self-direction and student expertise should not be viewed as an attribute of a child: rather the process of self direction depends on the 'fit' between the demands of the situation and the ability and interests of the student" (1998, p. 54). Students like my granddaughter Abigail (whose story I told in the preface) are a very hard sell when it comes to reading a lot. I am hopeful that this final intervention strategy will inspire you to seek out the most reluctant readers in your classroom and see if you can build some reading success into the year they spend with you. Just one successful experience increases students' willingness to work harder and endure some frustration.

Background Knowledge

Unfortunately, the students who need the most reading practice actually get the least during an average school day, especially when compared to their more accomplished peers (Allington, 1977, 1980). Children in low reading groups read as few as 16 words in a week, while their "linguistically rich" classmates in higher reading groups read as many as 1933 words per week (Allington, 1984). Nagy and Anderson (1984) reported that proficient readers read about 1,000,000 words per year in and out of school, while their less-skilled classmates are reading as few as 100,000 during a year. Cunningham and Stanovich (1998) found a similar chasm between the reading volume of good and poor readers. A student at the 90th percentile of reading ability may read as many words in two days as a child at the 10th percentile reads in an entire school year outside the school setting. Closing the achievement gap will be impossible unless we find ways to increase reading volume for readers at risk. Allington (2006) suggests that a critical step in designing interventions for struggling readers should begin with making sure they have as many real reading experiences in school as their more successful peers.

Sample Lesson for Choosing Comfort Zone Books

As you work with this group of reluctant readers, take off your teacher hat and put on your psychologist/salesperson hat. Find a way to meet with this small group when there is nobody else around. Ask the reading specialist or interventionist to do some informal testing to determine where these students have gaps in their reading knowledge to give you a sense of each student's independent reading level. Find a way to "sell" easy reading to these students while simultaneously giving them the skills they need to become better readers. They are caught in a vicious cycle.

Meet with your target students for twenty minutes every other day to communicate the importance of reading on their *comfort level*, the term I have given to a student's independent reading level. You are free to change the amount of time you require students to spend reading, but start with a short period. Students who find an interesting book at their comfort level will likely find themselves reading for longer periods. However, let them discover that for themselves, rather than forcing them. Each student will bring to the group the book the group is reading. You should also bring a book you are reading, and you should make it an easy book so your students can see that adults choose easy books, too. Your goal is to sell them on the benefits of reading a lot while at the same time teaching them how to read a lot. Figure 40.1 contains a sample lesson for explaining and modelling how students can choose books that are in their "comfort zone" (books at their independent reading level). (See also Intervention 17.) Figure 40.2 is a student handout containing the directions for choosing a comfort zone book.

Figure 40.1: Sample lesson for choosing comfort zone books.

Lesson Objective	Students will be able to choose books for recreational reading that are in their comfort zone.
Materials Needed for the Lesson	You'll need copies of the comfort zone guidelines in figure 40.2.
Advance Organiser	**Teacher Says:** Today I'm going to teach you a strategy for selecting books that you can understand and enjoy. You may remember strategies you learned in year one, and they worked well for books that did not have many words on a page, but the books you read now have many more words on a page. I am going to teach you a strategy in which you will find books in your comfort zone. Everyone's comfort zone will be different. First I will show you the steps. Then you will do the steps with me. Finally you will try them on your own with your recreational reading books. I will check how you're doing by inviting you to read to me.
I Do It: Teacher Models	**Teacher Says:** The steps to finding your comfort zone are on the sheet I passed out to you. Follow along as I show you how to do it. First, I have to pick a book that looks interesting to me. This book looks interesting. John Jakes, one of my favourite authors, wrote it. He writes historical fiction, which is my favourite genre. The title of this book is *Charleston*. The front cover summarises the book. So far it looks good, but it has over five hundred pages. I am going to look through the book at the font—the type size—and the white space. The font is small, and there are no pictures and not very much white space. I do not think I want to read this book now. It's just too much for me. I am going to try another book.
We Do It: Teacher and Students Work Together	**Teacher Does:** Provide a variety of novels and nonfiction titles for students to examine. It may be necessary to go through this step several times until students are comfortable with the sequence. **Teacher Says:** I am going to give you a book from the library. You each will have a different book. We are going to walk through the comfort zone steps together. I will read the step, and you will do what the step says to do.
You Do It: Students Work Independently	**Teacher Says:** Now it's your turn. Take some time with the books and follow the comfort zone steps. When you are ready and have chosen a book, bring it to me and read part of it aloud. We will talk about whether the book seems to be in your comfort zone.

Source: McEwan & Bresnahan, 2008a.

Figure 40.2: Student directions for choosing a comfort zone book.

✔	Steps
	1. Select a book that seems interesting. Read the title and front and back covers. Look at the size of the font, the illustrations, the white space and the number of pages. If the book still seems interesting to you, continue with the following steps or choose another book.
	2. Choose three sections in the book to test: one near the beginning, one near the middle and one near the end.
	3. Count out about twenty words in the first section, or about three lines of text.
	4. Read the passage in a low, whispering volume.
	5. Mark any words you have trouble with or do not understand with a sticky note. I will give you some to use. Do not count names of people.
	6. Look away from the passage and tell yourself what you just read.
	7. If you missed more than one word, the passage was too hard.
	8. If you could not explain what the passage was about, the passage was too hard.
	9. Repeat steps 3–8 for the middle and ending sections of the book.
	10. If you missed only one word in each passage, or no words, and you could explain each passage, the book is in your comfort zone. Read and enjoy! If two or more passages are too hard, save the book for later in the year.

Source: McEwan & Bresnahan, 2008b. Used with permission.

Copyright © Hawker Brownlow Education. All rights reserved. Reprinted from *40 Reading Intervention Strategies for P–6 Students*, by Elaine K. McEwan-Adkins. Melbourne, Vic: Hawker Brownlow Education, www.hbe.com.au. Reproduction authorised only for use in the school site that has purchased the book.

Conclusion

Although you may not have thoroughly reviewed or taught all 40 of the intervention strategies at this point, I hope that what you have read has fulfilled the expectations you had when you purchased the book. The following big ideas were foremost in my mind as I wrote, and I hope they will guide you as you seek to use these strategies with your struggling students:

- If struggling students at any year level are to achieve that often elusive goal of year-level proficiency in reading, they will need enhanced opportunities to learn. You can no longer afford to wait and see if students will catch on or develop as they get older. You must intervene as soon as a student starts to fail.

- The key to teaching all students to read lies in effective teaching as described in the introduction. The ideas in this book hold promise for meeting the needs of struggling students much sooner and with more prescriptive interventions. However, without highly effective instruction, they could become just another failed innovation. You and your colleagues hold the keys to success.

- Teaching all students to read is best done in a professional learning community where *all* teachers assume the responsibility for *all* students. Implementing the intervention strategies in this book within the framework of a collaborative team will build instructional capacity, as well as result in increased academic achievement on the part of your students.

- The intervention strategies in this book are not prescriptions or things you absolutely have to do. They offer suggestions and possibilities. Although each one has a solid research base, when combined with your creativity and instructional expertise, the interventions will become even more effective.

I wish you great success in your ongoing endeavour to teach all of your students to read.

Glossary

accessible text—Text that the reader can read independently (95 per cent accuracy) without scaffolded assistance from the teacher

accountability—The process of holding students responsible for gaining meaning during reading

activating—A cognitive strategy in which readers "prime the cognitive pump" to recall relevant prior knowledge and experiences from long-term memory to extract and construct meaning from the text

affirming—A teaching move that includes encouraging, praising or rewarding students' actions, attitudes, thinking processes, verbal statements and work products

alphabetic principle—An understanding by the reader that letters either singly or in combination represent various sounds

analogy—Identifying (reading) words by drawing on a memorised body of analogous keywords

anaphora—Words or phrases in a text that stand for other words such as pronouns, synonyms, or descriptive words and phrases

annotating—A teaching move in which the teacher adds additional information during the course of reading or discussion; information that students do not have but need to make sense of the discussion of the text

assessing—Determining both formally (through testing) and informally (through questioning) what students have learned and where instruction needs to be adjusted and adapted for students to achieve mastery

assisted reading—Oral reading done with a tutor or teacher

attributing—Communicating to students that their accomplishments are the result of effort, wise decision making, attending to the task, exercising good judgment and perseverance, rather than their intelligence or ability

background knowledge—Knowledge that the reader has acquired through previous reading or life experiences

basal readers—See **core program**

blending—The rapid combination of individual sounds corresponding to letters in a word that enables readers to decode and thereby identify words

choral reading—Oral reading by a group of students or by the entire class

choral responses—Oral responses by students to questions or prompts by the teacher

coaching—Asking students to think aloud, cueing them to choose strategies that have been taught, and generally encouraging their efforts

coding—The physical marking of text by students to monitor their reading through making notes, underlining or highlighting, as well as the application of sticky notes and flags to signify various aspects of their interaction with the text

cognitive apprenticeship—An instructional process by which teachers provide and support students with scaffolds as students acquire cognitive strategies

cognitive load—The total amount of mental activity imposed on working memory at specific times during instruction, often defined as the number of elements, ideas, concepts or directions to which students need to attend

cognitive processing—Brain activity of students during learning in which they process new information and make connections between prior learning and experiences, and new learning by writing, talking, acting out, or developing visual organisers to aid in understanding and retention

cognitive strategies—Mental processes or physical acts students use during reading and writing to aid in the understanding and retention of text

comfort zone (See also **independent reading level**)—An expression communicating students' ease with reading text of a certain level of difficulty

comprehension—Understanding what is read or extracting or constructing meaning during the act of reading

constructing meaning—Working collaboratively with students to extract and construct multiple meanings from conversations, discussions and the reading together of text

context—The words and phrases in a sentence, paragraph or conversation surrounding a specific word or phrase that can help readers and listeners determine its meaning

contextual guessing (See also **guessing syndrome**)—The identification of a word by guessing

core program—A published series of materials specifically designed to teach the various components of reading usually accompanied by comprehensive teachers' manuals and support materials

cumulative review—Maximised opportunities for practice ensuring that previously introduced skills are constantly included with new material during practice

decodable text—Text written to provide practice with certain letter-sound correspondences that have been previously taught

decoding (See also **word identification**)—Mapping sounds to their corresponding letters to identify (read) words

differentiation—An approach to meeting the needs of students who have failed to respond in whole-group instruction through offering more time and more individualised, more intensive or more specialised instruction

direct instruction—When written in lowercase (such as direct instruction), refers to a style of teaching in which the teacher is "in charge" and has carefully structured the presentation as well as the responses desired from students. When the term is capitalised (such as *Direct Instruction*), it refers to a specific teaching style originally developed at the University of Oregon or to a published curriculum that incorporates the direct instruction teaching approach.

dysfluency—Lack of fluency during oral reading

encode—To write the spoken or thought word with accurate spelling

error correction—Providing immediate corrective feedback to students through modelling the correct answer and then asking the corrected student to provide the answer independently shortly thereafter

exception words—Words in the English language that cannot be sounded out (for example, *was, the, one, of, shoe* and *said*) and must be memorised by students

explaining—A teaching move that provides verbal input about what will happen in a lesson, what the goals are, why it's being done, how it will help students, and what the roles of the teacher and students will be during the lesson

explicit instruction—Instruction that is clearly stated and distinctly expressed and offers students adequate time and opportunities to elaborate, review and summarise new learning on multiple occasions and in varying ways

expository text—Text (nonfiction) that is written to explain and convey information about a specific topic as opposed to narrative text (fiction)

facilitating—A teaching move in which the teacher thinks along with students and helps them to develop their own ideas, rather than managing their thinking, explaining ideas and telling them what and how to do something

fluency—Automaticity, accuracy and prosody in the act of oral reading

frustration reading level—The point in the act of reading in which students' reading skills break down, resulting in dysfluency, frequent errors in word recognition, lack of comprehension and recall, and emotional distress

giving directions—A teaching move that provides unambiguous and concise verbal input that gives students a way to get from where they are at the beginning of the lesson, task or unit to the achievement of a specific task or outcome while providing wait time for students to process directions, respond or ask clarifying questions

grapheme—A unit of written language (one or more letters) that represents phonemes in the spellings of words

graphic organiser—A visual representation that provides a framework for remembering important information about a word, concept or big idea

guessing syndrome (See also **contextual guessing**)—A way of describing a pattern of reading used by struggling students who have not fully mastered the forty-four sound-spelling correspondences

guided reading—A scaffolded reading experience in which a teacher works with a small group of students who read at about the same instructional level

heterogeneous group—A group of students with widely varying characteristics or skill levels

high-frequency word—The most frequently encountered words in written English

homogeneous group—A group of students with similar characteristics or skill levels

independent reading level—The highest level of text difficulty at which students can read fluently with comprehension and recall

inferring—A cognitive strategy in which the reader brings together what is spoken (written) in the text, what is unspoken (unwritten) in the text, and what the reader already knows from relevant prior experiences and learning to extract and construct meaning from text

instructional reading level—The highest level of text difficulty at which students can read and comprehend satisfactorily, provided they receive preparation and supervision from a teacher

intervention—The implementation of a specific research-based strategy to meet the needs of one or more struggling students in a whole class

irregular words—See **exception words**

judicious teacher talk—A conscious effort by the teacher to use language that students can understand, as well as to limit verbose explanations or comments unrelated to the lesson

key word—A set of 100-120 words with common phonogram patterns and word parts that students learn as a way of decoding words they don't know from words and word parts they do know

lesson—A written plan for delivering instruction to students

letter-sound correspondence—How a particular sound is represented either by a single letter or a cluster of two or more letters; the word *relationship* is sometimes used in place of the word *correspondence*

mental orthographic image (MOI)—A mental visualisation of a word that enables students to read and spell that word automatically and accurately

metacognition—The process of thinking about one's own thinking that is required for teacher think-alouds

miniroutine—A set of prompts and responses used for practising word meanings, blending, serial processing, and other discrete reading tasks

modelling—Teachers' thinking aloud regarding their personal cognitive processing of text (for example, making connections with prior knowledge to something that is read in the text; showing how an inference was made; or demonstrating how to write a summary) or in other contexts demonstrating how to produce, blend or segment sounds, or engage in an action in the classroom

monitoring-clarifying—A cognitive strategy in which readers think about how and what they are reading both during and after the act of reading for purposes of determining if they are comprehending the text combined with the ability to clarify and fix mix-ups if necessary

motivating–connecting—Teacher actions to generate interest, activate prior knowledge and connect instruction to the real world or the solutions of real problems

narrative text—Text written to tell a story or relate a sequence of events including fiction

onset-rhyme—The part of the syllable that precedes the vowel of the syllable and the part of a syllable (not a word) that consists of its vowel and any consonant sounds that come after it

oral reading fluency (ORF)—The ability to read accurately, automatically and with prosody

orthographic image—See **mental orthographic image**

phoneme—The most basic element of the language system: a sound

phonemic awareness— The ability to hear and manipulate the individual sounds of the language coupled with the ability to recognise individual sounds in words (for example, rhyming, blending spoken sounds into words, counting phonemes)

phonemic decoding—See **decoding**

phonics—Either the sounds that various letters represent or a teaching method for helping students to fluently map specific sounds of English pronunciation with letters

phonological awareness—Readers' knowledge that words can be divided into segments of sound smaller than a syllable (phonemes) and the skill to know how the phonemes sound in the words they encounter during reading

practice—Repetition of a discrete skill or strategy until it has been mastered

preventive interventions—The implementation of instructional activities and approaches that are known to be effective with students at risk from the moment they enrol in school to avoid early failure

prosody—Appropriate intonation and expression during oral reading

questioning—A cognitive strategy in which readers engage in learning dialogues with text (authors), peers and teachers through self-questioning, question generation and question answering

read-aloud—Text read orally by either the student or teacher

reading—A process in which information from the text and the reader's knowledge interact to create meaning

reading a lot—The mindful and engaged reading of a large volume of text both in and out of school, at increasing levels of difficulty, with personalised accountability

reading culture—The collective attitudes, beliefs and behaviours of all of the stakeholders in a school regarding any and all of the activities associated with enabling all students to read at the highest level of attainment possible for both their academic and personal gain

recapping—Teacher summarising what has been concluded, learned or constructed during a given discussion or class period, as well as providing statements regarding why it is important and where it can be applied or connected in the future

recursive teaching—The cyclical teaching of key skills and concepts to ensure mastery

redirecting—A teaching move in which the teacher monitors the level of student attention and engagement, using a variety of techniques, prompts and signals to regain or redirect students' attention and focus on the learning task, transitioning students from one activity to another with minimal time loss

repeated reading—The oral reading of a section of text repeatedly to develop accuracy and speed in oral reading

routine—A desired pattern of behaviour; a procedure that is habitually executed by either students or their teachers

rubric—A performance-based assessment that includes checklists and rating scales useful for conveying behavioural, social and academic expectations to students

scaffolded instruction—Instruction in which students are given tasks that are graduated in difficulty, with each one being only slightly more difficult than the last

scaffolded silent reading—Silent reading either individually or in a small group that is led by a tutor or teacher who models cognitive strategy usage, offers periodic comprehension checks to refocus readers' attention and continually coaches them in the use of cognitive strategies

scaffolding—Providing instructional support—for example, further explanation, modelling, coaching or additional opportunities to learn—that enables students to solve problems, carry out tasks, master content and skills, or achieve goals that would otherwise be impossible without teacher support

schwa—The vowel sound in many unaccented syllables of words with more than one syllable

searching–selecting—A cognitive strategy in which readers search a variety of sources to select appropriate information to answer questions, define words and terms, clarify misunderstandings, solve problems or gather information

segmenting—Dividing words into individual phonemes (sounds), parts (prefixes, root words and suffixes), syllables, or onsets and rhymes

self-collection strategy—An instructional approach that teaches and motivates students to seek out and acquire new words from their environment either through reading or listening

serial processing—Orally reading a group of words from left to right in rows rather than top to bottom in lists

sight words—Words that have been decoded a sufficient number of times by a reader to become words that are recognised in under one second by that reader, or exception words that have been memorised

signaling—A visual, verbal, or other auditory cue given by the teacher telling students when to make a response

silent reading (See also **scaffolded silent reading**)—Unvocalised reading of text

sound-letter correspondence—How a particular letter or group of letters is represented by a sound; the word *relationship* is sometimes used in place of the word *correspondence*

spelling—The ability to recognise, recall, reproduce, or obtain orally or in written form the correct sequence of letters in words (Graham & Miller, 1979)

suffix—A letter or group of letters known as a morpheme added to the end of a word or word part to make a new word (for example, child/childish) or to function as an inflectional ending (for example, run/runs; treat/treated)

summarising—A cognitive strategy in which readers summarise text in their own words—different words from those used in the original text

supportive instruction (See **scaffolded instruction**)—Instruction that provides scaffolding for students in a multitude of ways: further explanation, modelling, coaching or additional opportunities to learn at students' independent learning levels

systematic instruction—Instruction that is characterised by the use of a method or plan; organised and sequential instruction

text—Reading material, whether expository or narrative, that an individual reads

unison responses—See **choral responses**

verbal protocols—Scripts recording the spoken thoughts of skilled readers regarding their cognitive processing

visualising–organising—A cognitive strategy in which readers construct a mental image or graphic organiser for the purpose of extracting and constructing meaning from text

vocabulary—A term used to describe the body of words that students acquire through listening and reading

wait time—A thinking pause provided by the teacher immediately after giving directions or asking questions so that students have time to think about what they want to say

word identification—The ability of readers to visually recognise or "read" words on the printed page

© 2009 Hawker Brownlow Education • SOT4749

working memory—Hypothesised to be the central processing unit of the brain in which information is either processed or transmitted to other parts of the brain for either temporary or long-term storage

world knowledge—See **background knowledge**

References

Adams, G., & Carnine, D. (2003). *Direct instruction*. In H. L. Swanson, K. R. Harris, & S. Graham (Eds.), *Handbook of learning disabilities* (pp. 403–416). New York: Guilford Press.

Adams, M. J. (1990). *Beginning to read*. Cambridge, MA: MIT Press.

Adams, M. J. (1991). A talk with Marilyn Adams. *Language Arts, 68,* 206–212.

Adams, M. J. (1998). The three-cueing system. In J. Osborn & F. Lehr (Eds.), *Literacy for all: Issues in teaching and learning* (pp. 73–99). New York: Guilford Press.

Adams, M. J., & Bereiter, C. (2002). *Open court reading*. New York: SRA/McGraw-Hill.

Adler, M. A., & Fisher, C. W. (2001). Early reading programs in high poverty schools. *Reading Teacher, 54*(6), 616–619.

Adler, M. J., & Van Doren, C. (1972). *How to read a book*. New York: Simon & Schuster.

Afflerbach, P. (1990). The influence of prior knowledge and text genre on readers' prediction strategies. *Reading Research Quarterly, 22,* 131–148.

Al-Jarf, R. (2001, March/April). Processing of cohesive ties by EFL Arab college students. *Foreign Language Annals, 34*(2), 2–23.

Allington, R. L. (1977). If they don't read much, how they ever gonna get good? *Journal of Reading, 21,* 57–61.

Allington, R. L. (1980). Poor readers don't get to read much in reading groups. *Language Arts, 57*(8), 872–876.

Allington, R. L. (1984). Content coverage and contextual reading in reading groups. *Journal of Reading Behaviour, 16,* 85–96.

Allington, R. L. (2006). Fluency: Still waiting after all these years. In S. J. Samuels & A. E. Farstrup (Eds.), *What research has to say about fluency instruction* (pp. 94–105). Newark, DE: International Reading Association.

Apel, K. (2007, March 20). *Word study: Using a five-block approach to improving literacy skills.* Presented to the Texas School Health Association, Austin, TX.

Archer, A. L., Gleason, M., & Vachon, V. (2005). *Multisyllabic word reading strat-egies: Teacher's guide*. Longmont, CO: Sopris West.

Armbruster, B. B., Lehr, F., & Osborn, J. (2001). *Put reading first: The research building blocks for teaching children to read*. Ann Arbor, MI: Centre for the Improvement of Early Reading Achievement.

Ball, E. W., & Blachman, B. A. (1991). Does phoneme awareness training in kindergarten make a difference in early word recognition and developmental spelling? *Reading Research Quarterly, 24*(1), 49–66.

Baumann, J. F. (1984). The effectiveness of a direct instruction paradigm for teaching main idea comprehension. *Reading Research Quarterly, 20*(1), 93–115.

Baumann, J. F. (1986). Teaching third-grade students to comprehend anaphoric relationships: The application of a direct instruction model. *Reading Research Quarterly, 21*(1), 70–90.

Beck, I. L., & McKeown, M. G. (1991). Conditions of vocabulary acquisition. In R. Barr, M. L. Kamil, P. B. Mosenthal, & P. D. Pearson (Eds.), *Handbook of reading research, II* (pp. 789–914). White Plains, NY: Longman.

Beck, I. L., McKeown, M. G., Hamilton, R. L., & Kucan, L. (1997). *Questioning the author: An approach for enhancing student engagement with text.* Newark, DE: International Reading Association.

Beck, I. L., McKeown, M. G., & Kucan, L. (2002). *Bringing words to life: Robust vocabulary instruction.* New York: Guilford Press.

Becker, W. C. (1977). Teaching reading and language to the disadvantaged—What we have learned from field research. *Harvard Educational Review, 47*, 518–543.

Biemiller, A. (1999). *Language and reading success.* Cambridge, MA: Brookline.

Blevins, W. (2001). *Building fluency: Lessons and strategies for reading success.* Scranton, PA: Scholastic.

Bransford, J. D. (1979). *Human cognition: Learning, understanding, and remembering.* Belmont, CA: Wadsworth.

Brenner, D., Tompkins, R., Hiebert, E., Riley, M., & Miles, R. (2007, May). *Eyes on the page: A large-scale intervention to increase time spent reading accessible texts.* Paper presented at the 2007 International Reading Association Annual Convention, Toronto, Ontario.

Brophy, J. (1999). *Teaching.* Brussels: International Academy of Education.

Brown, A. L., & Day, J. D. (1983). Macrorules for summarising texts: The development of expertise. *Journal of Verbal Learning and Verbal Behaviour, 22*, 1–14.

Buck, J., & Torgesen, J. (2003). *The relationship between performance on a measure of oral reading fluency and performance on the Florida Comprehensive Assessment Test* (Tech. Rep. No. 1). Tallahassee, FL: Florida Centre for Reading Research.

Bursuck, W. D., & Damer, M. (2007). *Reading instruction for students who are at risk or have disabilities.* New York: Pearson Education, Inc.

Bursuck, W., Smith, T., Munk, D., Damer, M., Mehlig, L., & Perry, J. (2004). Evaluating the impact of a prevention-based model of reading on children who are at risk. *Remedial and Special Education, 25*, 303–313.

Byrne, B., & Fielding-Barnsley, R. (1989). Phonemic awareness and letter knowledge in the child's acquisition of the alphabetic principle. *Journal of Educational Psychology, 81*, 313–321.

Caldwell, J. S., & Leslie, L. (2009). *Intervention strategies to follow informal reading inventory assessment. So what do I do now?* Boston: Allyn & Bacon.

Carnine, D. W., Silbert, J., & Kame'enui, E. J. (1997). *Direct instruction reading* (3rd ed.). Upper Saddle River, NJ: Prentice Hall.

Carnine, D. W., Silbert, J., Kame'enui, E. J., & Tarver, S. G. (2004). *Direct instruction reading* (4th ed.). Upper Saddle River, NJ: Merrill Prentice Hall.

Cecil, N. L. (1995). *The art of inquiry: Questioning strategies for K–6 classrooms.* Winnipeg, Manitoba: Peguis.

Chall, J. S., & Popp, H. M. (1996). *Teaching and assessing phonics: Why, what, when, how.* Cambridge, MA: Educators Publishing Service.

Chard, D. J., & Osborn, J. (1999). Phonics and word recognition instruction in early reading programs: Guidelines for accessibility. *Learning Disabilities Research and Practice, 14*(2), 107–117.

Cleary, B. (1994). *Dear Mr. Henshaw.* New York: HarperCollins.

Collins, A., Brown, J. S., & Holum, A. (1991). Cognitive apprenticeship: Mak-ing thinking visible. *American Educator, 15*(3), 6–11, 38–46.

Collins, A., Brown, J. S., & Newman, S. E. (1990). Cognitive apprenticeship: Teaching the crafts of reading, writing, and mathematics. In L. Resnick (Ed.), *Knowing, learning, and instruction: Essays in honor of Robert Glaser* (pp. 453–494). Hillsdale, NJ: Erlbaum.

Connor, C. M., Morrison, F. J., Fishman, B. J., Schatschneider, C., & Under-wood, P. (2007). Algorithm-guided individualized reading instruction. *Science, 315*(5811), 464–465.

Connor, C. M., Morrison, F. J., & Katch, L. E. (2004). Beyond the reading wars: Exploring the effect of child-instruction interactions on growth in early reading. *Scientific Studies of Reading, 8*(4), 305–336.

Connor, C. M., Morrison, F., & Petrella, J. N. (2004). Effective reading comprehension instruction: Examining child by instruction interactions. *Journal of Educational Psychology, 96*(4), 682–698.

Connor, C. M., Morrison, F., & Slominski, L. (2006). Preschool instruction and children's literacy skill growth. *Journal of Educational Psychology, 98*(4), 665–689.

Connor, C. M., Piasta, S. B., Glasney, S., Schatschneider, C., Crowe, E., Under-wood, P., et al. (2009). Individualizing student instruction precisely: Effects of child-by-instruction interactions on students' literacy. *Child Development, 80*(1), 77–100.

Connor, C. M., Schatschneider, C., Fishman, B., & Morrison, F. J. (2008, June). *Individualizing student literacy instruction: Exploring causal implications of child x instruction interactions.* Paper presented to the Institute of Education Sciences, Washington, DC.

Cooper, J. D., Chard, D. J., & Kiger, N. D. (2006). *The struggling reader: Inter-ventions that work.* New York: Scholastic.

© 2009 Hawker Brownlow Education • SOT4749

Coyne, M. D., Simmons, D. C., & Kame'enui, E. J. (2004). Vocabulary instruction for young children at-risk of experiencing reading difficulties: Teaching word meanings during shared storybook reading. In J. F. Baumann & E. J. Kame'enui (Eds.), *Vocabulary instruction: Research in practice* (pp. 41–58). New York: Guilford Press.

Crystal, D. (2007). *How language works: How babies babble, words change meaning, and languages live or die.* New York: Avery.

Cunningham, A. E. (1990). Explicit versus implicit instruction in phonemic awareness. *Journal of Experimental Child Psychology, 50,* 429–444.

Cunningham, A. E., & Stanovich, K. E. (1998). What reading does for the mind. *American Educator, 22*(1–2), 8–15.

Dansereau, D. F. (1988). Cooperative learning strategies. In C. E. Weinstein, E. T. Goetz, & P. A. Alexander (Eds.), *Learning and study strategies: Issues in assessment, instruction, and evaluation* (pp. 103–120). New York: Aca-demic Press.

Davey, B. (1983). Think aloud: Modelling the cognitive processes of reading comprehension. *Journal of Reading, 27*(1), 44–47.

Dewitz, P., & Dewitz, P. K. (2003). They can read the words, but they can't understand: Refining comprehension assessment. *Reading Teacher, 56,* 422–435.

Dewitz, P., Jones, J., & Leahy, S. (2007, November 30). *The research base of comprehension instruction in five basal reading programs.* Paper presented at the 57th National Reading Conference, Austin, TX.

DIBELS Data System (2009). *DIBELS word use fluency.* Accessed at https://dibels.uoregon.edu/measures/wuf.php on 28 January, 2009.

Dillon, J. T. (1988). *Questioning and teaching: A manual of practice.* New York: Teachers College Press.

Dixon, R., Carnine, D., & Kame'enui, E. (1992). *Curriculum guidelines for diverse learners* (Monograph for the National Centre to Improve the Tools of Educators). Eugene, OR: University of Oregon.

Dixon, R., Klau, K., Rosoff, A., & Conrad, L. (2002). *Reading success: Level A.* New York: SRA/McGraw-Hill.

Dowhower, S. L. (1987). Effects of repeated reading on second-grade transitional readers' fluency and comprehension. *Reading Research Quarterly, 22,* 389–406.

Duffy, G. G., & Roehler, L. R. (1987). Teaching reading skills as strategies. *Reading Teacher, 40,* 414–418.

Dunn, L. M., & Dunn, D. M. (2007). *Peabody picture vocabulary test* (4th ed.). San Antonio, TX: Pearson Assessments.

Edmonds, R. (1981). Making public schools effective. *Social Policy, 12,* 53–60.

Ehri, L. C. (1980). The development of orthographic images. In U. Frith (Ed.), *Cognitive processes in spelling* (pp. 85-116). London: Academic Press.

Ehri, L. C. (1995). Teachers need to know how word reading processes develop to teach reading effectively to beginners. In C. N. Hedley, P. Antonacci, & M. Rabinowitz (Eds.), *Thinking and literacy: The mind at work* (pp. 167–188). Hillsdale, NJ: Erlbaum.

Ehri, L. C. (1997). Sight word learning in normal readers and dyslexics. In B. A. Blachman (Ed.), *Foundations in reading acquisition and dyslexia: Implications for early interventions* (pp. 163–190). Mahwah, NJ: Erlbaum.

Ehri, L. C. (1998). Grapheme-phoneme knowledge is essential for learning to read words in English. In J. L. Metsala & L. C. Ehri (Eds.), *Word recognition in beginning literacy* (pp. 3–40). Hillsdale, NJ: Erlbaum.

Ehri, L. C., & Rosenthal, J. (2007). Spellings of words: A neglected facilitator of vocabulary. *Journal of Literary Research, 39*(4), 389–409.

Emmer, E. T., Evertson, C. M., & Anderson, L. (1980). Effective classroom management at the beginning of the school year. *Elementary School Journal, 80*(5), 219–231.

Feldman, K., & Kinsella, K. (2002). *Narrowing the gap: The case for explicit vocabulary instruction.* New York: Scholastic.

Fielding, L., Kerr, N., & Rosier, P. (2004). *Delivering on the promise of the 95% reading and maths goals.* Kennewick, WA: New Foundation Press.

Fielding, L., Kerr, N., & Rosier, P. (2007). *Annual growth for all students: Catch-up growth for those who are behind.* Kennewick, WA: New Foundation Press.

Fielding, L., & Roller, C. (1992). Making difficult books accessible and easy books acceptable. *Reading Teacher, 45*, 678–685.

Flood, J., Medearis, A. S., Hasbrouck, J. E., Paris, S., Hoffman, J. V., Stahl, S., et al. (2001). *Macmillan McGraw-Hill reading program.* New York: Macmillan, McGraw-Hill.

Frayer, D., Frederick, W. C., & Klausmeier, H. J. (1969). *A schema for testing the level of concept mastery* (Working Paper No. 16). Madison: University of Wisconsin.

Gardner, H. (1983). *Frames of mind: The theory of multiple intelligences.* New York: Basic Books.

Gaskins, I. W. (2005). *Success with struggling readers: The Benchmark School approach.* New York: Guilford Press.

Gaskins, I. W., Ehri, L. C., Cress, C., O'Hara, C., & Donnelly, K. (1996/1997). Procedures for word learning: Making discoveries about words. *Reading Teacher, 50*, 312–327.

Goldstein, R. (2002, October 14). Stephen Ambrose dies at 66. *The New York Times.* Accessed at www.nytimes.com/2002/10/14/obituaries/14AMBR.html?ex=104951880-0&en=818f908ec5b7befd&ei=5070 on April 3, 2003.

Good, R. H., & Kaminski, R. A. (Eds). (2000). *Dynamic indicators of basic early literacy skills (DIBELS)* (6th ed.) Eugene, OR: Institute for the Development of Educational Achievement.

Goodman, K. (Ed.). (2006). *The truth about DIBELS: What it is, what it does.* Portsmouth, NH: Heinemann.

Graham, S., & Miller, L. (1979). Spelling research and practice: A unified approach. *Focus on Exceptional Children, 12*(2), 75–91.

Grahame, K. (1908). *Wind in the willows*. New York: Grosset & Dunlap.

Graves, M. F., Cooke, C. L., & LaBerge, M. J. (1983). Effects of previewing difficult short stories on low ability junior high school students' comprehension, recall, and attitudes. *Reading Research Quarterly, 18*, 262–276.

Graves, M. F., Penn, M. C., & Cooke, C. L. (1985). The coming attraction: Previewing short stories. *Journal of Reading, 28*, 594–598.

Gregorc, A. F. (1985). *Inside styles: Beyond the basics—Questions and answers on style*. Maynard, MA: Gabriel Systems.

Hall, S. (2008). *Implementing response to intervention: A principal's guide*. Thousand Oaks, CA: Corwin Press.

Hansen, J. (1981). The effects of inference training and practice on young children's reading comprehension. *Reading Research Quarterly, 16*, 391–417.

Harris, A. J., & Sipay, E. R. (1985). *How to increase reading ability: A guide to developmental and remedial methods*. New York: Longman.

Harvey, S., & Goudvis, A. (2000). *Strategies that work: Teaching comprehension to enhance understanding*. York, ME: Stenhouse.

Hasbrouck, J., & Tindal, G. A. (2006). Oral reading fluency norms: A valuable assessment tool for reading teachers. *Reading Teacher, 59*(7), 636–644.

Herber, H. L., & Herber, J. N. (1993). *Teaching in content areas with reading, writing, and reasoning*. Boston: Allyn & Bacon.

Hiebert, E. (2003). *QuickReads*. Parsipanny, NJ: Pearson Learning Group.

Hiebert, E. H. (2008). The (mis)match between texts and students who depend on schools to become literate. In E. H. Hiebert & M. Sailors (Eds.), *Finding the right texts: What works for beginning and struggling readers* (pp. 1–22). New York: Guilford Press.

Hiebert, E. H., & Fisher, C. W. (2005). A review of the National Reading Panel's studies on fluency: On the role of text. *Elementary School Journal, 105*, 443–460.

Hudson, R. F., Mercer, C. D., & Lane, H. B. (2000). *Exploring reading fluency: A paradigmatic overview*. Unpublished manuscript, University of Florida, Gainesville.

Individuals with Disabilities Education Improvement Act of 2004, Pub. L. No.108-446, §§ 300.307, 300.309, 300.311 (2004).

Juel, C. (1988). Learning to read and write: A longitudinal study of fifty-four children from first through fourth grade. *Journal of Educational Psychology, 80*, 437–447.

Juel, C. (1990). Effects of reading group assignment on reading development in first and second grade. *Journal of Reading Behaviour, 22*, 233–254.

Just, M. A., & Carpenter, P. A. (1987). *The psychology of language and reading comprehension*. Newton, MA: Allyn & Bacon.

Kagan, S. (1997). *Cooperative learning*. San Clemente, CA: Author.

Kame'enui, E. J. (1986). Main idea instruction for low performers: A direct instruction analysis. In J. F. Baumann (Ed.), *Teaching main idea comprehension* (pp. 239–276). Newark, DE: International Reading Association.

Kamil, M., & Hiebert, E. H. (2005). The teaching and learning of vocabulary. In E. H. Hiebert & M. H. Kamil (Eds.), *Teaching and learning vocabulary* (pp. 1–23). Mahwah, NJ: Erlbaum.

Karon, J. (1996). *These high, green hills*. New York: Penguin Books.

Keene, E. O., & Zimmermann, S. (1997). *Mosaic of thought: Teaching comprehension in a reader's workshop*. Portsmouth, NH: Heinemann.

Kohl, H. (1998). *The discipline of hope: Learning from a lifetime of teaching*. New York: Simon & Schuster.

Lie, A. (1991). Effects of a training program for stimulating skills in word analysis for first-grade children. *Reading Research Quarterly, 26*(3), 263–284.

London, J. (1903). *Call of the wild*. New York: Tom Doherty Associates, Inc.

Lundberg, I., Frost, J., & Peterson, O. (1988). Effects of an extensive program for stimulating phonological awareness in pre-school children. *Reading Research Quarterly, 23*, 263–284.

Lyon, G. R. (1998, March). Why reading is not a natural process. *Educational Leadership, 55*(50), 14–18.

Marzano, R. J., Gaddy, B. B., & Dean, C. (2000). *What works in classroom instruction*. Aurora, CO: Mid-continent Research for Education and Learning.

Masterson, J. J., Apel, K., & Wasowicz, J. (2002). *SPELL-2: A multiple linguistic, prescriptive assessment, examiner's manual* (2nd ed.). Evanston, IL: Learning by Design, Inc.

McCarthy, B. (1997). A tale of four learners: 4MAT's learning styles. *Educational Leadership, 54*(6), 46.

McCormack, R. L., Paratore, J. R., & Dahlene, K. F. (2004). Establishing instruction congruence across learning settings: One path to success for struggling third grade readers. In R. L. McCormack & J. R. Paratore (Eds.), *After early intervention, then what: Teaching struggling readers in grades 3 and beyond* (pp. 117–136). Newark, DE: International Reading Association.

McEwan, E. K. (1991). *Project cockroach*. Elgin, IL: David C. Cook.

McEwan, E. K. (1994). *Murphy's mansion*. Elgin, IL: David C. Cook.

McEwan, E. K. (2002). *The ten traits of highly effective teachers: How to hire, coach, and mentor successful teachers*. Melbourne, Australia: Hawker Brownlow Education.

McEwan, E. K. (2004). *Seven strategies of highly effective readers: Using cognitive research to boost K–8 achievement*. Thousand Oaks, CA: Corwin Press.

McEwan, E. K. (2006). *How to survive and thrive in the first three weeks of school*. Thousand Oaks, CA: Corwin Press.

McEwan, E. K. (2007). *40 ways to support struggling readers in content classrooms, grades 6–12*. Thousand Oaks, CA: Corwin Press.

McEwan, E. K. (2008). *The ten traits of highly effective schools*. Melbourne, Australia: Hawker Brownlow Education.

McEwan, E. K. (2009). *Teach them all to read: Catching kids before they fall through the cracks* (2nd ed.). Melbourne, Australia: Hawker Brownlow Education.

McEwan, E. K., & Bresnahan, V. (2008a). *Vocabulary: Grades K–3*. Thousand Oaks, CA: Corwin Classroom Activity Books.

McEwan, E. K., & Bresnahan, V. (2008b). *Vocabulary: Grades 4–8*. Thousand Oaks, CA: Corwin Classroom Activity Books.

McEwan, E. K., & Damer, M. (2000). *Managing unmanageable students: Practical solutions for administrators*. Thousand Oaks, CA: Corwin Press.

McEwan, E. K., Dobberteen, K. W., & Pearce, Q. L. (2008a). *Fluency: Grades K–3*. Thousand Oaks, CA: Corwin Classroom Activity Books.

McEwan, E. K., Dobberteen, K. W., & Pearce, Q. L. (2008b). *Fluency: Grades 4–8*. Thousand Oaks, CA: Corwin Press.

McEwan, E. K., Judware, M., Carino, D., & Darling, C. (2008). *Comprehension: Grades K–3*. Thousand Oaks, CA: Corwin Press.

McEwan, E. K., Nielsen, L., & Edison, R. (2008). *Word analysis: Grades 4–8*. Thousand Oaks, CA: Corwin Press.

McKeown, M. G., Beck, I. L., Omanson, R. C., & Pople, M. T. (1985). Some effects of the nature and frequency of vocabulary instruction on the knowledge and use of words. *Reading Research Quarterly, 20*(5), 522–535.

Mehan, H. (1979). *Learning lessons: Social organisation in the classroom*. Cambridge, MA: Harvard University Press.

Mehta, P., Foorman, B. R., Branum-Martin, L., & Taylor, P. W. (2005). Liter-acy as a unidimensional construct: Validation, sources of influence and implications in a longitudinal study in grades 1 to 4. *Scientific Studies of Reading, 9*(2), 85–116.

Meichenbaum, D., & Biemiller, A. (1998). *Nurturing independent learners: Helping students take charge of their learning*. Cambridge, MA: Brookline.

Messiah, A. (1999). *Quantum mechanics*. North Chelmsford, MA: Courier Dover Publications.

Miller, G. (1956). The magical number seven, plus or minus two: Some limits on our capacity for processing information. *Psychological Review, 104*, 3–65.

Moats, L. C. (2000). *Speech to print: Language essentials for teachers*. Baltimore: Brookes.

Moats, L. C. (2001). Overcoming the language gap: Invest generously in teacher professional development. *American Educator, 25*(2), 5, 8–9.

Moats, L. C. (2006, September 29–October 1). *Implementing research-based reading instruction in high poverty schools: Lessons learned from a five year research program*. Presentation at Pathways to Literacy Achievement for High Poverty Children, University of Michigan School of Education. Ready to Read Program, Ann Arbor, MI.

Morgan, P. L., Farkas, G., Tufis, P. A., & Sperling, R. A. (2008). Are reading and behaviour problems risk factors for each other? *Journal of Learning Disabilities, 41*, 417–436.

Nagy, W. E. (2005). Why vocabulary instruction needs to be long-term and comprehensive. In E. H. Hiebert & M. L. Kamil (Eds.), *Teaching and learning vocabulary* (pp. 27–44). Mahwah, NJ: Erlbaum.

Nagy, W. E., & Anderson, R. C. (1984). How many words are there in printed school English? *Reading Research Quarterly, 19*, 304–330.

Nagy, W. E., & Scott, J. A. (2000). Vocabulary processes. In M. L. Kamil, P. Mosenthal, P. D. Pearson, & R. Barr (Eds.). *Handbook of reading research* (*Vol. 3*, pp. 269–284). Mahwah, NJ: Erlbaum.

National Early Literacy Panel. (2008). *Developing early literacy: Report of the National Early Literacy Panel*. Washington, DC: National Institute for Literacy.

National Institute of Child Health and Human Development (2000). *Report of the National Reading Panel: Teaching children to read—An evidence-based assessment of the scientific research literature on reading and its implications for reading instruction: Report of the subgroups* (NIH Publication No. 00-4769). Washington, DC: U.S. Government Printing Office.

New York Times Notable Books 2002. (2003). Review of *Blessings*. Accessed at www.nytimes.com/2002/12/08/books/review/2002/notablefiction.html?ex=1049605200&en=5d24c1bb36c3da09&ei=5070 on 4 April, 2003.

Nelson, J. R., Cooper, P., & Gonzalez, J. (2004). *Stepping stones to literacy*. Longmont, CO: Sopris West.

No Child Left Behind Act of 2001, Pub. L. No. 107-110, 115 Stat. 1425H.R.1 (2002). Accessed at www.ed.gov/nclb/landing.jhtml on 1 September, 2009.

Novak, J. D. (1998). *Learning, creating, and using knowledge: Concept maps as facilitative tools in schools and corporations*. Mahwah, NJ: Erlbaum.

Novak, J. D., & Gowin, B. (1984). *Learning how to learn*. Cambridge, UK: Cambridge University Press.

Oakhill, J., Cain, K., & Yuill, N. (1998). Individual differences in children's comprehension skill: Toward an integrated model. In C. Hulme & R. M. Joshi (Eds.), *Reading and spelling: Development and disorders* (pp. 343–367). London: Erlbaum.

O'Connor, R. E., Jenkins, J. R., & Slocum, T. A. (1993). *Unpacking phonological awareness: Two treatments for low-skilled kindergarten children*. Unpublished manuscript.

Opitz, M. F., & Rasinski, T. V. (1998). *Good-bye Round Robin: 25 effective oral reading strategies*. Portsmouth, NH: Heinemann.

Pany, D., & McCoy, K. M. (1988). Effects of corrective feedback on word accuracy and reading comprehension of readers with learning disabilities. *Journal of Reading Disabilities, 21,* 546–550.

Patterson, K. E., & Coltheart, V. (1987). Phonological processes in reading: A tutorial review. In M. Coltheart (Ed.), *Attention and performance: Vol. 12. The psychology of reading* (pp. 421–447). Hillsdale, NJ: Erlbaum.

Paulsen, G. (1987). *Hatchet*. New York: Simon & Schuster.

Pearson, P. D., Cervetti, G., Bravo, M., Hiebert, E. H., & Arya, D. J. (2005). *Reading and writing at the service of acquiring scientific knowledge and dispositions: From synergy to identity*. Paper presented at the Edmonton Regional Learning Consortium, Edmonton, Alberta.

Pearson, P. D., & Fielding, L. (1991). Comprehension instruction. In R. Barr, M. L. Kamil, P. B. Mosenthal, & P. D. Pearson (Eds.), *Handbook of reading research*, (Vol. 2, pp. 815–860). White Plains, NY: Longman.

Pearson, P. D., & Gallagher, M. C. (1983). The instruction of reading comprehension. *Contemporary Educational Psychology, 8,* 317–344.

Pearson, P. D., Hiebert, E., & Kamil, M. L. (2007). Vocabulary assessment: What we know and what we need to learn. *Reading Research Quarterly, 42*(2), 228–296.

Perfetti, C. (1985). *Reading ability*. New York: Oxford University Press.

Pickard, P. R. (2005, September 14). Conjuring Willa Cather: A teacher on the magic of good examples. *Education Week, 35,* 37.

Pikulski, J. J., & Chard, D. J. (2005). Fluency: Bridge between decoding and comprehension. *Reading Teacher, 58*(6), 510–519.

Pinker, S. (1999). *Words and rules: Ingredients of language*. New York: Harper Collins.

Pressley, M., & Afflerbach, P. (1995). *Verbal protocols of reading: The nature of constructively responsive reading*. Hillsdale, NJ: Erlbaum.

Pressley, M., El-Dinary, P. B., & Brown, R. (1992). Skilled and not-so-skilled reading: Good information processing and not so good information processing. In M. Pressley, K. R. Harris, & J. T. Guthrie (Eds.), *Promoting academic competence and literacy in school* (pp. 91–127). San Diego: Academic Press.

Pressley, M., El-Dinary, P. B., Gaskins, I., Schuder, T., Bergman, J. L., Almasi, J., et al. (1992). Beyond direct explanation: Transactional instruction of reading comprehension strategies. *Elementary School Journal, 92,* 513–556.

Pressley, M., Goodchild, F., Fleet, J., Zajchowski, R., & Evans, E. D. (1989). The challenges of classroom strategy instruction. *Elementary School Journal, 89*(3), 301–342.

Princeton University. (2006). *WordNet 3.0*. Accessed at http://wordnet.princeton.edu/perl/webwn?s=inference on 2 March, 2009.

Rack, J. P., Hulme, C., Snowling, J. J., & Wightman, J. (1994). The role of phonology in young children's learning of sight words: The direct mapping hypothesis. *Journal of Experimental Psychology, 57*, 42–71.

Raphael, T. (1984). Teaching learners about sources of information for answering questions. *Journal of Reading, 27*(4), 303–311.

Raphael, T. E., & Wonnacott, C. A. (1985). Heightening fourth-grade students' sensitivity to sources of information for answering comprehension questions. *Reading Research Quarterly, 25*, 285–296.

Rapp-Rudell, M., & Shearer, B. A. (2002). "Extraordinary," "tremendous," "exhilarating," "magnificent": Middle school at-risk students become avid word learners with vocabulary self-selection strategy (VSS). *Journal of Adolescent & Adult Literacy, 45*, 352–363.

Rasinski, T. V. (1990). Effects of repeated reading and listening-while-reading on reading fluency. *Journal of Educational Research, 83*, 147–150.

Rasinski, T. V., Padak, N., Linke, W., & Sturdevant, E. (1994). The effects of fluency development instruction on urban second graders. *Journal of Education Research, 87*, 158–164.

Rayner, K., & Pollatsek, A. (1989). *The psychology of reading.* Englewood Cliffs, NJ: Prentice Hall.

Reitsma, P. (1983). Printed word learning in beginning readers. *Journal of Experimental Child Psychology, 75*, 321–339.

Roehrig, A. D., Petscher, Y., Nettles, S. M., Hudson, R. F., & Torgesen, J. K. (2008). Accuracy of the DIBELS oral reading fluency measure for predicting third grade reading comprehension outcomes. *Journal of School Psychology, 46*(3), 343–366.

Rosenshine, B. (1986). Synthesis of research on explicit teaching. *Educational Leadership, 43*(7), 60–69.

Rosenthal, J., & Ehri, L. C. (2008). The mnemonic value of orthography for vocabulary learning. *Journal of Educational Psychology, 100*(1), 175–191.

Sachar, L. (1993). *Marvin Redpost: Is he a girl?* New York: Random House.

Samuels, S. J. (1979). The method of repeated readings. *Reading Teacher, 32*, 403–408.

Santa, C., Havens, L., & Valdes, B. (2004). *Project CRISS: Creating independence through student-owned strategies* (3rd ed.). Dubuque, IA: Kendall Hunt.

Santoro, L. E., Coyne, M. D., & Simmons, D. C. (2006). The reading-spelling connection: Developing and evaluating a beginning spelling intervention for children at risk of reading disability. *Learning Disabilities Research and Practice, 2*(2), 122–133.

Saphier, J., & Gower, R. (1997). *The skillful teacher: Building your teaching skills.* Acton, MA: Research for Better Teaching.

Say, A. (1993). *Grandfather's journey.* New York: Houghton Mifflin.

Schooler, J. W., Reichle, E. D., & Halpern, D. V. (2004). Zoning out while reading: Evidence for dissociations between experience and metaconsciousness. In D. T. Levin (Ed.), *Thinking and seeing: Visual metacognition in adults and children* (pp. 203–226). Cambridge, MA: MIT Press.

Scott, J. A., Jamieson-Noel, D., & Asselin, M. (2003). Vocabulary instruction throughout the day in 23 Canadian upper-elementary classrooms. *Elementary School Journal, 103*(3), 269–286.

Searfoss, L. (1975). Radio reading. *Reading Teacher, 29*, 295–296.

Seuss, Dr. (1990). *Oh, the places you'll go!* New York: Random House.

Share, D. L. (1999). Phonological recoding and orthographic learning: A direct test of the self-teaching hypothesis. *Journal of Experimental Child Psychology, 72*, 95–129.

Slavin, R. E. (1990). *Cooperative learning: Theory, research, and practice.* Englewood Cliffs, NJ: Prentice Hall.

Slavin, R. E. (1996). *Research on cooperative learning and achievement: What we know, what we need to know.* Accessed at www.aegean.gr/culturaltec/c_karagiannidis/2003-2004/collaborative/slavin1996.pdf on 28 July, 2006.

Spalding, R. B., & North, M. E. (2003). *The writing road to reading: The Spalding method of phonics for teaching speech, writing & reading* (5th rev. ed.). New York: HarperCollins.

Sprenger, M. (1999). *Learning and memory: The brain in action.* Alexandria, VA: Association for Supervision and Curriculum Development.

Stahl, S. A. (1999). *Vocabulary development.* Cambridge, MA: Brookline.

Stahl, S. (2005). Four problems with teaching word meanings and what to do to make vocabulary an integral part of instruction. In E. H. Hiebert and M.L. Kamil (Eds.), *Teaching and learning vocabulary* (pp. 95–114). Mahwah, NJ: Erlbaum.

Stahl, S. A., & Fairbanks, M. M. (1986). The effects of vocabulary instruction: A model-based meta-analysis. *Review of Educational Research, 56*(1), 72–110.

Stahl, S. A., & Heubach, K. M. (2005). Fluency-oriented reading instruction. *Journal of Literacy Research, 37*, 25–60.

Sternberg, R. (1996). *Successful intelligence: How practical and creative intelligence determine success in life.* New York: Simon & Schuster.

Summary of Duke-Kansas basketball game. (2003, 8 April). *USA Today*, p. 7C.

Swanson, H. L., & Hoskyn, M. (1998). Experimental intervention research on students with learning disabilities: A meta-analysis of treatment outcomes. *Review of Educational Research, 68*, 277–321.

Thernstrom, M. (2006, May 14). My pain, my brain. *New York Times.* Accessed at www.nytimes.com/2006/05/14/magazine/14pain.html?scp=1&sq=my%20pain,%20my%20brain&st=cse on 10 February, 2009.

Tierney, R. J., & Readence, J. E. (2000). *Reading strategies and practices: A compendium* (5th ed.). Boston: Allyn & Bacon.

Tompkins, G. (1998). *Fifty literacy strategies step by step.* Upper Saddle River, NJ: Merrill.

Torgesen, J. K. (2002). Lessons learned from intervention research in reading: A way to go before we rest. In R. Stainthorpe (Ed.), *Literacy: Learning and teaching* (pp. 89–104). (BJEP Monograph Series II, Vol. 11, No. 1). London: British Psychological Society.

Torgesen, J. K. (2005, September). *Multiple tiers of instruction and intervention: What it will take to leave no child behind in reading.* Presented at Nebraska Reading First, Lincoln, NE.

Torgesen, J. K. (2006). *Intensive reading interventions for struggling readers in early elementary school: A principal's guide.* Portsmouth, NH: RMC Research Corporation, Centre on Instruction.

Torgesen, J. K. (2007). *Using an RTI model to guide early reading instruction: Effects on identification rates for students with learning disabilities.* Tallahassee, FL: Florida Centre for Reading Research.

Torgesen, J. K. (2009, March). *Plain talk about reading.* Presented at the Plain Talk About Reading Institute, Chicago, IL.

Torgesen, J. K., Rashotte, C. A., & Alexander, A. W. (2001). Principles of fluency instruction in reading: Relationships with established empirical outcomes. In M. Wolf (Ed.), *Dyslexia, fluency, and the brain* (pp. 333–355). Timonium, MD: York.

Torgesen, J. K., Wagner, R. K., & Rashotte, C. A. (1997). The prevention and remediation of severe reading disabilities: Keeping the end in mind. *Scientific Studies of Reading, 1,* 217–234.

Tovani, C. (2000). *I read it but I don't get it: Comprehension strategies for adolescent readers.* Portland, ME: Stenhouse.

Trabasso, T., & Bouchard, E. (2002). Teaching readers how to comprehend text strategically. In C. C. Block & M. Pressley (Eds.), *Comprehension instruction: Research-based best practices* (pp. 176–200). New York: Guilford Press.

Twain, M. (1876). *The adventures of Tom Sawyer.* Leipzig: Bernhard Tauchnitz.

University of Washington Psychology Writing Centre. (2003). *Plagiarism and student writing.* Accessed at http://depts.washington.edu/psywc/handouts.shtml on 1 September, 2009.

van den Broek, P. (1994). Comprehension and memory of narrative texts: Inference and coherence. In M. A. Gernsbacher (Ed.), *Handbook of psycholinguistics* (pp. 539–588). San Diego: Academic Press.

Vaughn, S. (2005). *Interpretation of the 3-tier framework.* Accessed at http://texasrading.org/uctcrla/materias/3tier_letter.asp on 23 July, 2008.

Vellutino, F., & Scanlon, P. (1987). Phonological coding, phonological awareness, and reading ability: Evidence from a longitudinal and experimental study. *Merrill-Palmer Quarterly, 33,* 321–363.

Walberg, H. J., & Paik, S. J. (2003). *Effective educational practices*. Geneva: Geneva International Bureau of Education. Accessed at www.ibe.unesco.org on 22 March, 2009.

Walsh, K. (2003). Basal readers: The lost opportunity to build knowledge that propels comprehension. *American Educator, 27,* 24–27.

Wasowicz, J. (2007). *What do spelling errors tell us about language knowledge?* Evanston, IL: Learning by Design, Inc.

Wasowicz, J., Apel, K., Masterson, J., & Whitney, A. (2004). *SPELL—Links to reading & writing: A word-study curriculum*. Evanston, IL: Learning by Design, Inc.

Weinstein, C. E., & Mayer, R. E. (1986). The teaching of learning strategies. In M. C. Wittrock (Ed.), *Handbook of research on teaching* (pp. 315–327). New York: Macmillan.

Weisberg, P., Savard, P., & Christopher, F. (1993). Teaching preschoolers to read: Don't stop between the sounds when segmenting words. *Education and Treatment of Children, 16*(1), 1–18.

Wiggins, K. D. (1903). *Rebecca of Sunnybrook Farm*. New York: Grosset & Dunlap.

Willingham, D. (2004, Spring). Practice makes perfect: But only if you practice beyond the point of perfection. *American Educator*. Accessed at www.aft.org/pubs-reports/american_educator/spring2004/cogsci.html on 3 February, 2009.

Wilson, J. (2005). *The relationship of Dynamic Indicators of Basic Early Literacy Skills (DIBELS) oral reading fluency to performance on Arizona Instrument to Measure Standards (AIMS)*. Tempe, AZ: Assessment and Evaluation Department, Tempe School District No. 3.